DAVID LEIGH is one of Britain's best-known investigative journalists. He is Anthony Sampson professor of reporting at the journalism school of City University, London, and was investi-gations editor of the *Guardian* from 2000–2013. He is one of the founder members of the International Consortium of Investigative Journalists, a non-profit reporters' group head-quartered in Washington DC.

David handled the publication in 2010 of secret US military and diplomatic data from WikiLeaks. His books include *High Time*, a biography of international cannabis smuggler Howard Marks, and *The Wilson Plot*, a study of misconduct by western intelligence agencies. He has two children and lives in London with his wife, the lawyer Jeannie Mackie.

LUKE HARDING is an award-winning foreign correspondent with the *Guardian*. He has reported from Delhi, Berlin and Moscow and covered wars in Afghanistan, Iraq and Libya. He is the author of two other books: *Mafia State: How One Reporter Became an Enemy of the Brutal New Russia*, and *The Liar: The Fall of Jonathan Aitken*, written with David Leigh and nominated for the Orwell Prize. He has also written for *Granta* magazine.

He lives in Hertfordshire with his wife, the freelance journalist Phoebe Taplin, and their two children.

WikiLeaks

Inside Julian Assange's
War on Secrecy

David Leigh and Luke Harding
with Ed Pilkington, Robert Booth and Charles Arthur

Published in Great Britain in 2011 by Guardian Books

This revised and updated edition first published in 2013 by
Guardian Books, Kings Place, 90 York Way, London N1 9GU
and Faber and Faber Ltd, Bloomsbury House,
74–77 Great Russell Street, London WC1B 3DA

2 4 6 8 10 9 7 5 3 1

ISBN: 9781783350179

Designed and set by seagulls.net

Printed and bound in Great Britain by CPI Group (UK) Ltd, Croydon, CR0 4YY

FSC
www.fsc.org
MIX
Paper from
responsible sources
FSC® C008047

CONTENTS

CAST OF CHARACTERS

WikiLeaks

Julian Assange – WikiLeaks founder/editor

Sarah Harrison – aide to WikiLeaks founder Julian Assange

Kristinn Hrafnsson – Icelandic journalist and WikiLeaks supporter

James Ball – WikiLeaks data expert

Vaughan Smith – former Grenadier Guards captain, founder of the Frontline Club and Assange's host at Ellingham Hall

Jacob Appelbaum – WikiLeaks' representative in the US

Daniel Ellsberg – Vietnam war whistleblower, WikiLeaks supporter

Daniel Domscheit-Berg – German programmer and WikiLeaks technical architect (aka Daniel Schmitt)

Mikael Viborg – owner of WikiLeaks' Swedish internet service provider PRQ

Ben Laurie – British encryption expert, adviser to Assange on encryption

Mwalimu Mati – head of anti-corruption group Mars Group Kenya, source of first major WikiLeaks report

Rudolf Elmer – former head of the Cayman Islands branch of the Julius Baer bank, source of second major WikiLeaks report

Smári McCarthy – Iceland-based WikiLeaks enthusiast, programmer, Modern Media Initiative (MMI) campaigner

Birgitta Jónsdóttir – Icelandic MP and WikiLeaks supporter

Rop Gonggrijp – Dutch hacker-businessman, friend of Assange and MMI campaigner
Herbert Snorrason – Icelandic MMI campaigner
Israel Shamir – WikiLeaks associate
Donald Böstrom – Swedish journalist and WikiLeaks' Stockholm connection

The Guardian
LONDON

Alan Rusbridger – editor-in-chief
Nick Davies – investigative reporter
David Leigh – investigations editor
Ian Katz – deputy editor (news)
Ian Traynor – Europe correspondent
Harold Frayman – systems editor
Declan Walsh – Pakistan/Afghanistan correspondent
Alastair Dant – data visualiser
Simon Rogers – data editor
Jonathan Steele – former Iraq correspondent
James Meek – former Iraq correspondent
Rob Evans – investigative journalist
Luke Harding – Moscow correspondent
Robert Booth – reporter
Stuart Millar – news editor, guardian.co.uk
Janine Gibson – editor, guardian.co.uk
Jonathan Casson – head of production
Gill Phillips – in-house head of legal
Jan Thompson – managing editor

New York Times
New York, London

Max Frankel – former executive editor
Bill Keller – editor
Eric Schmitt – war correspondent
John F Burns – London correspondent
Ian Fisher – deputy foreign editor

Der Spiegel
Hamburg, London

Georg Mascolo – editor-in-chief
Holger Stark – head of German desk
Marcel Rosenbach – journalist
John Goetz – journalist

El País
Madrid, London

Javier Moreno – editor-in-chief
Vicente Jiménez – deputy editor

Bradley Manning

Bradley Manning – 23-year-old US army private and WikiLeaks source
Rick McCombs – former principal at Crescent high school, Crescent, Oklahoma
Brian, Susan, Casey Manning – parents and sister
Tom Dyer – school friend
Kord Campbell – former manager at Zoto software company
Jeff Paterson – steering committee member of the Bradley Manning support network

Adrian Lamo – hacker and online confidant
Timothy Webster – former US army counter-intelligence special agent
Tyler Watkins – former boyfriend
David House – former hacker and supporter
David Coombs – lawyer

Julian Assange

Christine Hawkins – mother
John Shipton – father
Brett Assange – stepfather
Keith Hamilton – former partner of Christine
Daniel Assange – Julian's son
Paul Galbally – Assange's lawyer during his 1996 hacking trial

Stockholm allegations / extradition

"Sonja Braun" – plaintiff; member of Brotherhood movement
"Katrin Weiss" – plaintiff; museum worker
Claes Borgström – lawyer for both women, former Swedish equal opportunities ombudsman and prominent Social Democrat politician
Marianne Ny – Swedish chief prosecutor and sex crimes specialist
Mark Stephens – Assange lawyer
Geoffrey Robertson, QC – Assange lawyer
Jennifer Robinson – lawyer in Mark Stephens' office
Gemma Lindfield – lawyer acting for the Swedish authorities
Howard Riddle – district judge, Westminster magistrates court
Mr Justice Ouseley – high court judge, London

INTRODUCTION
Alan Rusbridger

Mass digital leaking is something new in the world. The internet age is, of course, transforming many aspects of all our lives, but the extraordinary story of WikiLeaks is proving to be revolutionary in unexpected ways.

Back in 2011, I wrote in an introduction to the original edition of this book: "This is a compelling first chapter in a story which, one suspects, is destined to run and run." That prediction turned out to be accurate enough, but in a fashion far more dramatic than any of us would have imagined. For the WikiLeaks saga itself, with all its startling twists, is proving to be only the first act in what appears to be a stunning global phenomenon – the rise of what junior US soldier Bradley Manning called "hacktivism". It is a phenomenon that has put my own paper, the *Guardian*, on the front line.

Manning worked out how to scrape the entire contents of secret US government databases. He did so on a colossal scale, and he uploaded them to Julian Assange of WikiLeaks, who made them available for the *Guardian*'s analysis and publication, together with our other international media partners. Many of the subsequent revelations about the military behaviour of the world's biggest superpower were disturbing and sometimes shocking. A further set of disclosures from the state department's worldwide diplomatic archives were also, to say the least, highly educational. But three years later, as Manning faced the gravest charges a US army court martial could throw at him, his deeds were trumped by the even more sensational acts of Edward Snowden, a 29-year-old computer contractor for the super-secret US National Security Agency, which intercepts communications worldwide.

Snowden, as the world knows because he openly claimed authorship of the leak, turned over to us NSA documents classified "top secret". We decided it was important to publish them, and they have, to an even greater extent, caused worldwide uproar. Snowden has revealed that in recent years the NSA and its British junior partner GCHQ have been collecting all American phone records from such big companies as Verizon. Under a secret programme called PRISM, they are also gaining access to the internet data of companies like Google and Yahoo.

In Britain, GCHQ's contribution to the joint transatlantic spying effort is to ensure UK telecommunication firms install bulk taps on the fibre-optic submarine cables which carry more than 25 per cent of the world's internet traffic. In their TEMPORA project, they have developed means of storing and analysing those billions of internet searches, emails, text messages, credit card purchases and airline bookings. GCHQ has also been spying on friendly nations at the G20 summit held in Britain, using such outlandish devices as fake internet cafes, equipped to log delegates' keystrokes and steal their passwords. It seems no one's privacy is safe: these new technical abilities are not being used merely to combat terrorism, but for a wide range of intelligence purposes, all authorised, in both London and Washington, in what was intended to be complete secrecy.

Snowden, just like Manning and Assange, is young, male, computer-savvy – and disaffected. These three, like others in their world, operate on a global map connected by the internet, and they share a passion for what their opponents in the US establishment call "information anarchism". They have demonstrated what an unexpectedly powerful position such people now occupy.

All three men are currently paying a price for their insurrectionary activism. Manning, a young private who was serving in Iraq when he emptied out the contents of the State Department's central Washington database, is incarcerated in a US jail, serving a lengthy term. He fought off an unprecedented attempt by the US army to convict him at a court martial of treason, when they charged him with "aiding the enemy". But his full confession ensured he would nonetheless be convicted of a raft of other heavy charges, including theft of government property and offences under the espionage act.

Snowden was working as a contractor on the Pacific island of Hawaii when he decided to send data, obtained from the NSA's Fort Meade headquarters near Washington, to the *Guardian*'s Glenn Greenwald. He then fled to Hong Kong, and from there fell into the hands of the Russians. He was stranded at Moscow airport when he attempted to change planes, en route to hoped-for political asylum in Latin America. The US cancelled his passport, and signalled they would stop at little to get him back for his own trial and imprisonment. They even ensured the Bolivian president's private jet was blocked from European airspace and forced to land, when they mistakenly thought Snowden was on board. He was reduced to obtaining asylum in Putin's Russia.

As for the Australian Assange, who has a claim to be one of the founders of the ideology of "information anarchism", he has ended up – bizarrely – confined to a single room at Number 3, Hans Crescent in Knightsbridge, the central London home of the small embassy of Ecuador. He refuses to go to Sweden to face sexual assault allegations made by two women while he was visiting there. Instead, he has been granted asylum by Ecuador, which accepts Assange's claim that he fears extradition to the US were he to go and face the music in Sweden. The British government take a different view, and say they must arrest him on Sweden's behalf if he steps outside. Still unstoppably online, Assange claims to be helping Edward Snowden with advice and assistance as the NSA leaker tries to outrun a vengeful US government.

How did this amazing story start? Back in the days when almost no one had heard about WikiLeaks, regular emails starte arriving in my inbox from someone called Julian Assange. It was a memorable kind of name. All editors receive a daily mix of unso-licited tip-offs, letters, complaints and crank theories, but there was something about the periodic WikiLeaks emails that caught the attention.

Sometimes there would be a decent story attached to the emails. Or there might be a document which, on closer inspec-tion, appeared rather underwhelming. One day there might arrive a diatribe against a particular journalist – or against the venal cowardice of mainstream media in general. Another day this Assange person would be pleased with something we'd done, or would perambulate about the life he was living in Nairobi.

In Britain the *Guardian* was, for many months, the only paper to write about WikiLeaks or to use any of the documents they were publishing. In August 2007, for instance, we splashed on a remarkable secret Kroll report that claimed to show that former Kenyan President Daniel Arap Moi had been siphoning off hundreds of millions of pounds and hiding them away in foreign bank accounts in more than 30 different countries. It was, by any standards, a stonking story. This Asssange, whoever he was, was one to watch.

Unnoticed by most of the world, Assange was developing into a most interesting and unusual pioneer in using digital technolo-gies to challenge corrupt and authoritarian states. It's doubtful whether his name would have meant anything to Hillary Clinton at the time – or even in January 2010 when, as secretary of state, she made a rather good speech about the potential of what she termed "a new nervous system for the planet".

She described a vision of semi-underground digital publishing – "the samizdat of our day" – that was beginning to champion transparency and challenge the autocratic, corrupt old order of the world. But she also warned that repressive governments would "target the independent thinkers who use the tools". She had regimes like Iran in mind.

Her words about the brave samizdat publishing future could well have applied to the rather strange, unworldly Australian hacker quietly working out methods of publishing the world's secrets in ways which were beyond any technological or legal attack.

Little can Clinton have imagined, as she made this much-praised speech, that within a year she would be back making another statement about digital whistleblowers – this time roundly attacking people who used electronic media to champion transparency. It was, she told a hastily arranged state department press conference in November 2010, "not just an attack on America's foreign policy interests. It is an attack on the international community". In the intervening 11 months Assange had gone viral. He had just helped orchestrate the biggest leak in the history of the world – only this time the embarrassment was not to a poor East African nation, but to the most powerful country on earth.

Within a few short years of starting out Assange had been catapulted from obscurity, dribbling out leaks that nobody much noticed, to publishing a flood of classified documents that went to the heart of America's military and foreign policy operations. From being a marginal figure invited to join panels at geek conferences he was suddenly America's public enemy number one. A new media messiah to some, he was a cyber-terrorist to others. Each side projected onto him superhuman powers of good or evil. As if this wasn't dramatic enough, in the middle of it all, two women in Sweden very publicly accused him of rape. To coin a phrase, you couldn't make it up.

It is that story, the transformation from anonymous hacker to being one of the most discussed people in the world – at once reviled, celebrated and lionised; sought-after, imprisoned and shunned – that this book sets out to tell.

This new form of indestructible publishing brought sharp questions into focus for us on the *Guardian*. There might be cases where someone intended to use WikiLeaks to smear or destroy someone. That made Assange a very powerful figure. The fact that there were grumbles among his colleagues about his autocratic and secretive style did not allay the fears about this new media baron. The questions kept coming: who was this shadowy figure 'playing God'? How could he and his team be sure of a particular document's authenticity? Who was determining the ethical framework that decided some information should be published, and some not? All this meant that Assange was in many respects – more, perhaps, than he welcomed – in a role not dissimilar to that of a conventional editor.

A unique collaboration was born between several newspapers, the mysterious Australian nomad … and whatever his elusive organisation, WikiLeaks, actually was. That much never became very clear. Assange was, at the best of times, difficult to contact, switching mobile phones, email addresses and encrypted chat rooms as often as he changed his location. Occasionally he would appear with another colleague – it could be a journalist, a hacker, a lawyer or an unspecified helper – but, just as often, he travelled solo. It was never entirely clear which time zone he was in. The difference between day and night, an important consideration in most lives, seemed of little interest to him.

The extent of the redaction process we managed and the relatively limited extent of publication of actual cables by the newspapers was apparently overlooked by many commentators –

including leading American journalists – who spoke disparagingly of a "willy-nilly dump" of mass cables and the consequent danger to life. There was no "mass dump", initially at least. Barely 1,000 of the 250,000 cables were published. Much later, after the state department had completed a damage-limitation exercise, Assange made the unilateral decision to publish everything online – a move deplored by the five newspapers who were his original partners. It is fair to say, however, that even during Bradley Manning's 2013 court martial, no one was able to demonstrate any resulting damage to life or limb.

It's impossible to write this story without telling the story of Assange himself, though clearly the overall question of WikiLeaks and the philosophy it represents is of longer-lasting significance. More than one writer has compared him to John Wilkes, the rakish 18th-century MP and editor who risked his life and liberty in assorted battles over free speech. Others have compared him to Daniel Ellsberg, the source of the Pentagon Papers leak, described by the *New York Times*' former executive editor, Max Frankel, as " a man of incisive, devious intellect and volatile temperament".

Certainly, few people seem to find Assange an easy man with whom to collaborate. *Slate*'s media columnist, Jack Shafer, captured his character well in this pen portrait: "Assange bedevils the journalists who work with him because he refuses to conform to any of the roles they expect him to play. He acts like a leaking source when it suits him. He masquerades as publisher or news-paper syndicate when that's advantageous. Like a PR agent, he manipulates news organisations to maximise publicity for his 'clients', or, when moved to, he threatens to throw info-bombs like an agent provocateur. He's a wily shape-shifter who won't sit still, an unpredictable negotiator who is forever changing the terms of the deal."

We certainly had our moments of difficulty and tension during the course of our joint enterprise. They were caused as much by the difficulty of regular, open communication and by Assange's status as a sometimes confusing mix of source, intermediary and publisher. Encrypted instant messaging is no substitute for talking. And, while Assange was certainly our main source for the documents, he was in no sense conventional, being not the original source and certainly not a confidential one. Latterly, he was not even the only source. He was, if anything, a new breed of publisher-intermediary – a sometimes uncomfortable role in which he sought to have a degree of control of the source's material (and even a form of "ownership", complete with legal threats to sue for loss of income). When, to Assange's fury, WikiLeaks itself sprang a leak, the irony of the situation was almost comic. The ethical issues involved in this new status of editor/source became more complicated still when it was suggested to us that we owed some form of protection to Assange – as a "source" – by not inquiring too deeply into the sex charges levelled against him in Sweden. That did not seem a compelling argument to us, though there were those – it is not too strong to call them 'disciples' – who were not willing to imagine any narrative beyond that of the smear.

These wrinkles were mainly overcome – sometimes eased by a glass of wine or by matching Assange's extraordinary appetite for exhaustive and intellectually exacting conversations. As Sarah Ellison's *Vanity Fair* piece on the subject concluded: "Whatever the differences, the results have been extraordinary. Given the range, depth, and accuracy of the leaks, the collaboration has produced by any standard one of the greatest journalistic scoops of the last 30 years."

The challenge from WikiLeaks for media in general (not to mention states, companies or global corporations caught up in the dazzle of unwanted scrutiny) is not a comfortable one. Assange's initial instincts were to publish more or less everything, and he was – at first – deeply suspicious of any contacts between his colleagues on the newspapers and any kind of officialdom. Talking to the state department, Pentagon or White House, as the *New York Times* did before each round of publication, was fraught territory in terms of keeping the relationship with WikiLeaks on an even keel. By the time the cables were published, Assange himself, conscious of the risks of causing unintentional harm to dissidents or other sources, offered to speak to the state department – an offer that was rejected.

WikiLeaks and similar organisations are, it seems to me, generally admirable in their single-minded view of transparency and openness. What has been remarkable is how the sky has *not* fallen in despite the truly enormous amounts of information released over the months and years. The enemies of WikiLeaks have made repeated assertions of the harm done by the release. It would be a good idea if someone would fund some rigorous research by a serious academic institution about the balance between harms and benefits. To judge from the response we had from countries without the benefit of a free press, there was a considerable thirst for the information in the cables – a hunger for knowledge which contrasted with the occasional knowing yawns from metropolitan sophisticates who insisted that the cables told us nothing new. Instead of a kneejerk stampede to more secrecy, this could be the opportunity to draw up a score sheet of the upsides and drawbacks of forced transparency.

That approach – a rational assessment of new forms of disclosure – should accompany the inevitable questioning of how the US classification system could have allowed the private musings of kings, presidents and dissidents to have been so easily read by Bradley Manning in the first place.

One of the lessons from the WikiLeaks project is that it showed the possibilities of collaboration. It's difficult to think of any other comparable example of news organisations working together in the way the *Guardian*, *New York Times*, *Der Spiegel*,

Le Monde and *El País* have done. I think all five editors would like to imagine ways in which we could harness our resources again.

During Bradley Manning's court martial for "aiding the enemy", it was admitted that WikiLeaks' position in law seems identical to that of mainstream publishers like us. There appears to be, among the cooler legal heads in the US, an appreciation that it would be virtually impossible to indict Assange for the act of publication of the war logs or state department cables without also putting five newspaper editors in the dock, the *Guardian* and the *New York Times* included. That would be the media case of the century.

Each news organisation grappled with the ethical issues involved – and in the overall decision to publish – in different ways. I was interested, a few days after the start of the cables' release, to receive an email from Max Frankel, who had overseen the defence of the *New York Times* in the Pentagon papers case 40 years earlier. Now 80, he sent me a memo he had then written to the *New York Times* public editor. It is worth quoting as concise and wise advice to future generations who may well have to grapple with such issues further in future:

1. My view has almost always been that information which wants to get out will get out; our job is to receive it responsibly and to publish or not by our own unvarying news standards.

2. If the source or informant violates his oath of office or the law, we should leave it to the authorities to try to enforce their law or oath, without our collaboration. We reject collaboration or revelation of our sources for the larger reason that ALL our sources deserve to know that they are protected with us. It is, however, part of our obligation to reveal the biases and apparent purposes of the people who leak or otherwise disclose information.

3. If certain information seems to defy the standards proclaimed by the supreme court in the Pentagon papers case – ie that publication will cause direct, immediate and irreparable damage – we have an obligation to limit our publication appropriately. If in doubt, we should give appropriate authority a chance to persuade us that such direct and immediate danger exists. (See our 24-hour delay of discovery of Soviet missiles in Cuba as described in my autobiography, or our delay in reporting planes lost in combat until the pilots can perhaps be rescued.)

4. For all other information, I have always believed that no one can reliably predict the consequences of publication. The Pentagon papers, contrary to Ellsberg's wish, did not shorten the Vietnam war or stir significant additional protest. A given disclosure may embarrass government but improve a policy, or it may be a leak by the government itself and end up damaging policy. "Publish and be damned" ... It sounds terrible but as a journalistic motto, it has served our society well through history.

There have been many longer treatises on the ethics of journalism that have said less.

London, August 2013

Alan Rusbridger is editor of the *Guardian*

CHAPTER 1
The Hunt

Ellingham Hall, Norfolk, England
November 2010

"You can't imagine how ridiculous it was"
JAMES BALL, WIKILEAKS

Glimpsed in the half-light of a London evening, the figure might just have passed for female. She emerged cautiously from a doorway and folded herself into a battered red car. There were a few companions – among them a grim-visaged man with Nordic features and a couple of nerdy youngsters. One appeared to have given the old woman her coat. The car weaved through the light Paddington traffic, heading north in the direction of Cambridge. As they proceeded up the M11 motorway the occupants peered back. There was no obvious sign of pursuit. Nonetheless, they periodically pulled off the road into a lay-by and waited – lights killed – in the gloom. Apparently undetected, the group headed eastward along the slow A143 road. By 10pm they had reached the flatlands of East Anglia, a sepia landscape where the occasional disused sugar factory hulked out of the blackness.

Fifteen miles inland, at the unremarkable village of Ellingham, they finally turned left. The car skidded on a driveway, and drove past an ancient dovecote before stopping in front of a grand Georgian manor house. The woman stepped from the car. There was something odd about her. She had a kind of hump! If a CIA agent or some other observer were hidden in the woodland along with the pheasants, they could have been forgiven for a moment of puzzlement.

Close up, however, it was obvious that this strange figure was Julian Assange, his platinum hair concealed by a wig. At more than 6ft tall, he was never going to be a very convincing female. "You can't imagine how ridiculous it was," WikiLeaks' James Ball later said. "He'd stayed dressed up as an old woman for more than two hours." Assange was swapping genders in a pantomime attempt to evade possible pursuers. With him were also his young aide, Sarah Harrison, and his deputy, the Icelandic journalist Kristinn Hrafnsson. On that evening, this small team was the nucleus of WikiLeaks, the whistleblower website Assange had launched four years earlier.

In a breathtakingly short time, WikiLeaks had soared out of its previous niche as an obscure radical website to become a widely known online news platform. Assange had published leaked footage showing airborne US helicopter pilots executing two Reuters employees in Baghdad, seemingly as if they were playing a video-game. He had followed up this coup with another, even bigger sensation: an unprecedented newspaper deal, brokered with the *Guardian* newspaper in London, to reveal hundreds of thousands of classified US military field reports from the wars in Afghanistan and Iraq, many of them damning.

Assange, a 39-year-old Australian, was a computer hacker of genius. He could be charming, capable of deadpan humour and wit. But he could also be waspish, flaring into anger and recrimination. Assange's mercurial temperament spawned groupies and enemies, supporters and ill-wishers, sometimes even in the same person. Information messiah or cyber-terrorist? Freedom fighter or sociopath? Moral crusader or deluded narcissist? The debate over Assange would reverberate in the coming weeks in headlines the world over.

Assange and his team had fled here from the Frontline Club, a hang-out for foreign correspondents and other media types in west London. Since July and the launch of the Afghan war logs, Assange had slept, on and off, in the club's accommodation at Southwick Mews. The club's founder, Vaughan Smith, had become a sympathiser and ally, and invited Assange and his coterie to his ancestral home, Ellingham Hall, tucked away in a remote corner of East Anglia. And here these unlikely refugees had now arrived.

Smith was a former captain of the Grenadier Guards, an elite regiment of the British army, who went on to become a freelance video journalist with Frontline TV. His adventures in war zones – Iraq during the first Gulf war, where he bluffed his way in disguised as a British army officer; Bosnia, with its massacres and horrors; Afghanistan; and Iraq again – had demonstrated a spirit of maverick independence. Smith was no anarchist. His family had served in the British army for generations. His paper of choice was Britain's conservative, crusty *Daily Telegraph*. Smith was also brave. In Kosovo, his life was saved when a deadly bullet lodged in his mobile telephone.

But in common with other right-wing libertarians, he had a stubborn sense of fair play and believed in sticking up for the underdog. In this instance that meant Assange, who had become a hate figure for the bellicose US right. They wanted him arrested. Some were even calling for his assassination. Smith broadly supported Assange's crusade for transparency at a time when – as Smith saw it – journalism itself had moved uncomfortably close to government, and was in danger of becoming mere PR fluff.

When Assange settled in to work at Ellingham Hall, already living in the manor house were Pranvera Shema, Smith's Kosovo-born wife, and their two small children. Aged five and two, their bikes stood outside the hall's imposing porte-cochère entrance.

Also in residence on the estate were Vaughan's upper-class parents. Vaughan's father, too, had served in the Guards; a portrait of him as a young officer in a scarlet tunic hung in the dining room. Smith Sr could be seen holding a white pouch: a discreet reference to his career as a Queen's Messenger. The role involved travelling around the world on Her Majesty's business, hand-carrying diplomatic secrets. It was clear that Smith Sr took a dim view of Assange, who was believed to be in possession of an astonishingly large number of secret diplomatic dispatches.

Smith Sr would take to patrolling the estate – with its twin lakes and cedar trees – armed with a rifle. The rifle was fitted with a telescope sight. The sniper-sight was camouflaged. Normally he fired at partridge and grouse. The temptation, however, to take a shot at the paparazzi that would soon encamp themselves outside the manor – or indeed at the unwashed radicals inside it – must have been considerable. Asked two days before Christmas whether he was enjoying playing host to the group of international leakers who were here, he answered through gritted teeth. "I wish they weren't." It was one of many ironies that would pepper the tension-filled weeks.

Among the WikiLeakers at Ellingham was 24-year-old James Ball, whom Assange had recruited, one of the few collaborators to receive a salary. Ball's talent was for dealing with large data sets. A cool young man, he was experiencing a giddy rise. Within a matter of months he went from a job as reporter on the *Grocer* trade magazine to being a spokesman for WikiLeaks, and even debating with the US diplomat John Negroponte on BBC World's *Hardtalk* programme. Ball's first task was urgent: to go into Norwich, 15 miles away, and head for a branch of the John Lewis department store for technical equipment. He set off, carrying several thousand pounds in cash (Assange's preferred medium of exchange), emerging with several laptops, a router, and cabling – and leaving a bemused shop assistant in his wake.

"Have you ever tried spending £1,000 cash in John Lewis? Honestly, the assistant looked scared of £50 notes," Ball reflected. "It was a surreal experience."

The team began setting up an anonymous internet identity. Their connection was designed to give the electronic impression that the WikiLeaks team sitting in rustic England was actually based in Sweden. The preoccupation with security was paramount: WikiLeaks was believed to be a permanent target for US surveillance and potentially crippling cyber-attacks. On trips outside the manor house, the team used the same counter-surveillance techniques they had employed during the journey to Norfolk. This may have been prudent. But it meant Ball was sometimes left hanging round for several hours at minor B-roads and other freezing rendezvous points, waiting for a lift.

Ensconced in a grand living room with a log fire, decorated with more portraits of Vaughan Smith's forebears, Assange got to work. Typically, he would spend between 16 and 18 hours a day in front of his laptop, sometimes staying up for a 48-hour period before crashing out on the floor. Other WikiLeaks staff would rouse him, and prod him towards the upstairs bedrooms. He would sleep for a couple of hours. Then he would carry on. Assange's cycle was nocturnal. He was at his most accessible at 3am or 4am. "I found it easier to do stuff at night when you could sometimes get Julian's attention. He's entirely capable of ignoring someone for five minutes while they're calling at him, 'Julian! Julian!'," says Ball. Other WikiLeaks associates – Sarah Harrison and Joseph Farrell, both recent journalistic interns – managed his email and diary.

Assange saw his role as that of a chief executive. His job was to monitor WikiLeaks' vast footprint in cyberspace, and to keep in touch with the organisation's collaborators in the other jurisdictions and time zones. Smith says: "He is obsessed with his work. Julian needs to understand what is written about WikiLeaks and the story. He describes it as monitoring the temperature."

To the right of the fireplace was a striking portrait of Vaughan Smith's great-great-grandfather, "Tiger" Smith. Smith acquired his sobriquet after killing 99 tigers, lugging many of them back to Ellingham Hall. Two stuffed beasts sat in glass boxes; others had been chucked out after mouldering. The entrance lobby was decorated with crossed sabres, old rifles with bayonets and other memorabilia from forgotten colonial skirmishes. There was a stuffed deer head, a pair of antlers, and a large painting depicting two stags charging furiously towards each other against an unusual pistachio background. If an American film director wanted the quintessential English country pile for his period movie, he could hardly have done better than Ellingham.

The WikiLeaks team quickly adapted to the rituals of English country house life. Ellingham Hall had a housekeeper; there was a kitchen with a raised central square table where staff would make meals; chops and sausages were piled up in a cardboard box. The estate had an organic farm (whose produce was also served in the restaurant of the Frontline Club back in London). Vaughan Smith had a decent cellar – its contents selected by the former *Guardian* wine critic Malcolm Gluck. At mealtimes Assange and his co-workers sat in Smith's splendid dining room beneath a venerable circular table. There was port – passed to the left by the cyber-radicals, in accordance with English convention. Assange insisted that nobody drank more than a glass a night, forcing his companions to cut side deals with the kitchen staff.

Assange's own habits were ascetic: he paid little attention to what he ate. His otherworldliness extended to his wardrobe. He didn't appear to possess any clothes of his own. At one point the WikiLeaks team decided Assange needed to remove himself from his screen and take some exercise. They bought him a red Adidas top: once a day Assange would jog through the parkland – a flash of brightness in a rural palette of browns and greens. Soon, Smith would transmogrify Assange further into the more muted shades of a country gentleman: he lent him a green parka and the tweed jacket with asymmetrical pockets that Smith had worn as a (trimmer) young man of 19. Assange also tried his hand at fishing.

From the outside few would have guessed what was really going on inside Ellingham Hall's high bay windows. Assange had gone to ground in this way, like a fox, because he was preparing, along with the *Guardian* and four other major international papers, to broker publication of the most spectacular leak in history. He had confided he was a little scared. There had been nothing like it, not even the Pentagon papers – the publication of the secret record of America's war in Vietnam – almost 40 years earlier. At one point the local hunt clattered across the grounds of Ellingham Hall; huntsmen and hounds crashing through the Spion Kop woods. It was the kind of pursuit that Assange seemed to sense he was involved in. Was he, too, the hunted animal, with prosecutors and US intelligence agents the red-coated huntsmen, riding to the sound of a blowing bugle, surging closer and closer?

CHAPTER 2

Bradley Manning

Contingency Operating Station Hammer,
40 miles east of Baghdad, Iraq
November 2009

"I should have left my phone at home"
LADY GAGA

After the punishing heat of summer, Iraq in November is pleasantly warm. But for the men and women stationed at Camp Hammer, in the middle of the Mada'in Qada desert, the air was forever thick with dust and dirt kicked up by convoys of lorries that supplied the capital – a constant reminder that they were very far from home. One of those was Specialist Bradley Manning, who'd been sent to Iraq with the 2nd Brigade Combat Team, 10th Mountain Division a few weeks earlier. About to turn 22, he was the antithesis of the battle-hardened US soldier beloved of Hollywood. Blue-eyed, blond-haired, with a round face and boyish smile, he stood just five feet and two inches tall and weighed 105 pounds.

But he hadn't been sent to Iraq because of his bulk. He was there for his gift at manipulating computers. In the role of intelligence analyst Manning found himself spending long days in the base's computer room poring over top-secret information. For such a young and relatively inexperienced soldier, it was extremely sensitive work. Yet from his first day at Hammer, he was puzzled by the lax security. The door was bolted with a five-digit cipher lock, but all you had to do was knock on it and you'd be let in. His fellow intelligence workers seemed to have grown bored and disenchanted from the relentless grind of 14-hour days, seven days a week. They just sat at their workstations, watching music videos or footage of car chases. "People stopped caring after three weeks," Manning observed.

After a few months Manning had grown scathing about the culture of the base. "Weak servers, weak logging, weak physical security, weak counter-intelligence, inattentive signal analysis … a perfect storm," he would later write. He approached the National Security Agency officer in charge of protecting information systems and asked him whether he could find any suspicious uploads from local networks. The officer shrugged and said, "It's not a priority."

It was a culture, as Manning later described it, that "fed opportunities". For Manning, those opportunities presented themselves in the form of two dedicated military laptops which he was given, each with privileged access to US state secrets. The first laptop was connected to the Secret Internet Protocol Router Network (SIPR-Net), used by the department of defence and the state department to securely share information. The second gave him entry to the Joint Worldwide Intelligence Communications System (JWICS), which acts as a global funnel for top-secret dispatches.

That such a low-level serviceman could have had apparently unrestricted access to this vast source of confidential material should surely have raised eyebrows. That he could do so with virtually no supervision or safeguards inside the base was all the more astounding. He would spend hours drilling down into top-secret documents and videos, wearing earphones and lip-synching to Lady Gaga. The more he read, the more alarmed and disturbed he became, shocked by what he saw as the official duplicity and corruption of his own country. There were videos that showed the aerial killing from a helicopter gunship of unarmed civilians in Iraq, there were chronicles of civilian deaths and "friendly fire" disasters in Afghanistan. And there was a mammoth trove of diplomatic cables disclosing secrets from all around the world, from the Vatican to Pakistan. He started to become overwhelmed by the scale of the scandal and intrigue he was discovering. "There's so much," he would later write. "It affects everybody on earth. Everywhere there's a US post there's a diplomatic scandal that will be revealed. It's beautiful, and horrifying."

From there it was but a short step to thinking that he could do something about it. "If you had unprecedented access to classified networks 14 hours a day, seven days a week for eight-plus months, what would you do?" he asked. What he did was to take the rewritable CD which carried his Lady Gaga music and erase it, then copy onto the disc other, far more dangerous, digital material. He was about to embark on a journey that would lead to the largest leak of military and diplomatic secrets in US history.

Crescent, Oklahoma, is flat and off the beaten track, just like the Mada'in Qada desert. But there the likeness ends. A small town in the middle of a rural bread basket, 35 miles to the north of Oklahoma City, its skyline is dominated by a large white grain stack. "This is a tight-knit, very conservative community," says Rick McCombs, the recently retired principal of Crescent high school.

Born on 17 December 1987, Bradley Manning spent the first 13 years of his life in Crescent, benefiting from its small-town intimacy, suffering from the narrow-mindedness that went with it. He lived outside town in a two-storey house with his American father, Brian, his Welsh mother, Susan, and his elder sister, Casey. His parents had met when Brian was serving in the US navy and stationed at the Cawdor Barracks in south-west Wales.

Bradley's childhood and youth were highly distressing, according to the subsequent testimony of his family. His sister Casey would reveal that their mother became an alcoholic who drank heavily during her pregnancy. An army doctor subsequently confirmed that Bradley's underweight physique was among several signs he showed of having suffered early damage from Foetal Alcohol Syndrome. Susan would stay in bed until mid-day after he was born, and then start drinking again through the day. The 11-year-old Casey had to care for her little brother as best she could, she said. Their father Brian she also characterized as an alcoholic, who left the family in the isolated house 4 miles outside Crescent while away on business trips as a computer expert for his then employers, the Hertz Corporation. Bradley's aunt, Debra van Alstyne, who later befriended him, was to maintain: "He had a very hard start to his life".

From a young age, Bradley also displayed qualities that would set him apart from others. He possessed a lively, inquiring mind and a tendency to question the prevailing attitude. McCombs recalls that Bradley not only played a mean saxophone in the school band but also appeared in the school quiz team alongside much older children. "He was very, very smart. He was also very opinionated – but only up to a point. He never got in trouble. Not once was Bradley disciplined for any reason." Manning had an early passion for computer games, playing Super Mario Bros with a neighbour. He was also fiercely independent of spirit. He was one of very few inhabitants of Crescent who openly professed doubts about religion – not an easy position for a child to take in a devoutly Christian town with no fewer than 15 churches. He used to refuse to do homework that related to the Bible and remained silent during the reference to God in the Pledge of Allegiance. Crescent, Manning once quipped, had "more pews than people".

His father was by all accounts a strict parent. Neighbours reported that Brian's severity contributed to Bradley growing introverted and withdrawn. Such introversion deepened with puberty and Bradley's dawning realisation that he was gay. Aged 13, he confided his sexuality to a couple of his closest friends at Crescent school.

The entry to teenage years was a tumultuous time. In 2001, just as Manning was beginning to come to grips with his homosexuality, his father announced he was leaving. His mother took a bottleful of Valium and Bradley had to go with her to the hospital. Within months, Manning's life in Crescent was uprooted, his friendships torn asunder, and his life transplanted 4,000 miles to Haverfordwest in Wales, where his mother decided to return following the bitter break-up.

In Wales Manning had to acclimatise to his new secondary school, Tasker Milward, which, with about 1,200 pupils, was the size of his old home town. And he was its only American student.

"He was prone to being bullied for being a little bit different. People used to impersonate him, his accent and mannerisms," remembers Tom Dyer, a friend of Manning's at Tasker Milward. "He wasn't the biggest kid, or the most sporty, and they would make fun of him. At times he would rise to the provocation and lash out."

Perhaps as a means of reviving his self-esteem, he grew increasingly passionate about computers and geekery. He spent every lunchtime at the school computer club, where he built his own website.

"He was always doing something, always going somewhere, always with an action plan," says Dyer. "He would get exasperated if things went wrong, his mind always racing. That made him come across as a little bit quirky and hyperactive."

Dyer also notes that by the age of 15 Manning had begun to formulate a clear political outlook that, irrespective of his enduring patriotism, was increasingly critical of US foreign policy. When the invasion of Iraq happened in March 2003 they would have long conversations about it. "He would speak out and say it was all about oil and that George Bush had no right going in there."

That political sensibility developed further when, at the age of 17 and having left school, he was packed off back to Oklahoma to live with his father. He took up a job in Zoto, a photo-sharing software company.

"He struck me as wise beyond his years," recalls Manning's boss at Zoto, Kord Campbell. "This was the Bush era, and nobody in the computer software world liked that president. Brad would go on about his political opinions, which was unusual for a kid."

Campbell says that his employee "was smart. He learned like nobody's business." But the maverick side to Manning was also growing more pronounced. "He was quirky, there was no doubt about it. He was quirky as hell." On a couple of occasions he remembers Manning falling into what Campbell describes as a "thousand-mile stare". "He would be silent and wouldn't talk to me or recognise me." Four months in, concerned that Manning's personal issues were affecting his work, Campbell fired him.

After discovering that Bradley was homosexual, Brian Manning threw his son out of the house. Homeless, jobless, Bradley rambled around for a few months, moving from place to place, odd job to odd job. As Jeff Paterson of the Bradley Manning support network, puts it: "He needed a way of proving himself, to go out on his own, to establish himself."

Bradley eventually volunteered for the US Army. It may have seemed an unlikely step for such a gay nonconformist; but he said he badly wanted to go to college, and the GI Bill would fund it. The move also pleased his father. He enlisted in October 2007, and was put through specialist training for military intelligence work at Fort Huachuca in Arizona. In August 2008 he was posted to Fort Drum in upstate New York, awaiting dispatch to Iraq, armed with the security clearance that would give him access to those two top-secret databases.

For someone seeking a sense of purpose out of a career in the military, his experience of life in uniform was at times disillusioning. He complained of having been "regularly ignored ... except when I had something essential ... then it was back to 'bring me coffee, then sweep the floor' ... I felt like an abused workhorse." On another occasion, on Facebook, he wrote: "Bradley Manning is not a piece of equipment."

On top of feeling like a menial, there was Don't Ask, Don't Tell, the unhappy compromise thrashed out by the Clinton administration in 1993 that allowed gay personnel to serve in the military but only if they remained in the closet. Though Manning must have been aware of the restrictions when he enlisted, he quickly became infuriated and distressed by the policy. In an echo of his occasional outbursts at Tasker Milward school, he at times let his frustration show, coming close to flouting the Don't Tell half of the formula.

The motto he attached to his Facebook profile said it all: "Take me for who I am, or face the consequences." That devil-may-care approach was on display within weeks of his posting to Fort Drum, when he marched at a rally to protest against the Proposition 8 vote in California which prohibited same-sex marriage. His response to Don't Ask, Don't Tell, and his willingness to campaign against it semi-openly, was a presage of what was to come. Many gay people in the military took the view that, while they would quietly work to reform the policy from within, they would never disrespect an order. But Manning was too firm in his convictions – some say too hot-headed – to accommodate himself to a regulation that he believed to be unjust. As Jeff Paterson puts it: "He was willing to face retribution and ridicule within the army to fight something he knew was wrong."

There has been much discussion since Manning's arrest about the role that his sexuality played in the events that led up to the massive WikiLeaks disclosures. Timothy Webster is one who ridicules any correlation between Manning's sexuality and his leaking of state secrets. A former special agent with US army counter-intelligence, Webster played an important part in the Manning story. He acted as the go-between connecting Lamo, the hacker whom Manning had confided in, and the military, after Lamo decided to shop Manning to the authorities. Webster, who is himself gay, says, "A small but loud-mouthed sideshow of talking heads have tried to use the Manning case as leverage to impugn homosexuals serving in the military. But the notion that the Manning case has anything to do with his sexuality is categorically absurd. Many thousands of homosexual and bisexual men and women are serving honourably and to suggest that their sexuality renders them any less effective in the defence of our nation is bigoted nonsense."

Webster is obviously correct. But Manning's sexuality nonetheless does play a key role in his story. At the time of these events, he was experiencing not only resentment, but also great anguish and stress. He felt he was in the wrong sex – the well-recognised condition of "gender disphoria".

In the course of an online chat with the hacker Adrian Lamo shortly before his arrest Manning tells Lamo that he "wouldn't mind going to prison for the rest of my life, or being executed … if it wasn't for the possibility of having pictures of me … plastered all over the world press … as a boy." In another he complains that his CPU, or central processing unit, "is not made for this motherboard", an analysis using the language of computers from a man anguished by a brain that he felt did not fit his male frame. On home leave in January 2010 he tried living as a woman for a while, and was even eventually to send his sergeant a photo of this, captioned "My Problem".

Furthermore, it was through Manning's first serious boyfriend that he became introduced to the world of Boston hackers. The boyfriend in question was Tyler Watkins, a self-styled classical musician, singer and drag queen. They met in the autumn of 2008 while Manning was still stationed at Fort Drum. They must have made an unlikely couple, the flamboyant and extrovert Watkins and the quietly focused Manning. But judging by his status updates on Facebook, the soldier fell hard for the queen. Bradley Manning "is cuddling in bed tonight"; "is a happy bunny"; "is in the barracks, alone. I miss you Tyler!"

Watkins is a student of neuroscience and psychology at Brandeis University outside Boston. Manning would regularly make the 300-mile journey from Fort Drum to see him, and in so doing became acquainted with Watkins' wide network of friends from Brandeis, Boston University and Massachusetts Institute of Technology (MIT), the birthplace of computer geekery that has been described as the "Mesopotamia of hacker culture". For Manning, it was an entrée into a whole new way of thinking that was worlds apart from the small-town conservatism of Crescent or the buttoned-down rigidity of Fort Drum.

Typical of the new attitudes he was exploring was the "hackerspace" attached to Boston University that he visited in January 2010 while he was on leave back in the US and visiting Watkins. Known as Builds, it is a sort of 21st-century techy version of a 1960s artists' collective. Its members come together to work on a host of projects, from creating a red robot mouse, to designing a computer system that can record the miles run by athletes at a race track, to studying how to crack open door locks (strictly on their own property). It is part computer workshop, part electronics laboratory, part DIY clinic. What unites these multifarious activities is the hacker culture to which everyone subscribes.

David House, a Boston University graduate who set up the hackerspace there, says that hacking is not the shady skull-and-crossbones activity of breaking into computers that it is often assumed to be. Rather, it is a way of looking at the world.

"It's about understanding the environment in which we operate, taking it apart, and then expanding upon it and recreating it. Central to it is the idea that information should be free, combined with a deep distrust of authority."

House points to a book, *Hackers: Heroes of the Computer Revolution*, by Steven Levy, which chronicles the rise of the "hacker ethic" at MIT. "Hackers believe that essential lessons can be learned about ... the world from taking things apart, seeing how they work, and using this knowledge to create new and even more interesting things," Levy writes. "They resent any person, physical barrier, or law that tries to keep them from doing this. All information should be free. If you don't have access to the information you need to improve things, how can you fix them?"

House remembers meeting Manning when he came to the opening of his hackerspace in January 2010. They had a short conversation in which Manning said nothing out of the ordinary. "He did not strike me as someone who would be accused of working against the US government," House says.

That was the only occasion House met Manning before the soldier's arrest. Since then, however, House struck up a friendship with him, becoming one of only two people (the other is Manning's lawyer, David Coombs) allowed to visit him at Quantico. In the course of several visits, House developed a more intimate sense of what makes Manning tick.

"He's very professorial in his thinking. Talking to him is like having a drink with one of your old college professors. He's very interested in what underpins power, the underlying systems, in an abstract way. That's why he fit in so well with Boston hacker culture, which has the same academic line."

The other quality that struck House is what he calls Manning's "high moral integrity. He always draws a firm ethical line. There are certain things that he sees as basic human rights that he believes are inviolable."

One of those inviolable basics that Manning evidently believed in was the value to democratic society of free information. As he said in his web chats with Lamo, "information should be free. It belongs in the public domain. If it's out in the open ... it should be a public good ... I want people to see the truth ... regardless of who they are ... because without information, you cannot make informed decisions as a public." A statement that could have been taken straight out of the Boston hackers' manual.

It was a belief that came powerfully into play when Manning was deliberating about what to do with the vast hoard of state secrets he had been allowed to explore in Iraq. For most soldiers the answer to that conundrum would have been utterly simple: abide by the confidentiality with which you have been entrusted, and get on with your job. But for Manning it was more complicated than that. On the same trip back to Boston in which he visited House's hackerspace he talked to Tyler Watkins about his dilemma. As Watkins told Wired.com: "He wanted to do the right thing. That was something I think he was struggling with."

In the seven months he spent at the Contingency Operating Station Hammer in Iraq, there was one seminal moment that appears to have ignited Manning's anger. A dispute had arisen concerning 15 Iraqi detainees held by the national Iraqi police force on the grounds that they had been printing "anti-Iraqi literature". The police were refusing to work with the US forces over the matter, and Manning's job was to investigate and find out who the "bad guys" were. He got hold of the leaflet that the detained men were distributing and had it translated into English. He was astonished to find that it was in fact a scholarly critique against the Iraqi prime minister, Nouri al-Maliki, that tracked the corruption rife within his cabinet.

"I immediately took that information and *ran* to the officer to explain what was going on," Manning later explained. "He didn't want to hear any of it … He told me to shut up and explain how we could assist the [Iraqi] police in finding MORE detainees."

Manning noted that, thereafter, "everything started slipping … I saw things differently … I had always questioned the [way] things worked, and investigated to find the truth … but that was a point where I was a part of something, actively involved in something that I was completely against."

Slowly, surely, Manning began edging his way towards a position that many have denounced as traitorous and abhorrent, and others have praised as courageous and heroic. He was starting to think about mining the secret databases to which he had access, and dumping them spectacularly into the public domain. "It's important that it gets out … I feel for some bizarre reason," he said. "It might actually change something."

But first he needed a conduit, a secure pipe down which he could transmit the information that he had copied on to CDs labelled Lady Gaga. As he contemplated what route to use, his eye was caught by an exercise run by WikiLeaks on Thanksgiving 2009, about a month into his tour of duty in Iraq. Over a 24-hour period, WikiLeaks published a stream of more than 500,000 pager messages that had been intercepted on the day of the September 11 2001 attacks on New York and Washington in the order in which they had been sent. It provided an extraordinary picture of an extraordinary day. Manning was even more impressed, because with his specialist knowledge he knew that WikiLeaks must have somehow obtained the messages anonymously from a National Security Agency database. And that made him feel comfortable that he, too, could come forward to WikiLeaks without fear of being identified.

His search for a vessel through which to unload his mountain of top-secret material had succeeded. Within days of the WikiLeaks 9/11 spectacular, Manning took the first big step. He made contact with a man whom he described as "a crazy white-haired Aussie who can't seem to stay in one country very long". The game was on with Julian Assange.

CHAPTER 3
Julian Assange

Melbourne, Australia
December 2006

"Give him a mask, and he will tell you the truth"
Oscar Wilde

The unusual Australian who wrote up his dating profile for the OKCupid website used the name 'Harry Harrison'. He was 36 years old, 6ft 2ins tall and, said the site's test, "87% slut." He began:

"WARNING: Want a regular, down to earth guy? Keep moving. I am not the droid you are looking for. Save us both while you still can. Passionate, and often pig headed activist intellectual seeks siren for love affair, children and occasional criminal conspiracy. Such a woman should be spirited and playful, of high intelligence, though not necessarily formally educated, have spunk, class & inner strength and be able to think strategically about the world and the people she cares about.

"I like women from countries that have sustained political turmoil. Western culture seems to forge women that are valueless and inane. OK. Not only women!

"Although I am pretty intellectually and physically pugnacious I am very protective of women and children.

"I am DANGER, ACHTUNG, and ??????????????!"

"Harry" went on to say he was directing a "consuming, dangerous, human rights project which is, as you might expect, male dominated". He also suffered from "Asian teengirl stalkers". The question what "could [he] never do without" produced the answer, "I could adapt to anything except the loss of female company and carbon." The profile warned: "Do not write to me if you are timid. I am too busy. Write to me if you are brave."

Harry's stated activities were extraordinary. He described himself as "variously professionally involved in international journalism/books, documentaries, cryptography, intelligence activities, civil rights, political activism, white collar crime and the internet". His gallery of photographs showed a man with pale skin, sharp features and wind-blown silver-grey hair. In some he has a half-smile, in others he stares down the barrel of the camera.

Harry Harrison was a pseudonym, and the person behind the mask was Julian Assange, a computer hacker living in a crowded student house in Melbourne, dreaming up a scheme for an idealistic information insurgency which was eventually to become celebrated – and execrated – worldwide as WikiLeaks. Assange had a striking and, some critics would say, damaged personality. It was on peacock display in this dating profile, but probably rooted deep in his Australian childhood and youth.

His obsession with computers, and his compulsion to keep moving, both seemed to have origins in his restless early years. So too, perhaps, did the rumblings from others that Assange was somewhere on the autistic spectrum. Assange would himself joke, when asked if he was autistic: "Aren't all men?" His dry sense of humour made him attractive – perhaps too attractive – to women. And there was his high analytical intelligence. In a different incarnation,

Assange could perhaps have been the successful chief executive of a major corporation.

There were a few demerits OKCupid couldn't capture. Assange's social skills sometimes seemed lacking. The way his eyes flickered around the room was curious; one *Guardian* journalist described it as "toggling". And occasionally he forgot to wash. Collaborators who fell out with him – there was to be a long list – accused him of imperiousness and a callous disregard for those of whom he disapproved. Certainly, when crossed, Assange could get very angry indeed, his mood changing as if a switch had been flicked. But in one way the OKCupid profile, last modified in 2006, proved in the end to be dizzyingly accurate. Four years later, in 2010, nobody would be left in any doubt that Assange really did mean, DANGER, ACHTUNG!

Julian was born on 3 July 1971 in Townsville, in the state of Queensland, in Australia's sub-tropical north. His mother Christine was the daughter of Warren Hawkins, described by colleagues as a rigid and traditionalist academic who became a college principal; the family settled in Australia from 19th-century Scotland. Julian's biological father is absent from much of the record: at 17, Christine abruptly left home, selling her paintings to buy a motorcycle, a tent and a map. Some 1,500 miles later she arrived in Sydney and joined its counter-culture scene. According to the book *Underground*, a revealing docu-novel to which Assange contributed, his mother worked as an artist and fell in love with a rebellious young man she met at an anti-Vietnam war demonstration in 1970. He fathered Julian. But the relationship ended and he would apparently play no further role in Assange's life for many years. They had no contact until after Assange turned 25.

His father was not forgotten, though. In 2006, at the start of Julian's remarkable mission to uncover secrets, he registered the wikileaks.org domain name under what is, according to court records, his biological father's identity – John Shipton. After the birth of her child, Christine moved as a single mother to Magnetic Island, a short ferry ride across the bay from Townsville. Magnetic Island was primitive and bohemian. Its small population included hippies who slept on beaches and in rock caves. The local kids would fish, swim, and play cricket with coconuts. There were koalas, possums, and giant clams. The Great Barrier Reef was nearby, and the islanders were eco-pioneers who grew their own vegetables and helped themselves to what was in the sea – fish, prawns, crabs and crayfish.

Assange's mother later recalled, "I rented an island cottage for $12 a week in Picnic Bay ... I lived in a bikini, 'going native' with my baby and other mums on the island." She married Brett Assange, an actor and theatre director. The surname apparently derives from Ah Sang, supposedly a 19th-century Chinese settler. Their touring lifestyle was the backdrop to Assange's early years. His stepfather staged and directed plays, according to *Underground*, and his mother did the make-up, costumes and set design. She was also a puppeteer.

In 2010, Assange described his stepfather's productions as good preparation for WikiLeaks, a mobile organisation that could be rolled out or packed up in a matter of hours – "something that my family did do when they were involved in the theatre and movie business which is go to locations, set it up, bring all your people, get it all together, get ready for the production launch and – bang – you go."

The adult Assange became a shape-shifter: frequently changing hairstyles, and dressing up in other people's clothes. One day he was an English country gentleman; the next an Icelandic fisherman; or an old woman. Even his role at WikiLeaks seemed unclear. Was he a leaker, a publisher, a journalist, or an activist? When the show was over he would move on.

The Assanges lived for some of the time in an abandoned pineapple farm on Horseshoe Bay. Christine recalled slashing her way to the front door with a machete. She also claimed to have shot a taipan – a deadly snake – in the water tank. Royce Dalliston, who still lives on Magnetic Island, recalls Christine used to swim and paint under the banyan trees. The other boys would steal waste cooking fat from hotels, and smear it on the roof of the jetty's sheds to go sliding into the bubbling swell whenever the ferry pulled in from Townsville. Dalliston and the bigger boys called Assange a "raspberry" because the "scrawny little blond-haired kid" seemed too scared to go jetty jumping. But Assange told the *New Yorker* profile writer Raffi Khatchadourian: "I had my own horse. I built my own raft. I went fishing. I was going down mine shafts and tunnels."

By 1979 Christine was again living close to her parents in Lismore, in New South Wales, where local farmers and the hippies co-existed in a state of mutual incomprehension. Nimbin – the scene of the Age of Aquarius, a 1973 hippy music festival – was just up the road. She had a long swirly skirt and drove a green Volkswagen Beetle. Local hippies successfully stopped the logging of one of the area's surviving virgin rainforests at Terania. It was the first victory for Australia's nascent eco-movement. Old footage from the march shows a young woman wearing dungarees trudging along a track, together with a group of bearded activists and guitar-strummers. She looks remarkably like Assange's mother.

Christine did not want her son to have a conventional Lismore schooling. Lismore was a traditional place, with women banned in the local club from leaving the carpet area, apart from on dance nights. Jennifer Somerville, whose children went to a small rural primary with Assange, recalls: "She was a little bit alternative, and she didn't believe in terribly formal education. She apparently decided that it would be best if Julian went to a little country school."

His two-year stint there was one of his most sustained periods of education; according to his own account, during his childhood he attended 37 different schools, emerging with no qualifications whatsoever. "Some people are really horrified and say: 'You poor thing, you went to all these schools.' But actually during this period I really liked it," Assange later said. Classmates at the school in the hamlet of Goolmangar remember a quiet but sociable boy. His exceptional intelligence and blond, shoulder-length hair marked him out.

One former classmate, Nigel Somerville, says there were "always puppets hanging out of his window ... His mum was very artistic. I had a kite she'd made for many years. It was very colour-ful and had big eyes on it with oranges and reds and blues." He and Julian would talk about crystal radios and experiment by pulling things apart. Amid the laid-back anti-establishment times, there were paranoid moments. In Adelaide, when Assange was four, his mother's car had been menacingly pulled over, having left a meeting of anti-nuclear protesters. The police officer told her: "You have a child out at two in the morning. I think you should get out of politics, lady."

Christine's marriage was now also running into problems. Brett Assange, who ran the puppet theatre with her, was a good and close stepfather. Assange would in later life often quote sayings "from my father" such as, "Capable, generous men do not create victims: they nurture them." Brett Assange would later describe his stepson as "a very sharp kid" with a "keen sense of right and wrong". But according to transcripts of a court hearing Brett was, at the time, "plagued with difficulties with alcohol". When Assange was seven or eight, his stepfather was removed from his life, when he and Christine divorced.

Assange's mother then became tempestuously involved with a third, much younger man, Keith Hamilton. Hamilton was an amateur musician and a member of a New Age group, the Santi-niketan Park Association. He was also, according to Assange, a manipulative psychopath. Hamilton allegedly had five different identities. "His whole background was a fabrication, right down to the country of his birth," Assange claimed in *Underground*. Despite its respectable-sounding name, The Santiniketan Park Association was a notorious cult presided over by Anne Hamilton-Byrne, a yoga teacher who convinced her middle-class followers she was a reincarnation of Jesus. Keith Hamilton was not only associated with the cult. He may even have been Hamilton-Byrne's son. Hamilton-Byrne and her helpers collected children, often persuading teenage mothers to hand over their babies. She and her disciples – "the aunties" – lived together in an isolated rural property surrounded by a barbed wire fence and overlooking a lake near the town of Eildon, Victoria. Here, they administered a bizarre regime over their charges, who at one point numbered 28 children. There were regular beatings. Children had their heads held down in buckets of water.

Assange's mother tried to leave Keith Hamilton in 1982, a court transcript reports, resulting in a custody battle for Assange's half-brother, Jamie. Hamilton was an abusive partner who "had been physically violent", court documents allege. Assange says Hamilton now pursued his mother, forcing her to flee repeatedly with her children. Assange told an Australian journalist in 2010: "My mother had become involved with a person who seems to be the son of Anne Hamilton-Byrne, of the Anne Hamilton-Byrne cult in Australia, and we kept getting tracked down, possibly because of leaks in the social security system, and having to leave very quickly to a new city, and lived under assumed names."

For the next five or six years, the three lived as fugitives. Christine travelled to Melbourne, then fled to Adelaide for six months, and on to Perth. As a teenager, Assange returned to Melbourne, living with his mother in at least four different refuges. The WikiLeaks founder was to act out this pattern of evasive action all over again in 2010, believing he was being pursued by US intelligence because of his WikiLeaks exposures.

Court files from the teenage Assange's eventual hacking trial in Melbourne – of which more later – document some of the effects of such a strange life on a gifted teenager with a strong aptitude for mathematics. His lawyer said Assange was deprived of the chance to make friends or associate normally with his peers. "His background is quite tragic in a way." *Underground* describes a "dead boring" Melbourne suburb: "merely a stopping point, one of dozens, as his mother shuttled her child around the continent trying to escape from a psychopathic former de facto [spouse]. The house was an emergency refuge for families on the run. It was safe and so, for a time ... his exhausted family stopped to rest before tearing off again in search of a new place to hide."

When Assange was 13 or 14, his mother had rented a house across the street from an electronics shop. Assange began going there and working on a Commodore 64. His mother saved to buy the computer for her older son as a present. Assange began teaching himself code. At 16 he got hold of his first modem. He attended a programme for gifted children in Melbourne, where he acquired "an introverted and emotionally disturbed" girlfriend, as he put it. Assange grew interested in science and roamed around libraries. Soon he discovered hacking. By the age of 17 he suspected Victoria police were about to raid his home. According to *Underground*: "He wiped his disks, burnt his print-outs, and left" to doss temporarily with his girlfriend. The pair joined a squatters' union, and when Assange was 18 she became pregnant. They married and had a baby boy, Daniel. But as Assange's anxiety increased, and police finally closed in on his outlaw circle of hackers, his wife moved out, taking their 20-month-old son Daniel with them. Assange was hospitalised with depression. For a period he slept outdoors, rambling around the eucalyptus forests in Dandenong Ranges national park.

*

Human relationships must have seemed unstructured for the teenage Assange, prone to abandonment, confusion and reversals. The world of computers, on the other hand, was predictable. Algorithms – the key to Assange's later skill as a cryptographer – were reliable. People were not. Assange would later tell the *New Yorker* the "austerity" of interaction with computers appealed to him. "It is like chess ... There is no randomness." During his 1996 hacking trial his defence lawyer, Paul Galbally, said in mitigation that his computer became "his only friend". As Assange shifted from school to school he was targeted by bullies as the outsider: "His only real saviour in life or his own bedrock in life was this computer. His mother, in fact, encouraged him to use this computer ... It had become an addictive instrument to him at a very early age." Galbally describes Assange as "super smart"; not a nerdy hacker but someone unusual and flamboyant.

Interestingly, some of the world's most talented programmers come from broken families. Jacob Appelbaum, who would become WikiLeaks' representative in the US, says he was the son of a paranoid schizophrenic mother and heroin addict father. He spent much of his boyhood in a children's home. As a boy, he discovered a woman convulsing in his father's bathroom with a needle sticking out of her arm. Appelbaum told *Rolling Stone* magazine that programming and hacking allowed him, however, "to feel like the world is not a lost place. The internet is the only reason I'm alive today."

Melbourne's hacking underground in the 1980s, in which Assange became prominent, was a small, almost entirely male group of self-taught teenagers. Many came from educated but poor suburban homes; all were of above average intelligence. They experimented on Commodore 64s, and the Apple IIe. They wrote code and used painfully slow modems. There was no internet yet, but there were computer networks and bulletin board systems, known as BBSs. In his "real" life Assange might have been considered a failure. He failed to complete his Higher School Certificate via a correspondence course. He also studied computers and physics inconclusively at an adult further education college.

But in his electronic life, Assange was a god. These geeky and socially awkward young men could reinvent themselves as swaggering heroes with names like Phoenix, Gandalf or Eric Bloodaxe. Assange used the pseudonym Mendax. Lewis and Short's Latin dictionary says that means "given to lying" – the root for the English word mendacious. But Assange was more specifically inspired by Horace's *Odes*. Assange's mother had enthusiastically introduced him to the Greek and Latin classics. In book III, xi, Horace tells the story of the 50 daughters of Danaus. Their father is angry that they are being forced to marry their cousins, the sons of Aegyptus. He makes them swear to kill their husbands on their wedding night. Forty-nine carry out his order, but the 50th, Hypermnestra, tips off her husband, Lynceus, and they escape. (In some versions they go on to found a dynasty.) For this Horace calls her *splendide mendax* or "splendidly deceiving". Another translation could be "deceitful with glory". The name was well picked. It evoked what the intensely ambitious Assange would do next, something both deceitful and glorious: hack into the US's military network.

Underground: tales of hacking, madness & obsession on the electronic frontier appeared in 1997. Published under the byline of Suelette Dreyfus, a Melbourne academic, Assange is credited as researcher, but his imprint his palpable – in parts it reads like an Assange biography. The book depicts the international computer underground of the 90s: "a veiled world populated by characters slipping in and out of the half-darkness. It is not a place where people use their real names." Assange chose an epigraph from Oscar Wilde: "Man is least himself when he talks in his own person. Give him a mask, and he will tell you the truth."

"Sometimes Mendax went to school," runs the story in *Underground*. "Often he didn't. The school system didn't hold much interest for him. It didn't feed his mind ... The Sydney computer system was a far more interesting place to muck around in than the rural high school."

In 1988, Assange (Mendax) is busy trying to break into Minerva, a system of mainframes in Sydney belonging to the government-owned Overseas Telecommunications Commission, or OTC. For the computer underground, hacking into OTC was a sort of rite of passage.

Mendax phones an OTC official in Perth posing as an operator from Sydney, *Underground* describes. To add authenticity, he records his home printer chattering in the background, and even mumbles passages from *Macbeth* to simulate office noise. The official innocently reveals his password – LURCH. Mendax is in! It is one of the dramatic moments in the book. In 2010, recalling his hacker exploits as a teenager, Assange said, "You were young. You hadn't done anything for criminal gain. You had done this for curiosity, challenge, and some activism. We hadn't destroyed anything. If you were a teenager in a suburb of Melbourne this was an incredibly intellectually liberating thing."

In 1989 Melbourne hackers carried out a spectacular stunt, launching a computer worm against Nasa's website. Bemused Nasa staff read the message: "Your system has been officially WANKed." The acronym stood for Worms Against Nuclear Killers. Was Assange behind WANK? Possibly. But his involvement was never proved. By 1991 Assange was probably Australia's most accomplished hacker. He and two others, using the names Prime Suspect and Trax, founded *International Subversives* magazine, offering tips on "phreaking" – how to break into telephone systems illegally and make free calls. The magazine had an exclusive readership: its circulation was just three, the hackers themselves.

Assange next set about hacking into the master terminal of Nortel, a big Canadian company that manufactured and sold telecommunications equipment. He also penetrated the US military-industrial complex, using his own sophisticated password-harvesting program, Sycophant. He hacked the US Airforce 7th Command Group Headquarters in the Pentagon, Stanford Research Institute in California, the Naval Surface War Center in Virginia, Lockheed Martin's Technical Aircraft Systems plant in California, and a host of other sensitive military institutions. In the spring of 1991, the three hackers found an exciting new target: MILNET, the US military's own secret defence data network. Pretty quickly, Assange discovered a back door. He got inside. "We had total control over it for two years," he later claimed. The hackers also routinely broke into the computer systems at Australia's National University.

But the Australian federal police's computer crime unit was on their trail. They tapped the hackers' phone lines and eventually raided Assange's home. He confessed to police what he had done. But it wasn't until 1994 that he was finally charged, with the case only being heard in 1996. He pleaded guilty in Melbourne's Victoria County Court to 24 counts of hacking. The prosecution described Assange as "the most active" and "most skilful" of the group, and pressed for a prison sentence. Assange's motive, according to the prosecution, was "simply an arrogance and a desire to show off his computer skills".

At one point Assange turned up with flowers for one of the prosecution lawyers, Andrea Pavleka (described in *Underground* as "tall, slender and long-legged, with a bob of sandy blonde curls, booky spectacles resting on a cute button nose and an infectious laugh"). It was a courtly gesture. Galbally felt obliged to point out to Assange: "She doesn't want to date you, Julian. She wants to put you in jail."

Judge Leslie Ross said he regarded Assange's offences as "quite serious". But there was no evidence to suggest he had sought personal gain. He was indeed a "looksee" rather than a malicious hacker, and had acted, the judge said, out of "intellectual inquisitiveness".

"I accept what your counsel said about the unstable personal background that you have had to endure during your formative years and the rather nomadic existence that your mother and yourself were forced to follow and the personal disruption that occurred within your household ... That could not have been easy for you. It has had its impact on you obtaining formal educational qualifications which it seems were certainly not beyond you, and the submission that you are a highly intelligent individual seems to be well founded."

The judge fined Assange $2,100. He warned him that if he carried on hacking he would indeed go to jail. Despite the fact the case was over, Assange got up to speak. The court transcript reads as follows:

PRISONER: Your Honour, I believe the prosecution has made several misleading claims in terms of the charges and therefore I elect to continue this defence if Your Honour would so let me.

HIS HONOUR: No, you have pleaded guilty, the proceedings are over. You would be well advised to come forward and sit down behind Mr Galbally.

PRISONER: Your Honour, I feel a great misjustice has been done and I would like to record the fact that you have been misled by the prosecution in terms of the charges of [*indistinct*] and a number of other matters.

HIS HONOUR: Mr Galbally, do you want to have a word with your client?

MR GALBALLY: Yes, Your Honour.

HIS HONOUR: Yes, go and have a word with him.

Assange considered himself the victim of a Solzhenitsyn-style injustice. A decade later, he would blog: "If there is a book whose feeling captures me it is *First Circle* by Solzhenitsyn. To feel that home is the camaraderie of persecuted, and in fact, prosecuted, polymaths in a Stalinist slave labour camp! How close the parallels to my own adventures! ... Such prosecution in youth is a defining peak experience. To know the state for what it really is! To see through that veneer the educated swear to disbelieve in but still slavishly follow with their hearts! ... Your belief in the mendacity of the state ... begins only with a jackboot at the door. True belief forms when led into the dock and referred to in the third person. True belief is when a distant voice booms 'the prisoner shall now rise' and no one else in the room stands."

Convicted but leniently treated, Assange was now an unemployed father in Melbourne surviving on a single parent pension. The family courts had given him sole custody of his son. Assange and his mother would spend years battling his former wife over access to Daniel; this developed into a bitter fight with the state over access to information in the case. Assange was also working unpaid as a computer programmer. He set up a site on the internet giving advice on computer security, called Best of Security. By 1996 it had 5,000 subscribers. Assange's early commitment to free information, and free software, would slowly evolve into WikiLeaks. In words that now seem prophetic, Galbally had told the judge in 1996: "He is clearly a person who wants the internet to provide material to people that isn't paid for, and he freely gives his services to that."

Assange co-authored several free software programs as part of what would become the open source movement. (They included the Usenet caching software NNTPCache, and Surfraw, a command-line interface for web-based search engines.) He and a couple of collaborators invented the Rubberhose deniable encryption system. The idea was quite simple: that human rights activists who faced torture could surrender a password to one layer of information. Their torturers would not realise another layer was beneath.

According to the Rubberhose website, Assange conceived the software after meeting human rights workers, and hearing tales of abuse from repressive regimes such as East Timor, Russia, Kosovo, Guatemala, Iraq, Sudan and the Democratic Republic of the Congo. The website gives a flavour of Assange's activist philosophy: "We hope that Rubberhouse will protect your data and offer a broader kind of protection for people who take risks for just causes ... Our motto is: 'Let's make a little trouble.'"

As early as 1999 he came up with the idea of a leakers' website, he says, and registered the domain name wikileaks.org. But otherwise he didn't do much about it. Assange was living in Melbourne and quietly raising his son. The custody battle over, it was probably the most stable period in his life. Daniel – today a computer programmer – went to Box Hill high school in Melbourne's eastern suburbs. Between 2003 and 2006 Julian studied physics and maths at Melbourne University as well as philosophy and neuroscience. He still didn't manage to graduate. But the WikiLeaks idea stayed with him.

Assange drafted on his bravely named blog, IQ.org, an apparently fanciful theory for overthrowing injustice in the world: "The more secretive or unjust an organisation is, the more leaks induce fear and paranoia in its leadership and planning coterie. This must result in minimisation of efficient internal communications mechanisms (an increase in cognitive 'secrecy tax') and consequent system-wide cognitive decline resulting in decreased ability to hold on to power ... Since unjust systems, by their nature, induce opponents, and in many places barely have the upper hand, mass leaking leaves them exquisitely vulnerable to those who seek to replace them with more open forms of governance. Only revealed injustice can be answered; for man to do anything intelligent he has to know what's actually going on."

Assange spoke of a high-flown calling: "If we can only live once, then let it be a daring adventure that draws on all our powers … The whole universe … is a worthy opponent, but try as I may I can not escape the sound of suffering … Men in their prime, if they have convictions, are tasked to act on them."

Those on his mailing list soon learned more detail. John Young, of the Cryptome intelligence-material site, was one of those asked (unsuccessfully) to "front" a new WikiLeaks organisation. Secrecy was built in, including the avoidance of the secret word itself: "This is a restricted internal development mailing list for w-i-k-i-l-e-a-k-s-.-o-r-g. Please do not mention that word directly in these discussions; refer instead to 'WL'." On 9 December 2006, an email signed "WL" also arrived out of the blue for Daniel Ellsberg, the whistleblower of Vietnam war renown. Assange boldly invited Ellsberg to become the public face of a project "to place a new star in the firmament of man". Governance "by conspiracy and fear" depended on concealment, Assange wrote. "We have come to the conclusion that fomenting a worldwide movement of mass leaking is the most cost effective political intervention." Ellsberg, who eventually became an enthusiastic supporter, originally feared it was "a very naive venture, to think that they can really get away with it".

In the new year, Assange went public for the first time. Canada's CBC News was one of the few who reported the news:

"Deep Throat may be moving to a new address – online. A new website that will use Wikipedia's open-editing format is hoping to become a place where whistleblowers can post documents without fear of being traced. WikiLeaks, according to the group's website, will be 'an uncensorable version of Wikipedia for untraceable mass document leaking and analysis. Our primary interests are oppressive regimes in Asia, the former Soviet bloc, sub-Saharan Africa and the Middle East, but we also expect to be of assistance to those in the west who wish to reveal unethical behaviour in their own governments and corporations,' the group said."

Most of the mainstream media (MSM), however, paid very little attention to this news. For hackers, who had long lamented the inadequacies of the MSM, that came as no surprise.

CHAPTER 4

The rise of WikiLeaks

Annual congress of the Chaos Computer Club,
Alexanderplatz, Berlin
December 2007

*"How do you reveal things about powerful people
without getting your arse kicked?"*
BEN LAURIE, ENCRYPTION EXPERT

Julian Assange can be seen on the conference video giving
an enthusiastic raised-fist salute. Alongside him stands a thin,
intense-looking figure. This is the German programmer Daniel
Domscheit-Berg, who has just met Assange at the 24th Chaos
Communication Congress, the European hackers' gathering, and
is about to become a key lieutenant. Domscheit-Berg eventually
gave up his full-time job with US computer giant EDS, and
devoted himself to perfecting WikiLeaks' technical architecture,
adopting the underground nom de guerre "Daniel Schmitt".

Domscheit-Berg's friendship with Assange was to end in bitter
recriminations, but the relationship marked a key step in the
Australian hacker's emergence from the chrysalis of his Melbourne
student milieu. "I heard about WikiLeaks in late 2007 from a
couple of friends," says Domscheit-Berg. "I started reading about

it a bit more. I started to understand the value of such a project to society."

The Chaos Computer Club is one of the biggest and oldest hacker groups in the world. One of its co-founders in 1981 was the visionary hacker Herwart "Wau" Holland-Moritz, whose friends set up the Wau Holland Foundation after his death. This charity was to become a crucial channel to receive worldwide WikiLeaks donations. Chaos Computer Club members at the Berlin congress such as Domscheit-Berg, along with his Dutch hacker colleague Rop Gonggrijp, had mature talents that proved to be crucial to the development of Assange's guerrilla project. (Assange himself nevertheless later tried to reject the hacker label. He told an Oxford conference that "hacking" has now come to be regarded as an activity "mostly deployed by the Russian mafia in order to steal your grandmother's bank accounts. So this phrase is not as nice as it used to be.")

Domscheit-Berg was fired up with social idealism, and preached the hacker mantra that information should be free: "What attitude do you have to society?" he would later exhort. "Do you look at what there is and do you accept that as god-given, or do you see society as something where you identify a problem and then you find a creative solution? ... Are you a spectator or are you actively participating in society?" He and Assange wanted to develop physical havens for WikiLeaks' servers across the globe. Domscheit-Berg whipped up his fellow hackers at Berlin, urging them to identify countries which could be used as WikiLeaks bases:

"A lot of the countries in today's world do not have really strong laws for the media any more. But a few countries, like for instance Belgium, the US with the first amendment, and especially for example Sweden, have very strong laws protecting the media and the work of investigative or general journalists. So ... if there are any Swedes here, you have to make sure your country [remains] one of the strongholds of freedom of information."

Sweden did eventually become the leakers' safe haven – ironically, in view of all Assange's subsequent trouble with Swedish manners and morals. The hackers in Berlin had links to the renegade Swedish file-sharing site The Pirate Bay. And from there the trail led to a web-hosting company called PRQ, which went on to provide WikiLeaks with an external face. The bearded owner of the internet service provider (ISP), Mikael Viborg, was later to demonstrate his operation, located in an inconspicuous basement in a Stockholm suburb, on Swedish TV. "At first they wanted to tunnel traffic through us to bypass bans in places where they don't like WikiLeaks." he says. "But later they put a server here."

PRQ offers its customers secrecy. They say their systems prevent anyone eavesdropping on chat pages, or finding out who sent what to whom.

"We provide anonymity services, VPN [virtual private network] tunnels. A client connects to our server and downloads information. If anyone at the information's source tries to trace them, they can only get to us – and we don't disclose who was using that IP [internet protocol] number. We accept anything that is legal under Swedish law, regardless of how objectionable it is. We don't make moral judgments."

This uncompromising attitude appealed to Domscheit-Berg: "PRQ has a track record of being the hardest ISP you can find in the world. There's just no one that bothers less about lawyers harassing them about content they're hosting."

WikiLeaks' own laptops all have military-grade encryption: if seized, the data on them cannot be read, even directly off the disk. The volunteer WikiLeaks hacker, Seattle-based Jacob Appelbaum, boasts that he will destroy any laptop that has been let out of his sight, for fear that it might have been bugged. None of the team worries deeply about the consequences of losing a computer, though, because the lines of code to control the site are stored on remote computers under their control –

"in the cloud" – and the passwords they need for access are in their heads.

Popular for day-by-day in-house conversations is the internet phone service Skype, which also uses encryption. Because it was developed in Sweden rather than the US, the team trusts it not to have a "back door" through which the US National Security Agency can peer in on their discussions.

As its name suggests, WikiLeaks began as a "wiki" – a user-editable site (which has sometimes led to confusion with the user-editable Wikipedia; there is no association). But Assange and his colleagues rapidly found that the content and need to remove dangerous or incriminating information made such a model impractical. Assange would come to revise his belief that online "citizen journalists" in their thousands would be prepared to scrutinise posted documents and discover whether they were genuine or not.

But while the "wiki" elements have been abandoned, a structure to enable anonymous submissions of leaked documents remains at the heart of the WikiLeaks idea. British encryption expert Ben Laurie was another who assisted. Laurie, a former mathematician who lives in west London and among other things rents out bomb-proof bunkers to house commercial internet servers, says when Assange first proposed his scheme for "an open-source, democratic intelligence agency", he thought it was "all hot air". But soon he was persuaded, became enthusiastic and advised on encryption. "This is an interesting technical problem: how do you reveal things about powerful people without getting your arse kicked?"

As it now stands, WikiLeaks claims to be uncensorable and untraceable. Documents can be leaked on a massive scale in a way which "combines the protection and anonymity of cutting-edge cryptographic technologies". Assange and co have said they use OpenSSL (an open source secure site connection system, like that used by online retailers such as Amazon), FreeNet (a peer-to-peer method of storing files among hundreds or thousands of computers without revealing where they originated or who owns them), and PGP (the open source cryptographic system abbreviated from the jocular name "Pretty Good Privacy").

But their main anonymity protection device is known as Tor. WikiLeaks advertises that "We keep no records as to where you uploaded from, your time zone, browser or even as to when your submission was made." That's a classic anonymisation via Tor.

US intelligence agencies see Tor as important to their covert spying work and have not been pleased to see it used to leak their own secrets. Tor means that submissions can be hidden, and internal discussions can take place out of sight of would-be monitors. Tor was a US Naval Research Laboratory project, developed in 1995, which has been taken up by hackers around the world. It uses a network of about 2,000 volunteer global computer servers, through which any message can be routed, anonymously and untraceably, via other Tor computers, and eventually to a receiver outside the network. The key concept is that an outsider is never able to link the sender and receiver by examining "packets" of data.

That's not usually the case with data sent online, where every message is split into "packets" containing information about its source, destination and other organising data (such as where the packet fits in the message). At the destination, the packets are reassembled. Anyone monitoring the sender or receiver's internet connection will see the receiver and source information, even if the content itself is encrypted. And for whistleblowers, that can be disastrous.

Tor introduces an uncrackable level of obfuscation. Say Appelbaum in Seattle wants to send a message to Domscheit-Berg in Berlin. Both men need to run the Tor program on their machines. Appelbaum might take the precaution of encrypting it first using the free-of-charge PGP system. Then he sends it via

Tor. The software creates a further encrypted channel routed through the Tor servers, using a few "nodes" among the world-wide network. The encryption is layered: as the message passes through the network, each node peels off a layer of encryption, which tells it which node to send the payload to next. Successive passes strip more encryption off until the message reaches the edge of the network, where it exits with as much encryption as the original – in this case, PGP-encrypted.

An external observer at any point in the network tapping the traffic that is flowing through it cannot decode what is being sent, and can only see one hop back and one hop forward. So monitoring the sender or receiver connections will only show a transmission going into or coming out of a Tor node – but nothing more. This "onion" style encryption, with layer after layer, gave rise to the original name, "The Onion Router" – shortened to Tor.

Tor also allows users to set up "hidden services", such as instant messaging, that can't be seen by tapping traffic at the servers. They're accessed, appropriately, via pseudo-top-level domains ending in ".onion". That provides another measure of security, so that someone who has sent a physical version of an electronic record, say on a thumb drive, can encrypt it and send it on, and only later reveal the encryption key. The Jabber encrypted chat service is popular with WikiLeakers.

"Tor's importance to WikiLeaks cannot be overstated," Assange told *Rolling Stone*, when they profiled Appelbaum, his west coast US hacker associate. But Tor has an interesting weakness. If a message isn't specially encrypted from the outset, then its actual contents can sometimes be read by other people. This may sound like an obscure technical point. But there is evidence that it explains the true reason for the launch of WikiLeaks at the end of 2006 – not as a traditional journalistic enterprise, but as a piece of opportunistic underground computer hacking. In other words: eavesdropping.

On the verge of his debut WikiLeaks publication, at the beginning of 2007, Assange excitedly messaged the veteran curator of the Cryptome leaking site, John Young, to explain where his trove of material was coming from:

"Hackers monitor chinese and other intel as they burrow into their targets, when they pull, so do we. Inexhaustible supply of material. Near 100,000 documents/emails a day. We're going to crack the world open and let it flower into something new ...We have all of pre 2005 afghanistan. Almost all of india fed. Half a dozen foreign ministries. Dozens of political parties and consulates, worldbank, opec, UN sections, trade groups, tibet and falun dafa associations and ... russian phishing mafia who pull data everywhere. We're drowning. We don't even know a tenth of what we have or who it belongs to. We stopped storing it at 1Tb [one terabyte, or 1,000 gigabytes]."

A few weeks later, in August 2007, a Swedish Tor expert, Dan Egerstad, told *Wired* magazine that he had confirmed it was possible to harvest documents, email contents, user names and passwords for various diplomats and organisations by operating a volunteer Tor "exit" node. This was the final server at the edge of the Tor system through which documents without end-to-end encryption were bounced before emerging. The magazine reported that Egerstad "found accounts belonging to the foreign ministry of Iran, the UK's visa office in Nepal and the Defence Research and Development Organisation in India's Ministry of Defence. In addition, Egerstad was able to read correspondence belonging to the Indian ambassador to China, various politicians in Hong Kong, workers in the Dalai Lama's liaison office and several human rights groups in Hong Kong. "It kind of shocked me," he said. "I am absolutely positive that I am not the only one to figure this out."

The speculation was largely confirmed in 2010, when Assange gave Raffi Khatchadourian access to write a profile. The *New*

Yorker staffer wrote: "One of the WikiLeaks activists owned a server that was being used as a node for the Tor network. Millions of secret transmissions passed through it. The activist noticed that hackers from China were using the network to gather foreign governments' information, and began to record this traffic. Only a small fraction has ever been posted on WikiLeaks, but the initial tranche served as the site's foundation, and Assange was able to say, 'We have received over one million documents from 13 countries.' In December, 2006, WikiLeaks posted its first document: a 'secret decision', signed by Sheikh Hassan Dahir Aweys, a Somali rebel leader for the Islamic Courts Union, that had been culled from traffic passing through the Tor network to China."

The geeky hacker underground was only one part of the soil out of which WikiLeaks grew. Another was the anti-capitalist radicals – the community of environmental activists, human rights campaigners and political revolutionaries who make up what used to be known in the 1960s as the "counter-culture". As Assange went public for the first time about WikiLeaks, he travelled to Nairobi in Kenya to set out their stall at the World Social Forum in January 2007. This was a radical parody of the World Economic Forum at Davos, Switzerland, where rich and influential people gather to talk about money. The WSF, which originated in Brazil, was intended, by contrast, to be where poor and powerless people would gather to talk about justice.

At the event, tens of thousands in Nairobi's Freedom Park chanted, "Another world is possible!" Organisers were forced to waive entry fees after Nairobi slum dwellers staged a demonstration. The BBC reported that dozens of street children who had been begging for food invaded a five-star hotel tent and feasted on meals meant for sale at $7 a plate when many Kenyans lived on $2 a day: "The hungry urchins were joined by other participants who complained that the food was too expensive and police, caught unawares, were unable to stop the free-for-all that saw the food containers swept clean."

Assange himself spent four days in a WSF tent with his three friends, giving talks, handing out flyers and making connections. He was so exhilarated by what he called "the world's biggest NGO beach party" that he stayed on for much of the next two years in a Nairobi compound with activists from Médecins Sans Frontières and other foreign groups.

"I was introduced to senior people in journalism, in human rights very quickly," he told an Australian interviewer later. "[Kenya] has got extraordinary opportunities for reforms. It had a revolution in the 1970s. It has only been a democracy since 2004." He wrote that he met in Africa "many committed and courageous individuals – banned opposition groups, corruption investigators, unions, fearless press and clergy". These brave people seemed like the real deal to him: his mail-out contrasted them witheringly with western fellow-travellers. "A substantial portion of Social Forum types are ineffectual pansies who specialise in making movies about themselves and throwing 'dialogue' parties for their friends with foundation money. They ... love cameras."

Assange cast himself in contrast to these people, as a man of courage. He invoked one of his personal heroes in that WikiLeaks mail-out: "This quote from Solzhenitsyn is increasingly germane: 'A decline in courage may be the most striking feature that an outside observer notices in the west today. The western world has lost its civic courage ... Such a decline in courage is particularly noticeable among the ruling and intellectual elites.'" Assange would often pronounce to those around him: "Courage is infectious."

It was Kenya that gave WikiLeaks its first journalistic coup. A massive report about the alleged corruption of former president Daniel Arap Moi had been commissioned from the private inquiry firm Kroll. But his successor, President Mwai Kibaki, who commissioned the report, subsequently failed to release it, allegedly for political reasons. "This report was the holy grail of Kenyan journalism," Assange later said. "I went there in 2007 and got hold of it."

The actual circumstances of publication were more complex. The report was leaked to Mwalimu Mati, head of Mars Group Kenya, an anti-corruption group. "Someone dumped it in our laps," he says. Mati, prompted by a contact in Germany, had previously registered as a volunteer with WikiLeaks. The fear of retribution made it too dangerous to post the report on the group's own website: "So we thought: can we not put it on WikiLeaks?" The story appeared simultaneously on 31 August on the front page of the *Guardian* in London. The full text of the document was posted on WikiLeaks' website headed, "The missing Kenyan billions". A press release explained, "WikiLeaks has not yet publicly 'launched'. We are open only to submissions from journalistic and dissident contacts. However, given the political situation in Kenya we feel we would be remiss to withhold this document any longer." The site added: "Attribution should be to ... 'Julian A, WikiLeaks' spokesman'."

The result was indeed sensational. There was uproar, and Assange was later to claim that voting shifted 10% in the subsequent Kenyan elections. The following year, his site ran a highly praised report on Kenyan death squads, "The Cry of Blood – Extra-Judicial Killings and Disappearances". It was based on evidence obtained by the Kenyan National Commission on Human Rights. Four people associated with investigating the killings were themselves subsequently murdered, including human rights activists Oscar Kingara and John Paul Oulu.

Assange was invited to London to receive an award from the human rights organisation Amnesty: it was a moment of journalistic respectability. Characteristically, he arrived in town three hours late after a convoluted series of flights from Nairobi which involved withholding his passport details from the authorities until the last minute. His acceptance speech was generous, if a little grandiose: "Through the courageous work of organisations such as the Oscar foundation, the KNHCR [Kenya National Commission on Human Rights], Mars Group Kenya and others we had the primary support we needed to expose these murders to the world. I know that they will not rest, and we will not rest, until justice is done." Again, there was a symbiotic relationship with the MSM, the mainstream media: the Kenyan story only gained global traction when followed up by Jon Swain of the London *Sunday Times*.

A coda to the Kenya episode left a bad taste. In March 2009, journalist Michela Wrong published a book on corruption in the east African nation, called *It's Our Turn to Eat*, which took her three years to write. Nairobi bookshops proved nervous about stocking it, but she was startled to find a pirated copy posted worldwide on WikiLeaks without consultation. "This was a violation of copyright, involving a commercial publication, a book not banned by any African government, not a secret document. It left me feeling pretty jaundiced."

She wrote protesting: "I was delighted when WikiLeaks was launched, and benefited personally from its fearlessness in publishing leaked documents exposing venality in countries like Kenya. This strikes me as a totally different case." In what she terms a "gratingly self-righteous" reply, WikiLeaks, who eventually agreed to take the book down, wrote: "We are not treating document as a leak; it has been treated as a censored work that must be injected into the Kenyan political sphere. We thought you ... had leaked the PDF for promotional reasons. That said, the importance of the work in Kenya as an instrument of political struggle eclipses your individual involvement. It is your baby, and I'm sure it feels like that, but it is also its own adult – and Kenya's son."

*

Assange and his group were by now starting to see a flow of genuinely leaked documents, including some from UK military sources. Assange sought to market them. He wrote several times to the *Guardian*, calling himself the "editor" or the "investigative editor" of WikiLeaks, trying to get the paper's editor, Alan Rusbridger, to take up his stories. He seemed unable to accept that sometimes his leaks might just not be that interesting – no, the lack of response was always due to a failure of nerve, or worse, on the part of the despised MSM.

In July 2008, for instance, he declared: "[Have] the *Guardian* and other UK press outlets lost their civic courage when dealing with the Official Secrets Act?" He was offering the media access to a leaked copy of the 2007 UK counter-insurgency manual, but no one had signed up to his proffered "embargo pool": "I suggest the UK press has lost its way … Provided all are equally emasculated, all are equally profitable. It is time to break this cartel of timidity."

Those who recalled his Melbourne dating-site entry would have been intrigued by his remark that running combative journalistic exposures as he did was also, in fact, an excellent way to get laid: "In Kenya, where we are used to newspaper raids and manageable arrests, we don't care too much. These hamfisted attempts drive home the story that ignited them, sell newspapers, look good on the CV, and attract lovers like knighthoods."

A further Assange experiment in media manipulation in 2008 saw him try to auction a cache of what were claimed to be thousands of emails from a speechwriter to Venezuelan leader Hugo Chávez. The winning bidder was to get exclusive access, for a time, to the documents. The auction was based on his theory that nobody took material seriously if it was provided free of charge. He pointed out: "*People* magazine notoriously paid over $10 [million] for Brad Pitt and Angelina Jolie's baby photos." Bafflingly, the minutiae of Venezuelan politics did not prove as saleable as celebrities' baby pics: nobody bid.

Assange had by now discovered, to his chagrin, that simply posting long lists of raw and random documents on to a website failed to change the world. He brooded about the collapse of his original "crowd-sourcing" notion: "Our initial idea was, 'Look at all those people editing Wikipedia. Look at all the junk that they're working on ... Surely all those people that are busy working on articles about history and mathematics and so on, and all those bloggers that are busy pontificating about ... human rights disasters ... surely *those* people will step forward, given fresh source material, and do something?' No. It's all bullshit. It's *all* bullshit. In fact, people write about things, in general (if it's not part of their career), because they want to display their values to their peers, who are already in the same group. Actually, they don't give a fuck about the material."

He carried on hunting vainly for a WikiLeaks model that could both bring in working revenue and gain global political attention. His published musings from that period are revealing: they show he saw the problem from the outside, but could not yet crack it:

"The big issue for WikiLeaks is first-rate source material going to waste, because we make supply unlimited, so news organisations, wrongly or rightly, refuse to 'invest' in analysis without additional incentives. The economics are counter-intuitive – temporarily restrict supply to increase uptake ... a known paradox in economics. Given that WikiLeaks needs to restrict supply for a period to increase perceived value to the point that journalists will invest time to produce quality stories, the question arises as to which method should be employed to apportion material to those who are most likely to invest in it."

There was only one, relatively limited, way in which the Assange model was beginning to gain the interest of the mainstream media: and that was by behaving not as the originally envisaged anonymous document dump, but as what he called "the publisher of last resort". A fascinating clash between WikiLeaks and a Swiss bank demonstrated that at least one of the key claims for Assange's new stateless cyberstructure was true – it could laugh at lawyers.

Rudolf Elmer ran the Cayman Islands branch of the Julius Baer bank for eight years. After moving to Mauritius, and vainly trying to interest authorities in what he said was outrageous tax-dodging by some of his former employer's clients, he contacted Assange to post his documents: "We built up contact over encrypted software and I received instructions on how to proceed … I wasn't looking for anonymity."

The fuming Zurich bankers then went to court in California to force WikiLeaks to take down the files, claiming "unlawful dissemination of stolen bank records and personal account information of its customers". The bank won a preliminary skirmish when California-based domain name hosters Dynadot were ordered to disable access to the name "wikileaks.org". But Baer very quickly lost the entire war: WikiLeaks retained access to other sites hosted in Belgium and elsewhere; many "mirror sites" sprang up carrying the offending documents; and the court ruling was reversed as a stream of US organisations rallied behind WikiLeaks in the name of free speech. They included the American Civil Liberties Union and the Electronic Frontier Foundation, as well as a journalistic alliance which included the Associated Press, Gannett News Service, and the *Los Angeles Times*.

The Swiss bank and its corrupt customers merely managed to shine more light on themselves, while WikiLeaks demonstrated that it was genuinely injunction-proof. It was WikiLeaks one, Julius Baer nil. Assange picked up another award in London from the free speech group Index on Censorship. One of the judges, poet Lemn Sissay, blogged about a typical piece of showmanship: "We did not know whether Julian Assange … was to turn up to accept. Thankfully he came, a tall, studious man with shock-blonde hair and pale skin. Seconds before stepping on stage he whispered, 'Someone may lunge at the stage to present me with a subpoena. I cannot allow them to do this, and shall leave if I see them.'"

The *Guardian* in London now saw the value in having its own sensitive documents posted on WikiLeaks. Lawyers for Barclays Bank had woken up a judge one morning at 2am to force the takedown of the *Guardian*'s leaked files detailing the bank's tax-avoidance schemes. But the files were promptly posted in full by Assange, rendering the gag futile. (In an entertaining blend of old and new anti-censorship techniques, the *Guardian* and all other British media were also at first legally gagged from saying that the files were available on WikiLeaks. It took a Liberal Democrat member of the House of Lords, speaking under the ancient device of parliamentary privilege, to blow that nonsense away.)

Similarly, WikiLeaks functioned as an online back-up, along with Dutch Greenpeace and Norwegian state TV, in posting in full a damning report on toxic waste dumped by the oil traders Trafigura. Trafigura's lawyers had gagged the *Guardian* in the UK from running the leaked report: their draconian moves were thus proved to be a waste of time in a digitally globalised world.

Yet Assange himself was still striving for a way to be more than a niche player. At the outset, in 2006, he had incurred the ire of John Young, of the parallel intelligence-material site Cryptome. Young deplored Assange's approaches to billionaire George Soros, who funded a variety of mostly eastern European media projects, and he broke off relations angrily when Assange talked of raising $5 million. "Announcing a $5 million fund-raising goal by July [2007] will kill this effort," he wrote. "It makes WikiLeaks appear to be a Wall Street scam. This amount could not be needed so soon except for suspect purposes. Soros will kick you out of the office with such over-reaching. Foundations are flooded with big talkers making big requests flaunting famous names and promising spectacular results."

Now, two years on from that false start, Assange made another attempt to raise a substantial sum. He and his lieutenant, Domscheit-Berg, approached the Knight Foundation in the US, which was running "a media innovation contest that aims to advance the future of news by funding new ways to digitally inform communities". Domscheit-Berg asked for $532,000 to equip a network of regional newspapers with what were, in effect, "WikiLeaks buttons". The idea, developed and elaborated by Domscheit-Berg, was that local leakers could make contact through these news sites, and thus generate a regular flow of documents. A rival project, Documentcloud, designed to set up a public database of the full documents behind conventional news stories, was backed by staff at the *New York Times* and the non-profit investigative journalism initiative ProPublica. They got $719,500. Assange got nothing. As 2009 ended, WikiLeaks was still struggling to make a name for itself.

CHAPTER 5

The Apache video

Quality Hotel, Tønsberg, Norway
3am, 21 March 2010

"It's their fault for bringing their kids into a battle"
US HELICOPTER PILOT

Even in March, there was still ice in the harbour, and snow lay on the Slottsfjellet hill where the old fortress stood. But down in the waterfront hotel ballroom, the Boogie Wonder Band were hard at it: they were pumping out sweaty dance rhythms for hundreds of Norwegian reporters celebrating the Jubileumsfest – the 20th anniversary shindig of SKUP, the lively association of investigative journalists. "Bring nice clothes and good humour," said the invitation; and although Assange had not changed out of his regular brown leather jacket zipped up to the neck, he was certainly in a good mood. In fact, he was excited, and with good reason: he was about to take the first step towards becoming a world celebrity.

The billing for his lecture read, "Some believe the WikiLeaks site has done more investigative journalism than the *New York Times* over the past 20 years." But Assange knew that the world had seen nothing yet, compared with what was about to come. After a night of reindeer steaks and repeated Viking-style toasts with raised glasses, he could contain himself no longer. "Want to see something?" he asked David Leigh, the *Guardian* journalist who was also speaking at the conference. Assange, with his lean frame and long silver hair, had a boyishly enticing grin that had already been having its effect on nearby women: his present invitation was also intriguing.

Up in Leigh's hotel bedroom, with the door locked and the chain on, Assange produced one of his little netbooks from the backpack he never let out of his sight. He punched in a series of what seemed like lengthy passwords, and after a while a black-and-white video began to run. It was one of the most shocking things Leigh had ever seen.

The money shot, later played again and again on YouTube from China to Brazil, was a view from the air: it showed clouds of dust erupting among a scattering group of men, as they were knocked down and killed by the cannon-shells of a helicopter gunship. One man, wounded, was trying to crawl away from the carnage off to the right of the screen. Later a driver can be seen trying to drag the wounded man into a van, which is shot up by more cannon-fire. Told on the radio traffic that children were hurt, a pilot transmits, defensively: "Well, it's their fault for bringing their kids into a battle."

The pictures had been taken by an AH-64 Apache's military camera as it hovered over a Baghdad suburb, firing its 30mm gun while virtually invisible to those on the ground. The helicopter was a kilometre up in the sky. Leigh watched, stunned, as the uncut video of these killings ran on the little laptop for nearly 39 minutes.

The video was, explained Assange, the classified record of a scandal. In July 2007, US army pilots, in a pair of circling helicopters, had managed to kill two innocent employees of the Reuters news agency: Saeed Chmagh and Namir Noor-Eldeen. Noor-Eldeen was a 22-year-old war photographer. Chmagh was a 40-year-old Reuters driver and assistant, who had been wounded and attempted to crawl away. Altogether 12 people died in that single encounter. The van driver's two young children were wounded, but survived.

Assange didn't say where the raw video had come from, other than that he had got hold of a cache of material from "military sources". But he did tell the *Guardian* journalist what he planned to do next. He was going to travel to Iceland, where he would arrange for this sensational leak to be verified and edited up into a properly captioned version. Then he would reveal it to the world.

Iceland, in the far north Atlantic, was not so weird a destination for Assange as might be thought. The nomadic WikiLeaks founder had recently become popular there, since agreeing to post a leaked secret document listing major Icelandic bank loans which had been made to bankers' cronies, and the bank's own large shareholders. Iceland's financial meltdown had left an angry and resentful populace behind, and they seemed to appreciate Assange's brand of transparency.

Kristinn Hrafnsson was one of many Icelanders impressed by Assange. He was so inspired that he subsequently became his close lieutenant. Hrafnsson, who was to travel to Baghdad with a cameraman to check out the Apache helicopter story on Assange's behalf, says: "The first I heard of WikiLeaks was at the beginning of August 2009. I was working as a reporter for state television when I got a tip this website had important documents just posted online. It was the loan book for the failed Kaupthing Bank ... They [the bank] got a gag order on the state TV – the first and only one in its history."

The scandal brought an invitation to Reykjavik for Assange and his colleague Daniel Domscheit-Berg, and the two campaigners found themselves urging the small country to promote its own free speech laws. Assange sat on the TV studio sofa and declared: "Why doesn't Iceland become the centre for publishing in the world?" Domscheit-Berg recalls: "Julian and I were just throwing that idea out, declaring on national TV that we thought this would be the next business model for Iceland. That felt pretty weird ... realising the next day that everyone wanted to talk about it."

Assange was like a pied piper, gathering followers around him in region after region. Another Iceland-based WikiLeaks enthusiast, programmer Smári McCarthy, told Swedish TV, "We had failed as a country because we had not been sharing the information that we needed. We were in an information famine ... WikiLeaks gave us the nudge that we needed. We had this idea but didn't know what to do with it. Then they came and told us, and that is an incredibly valuable thing. They are information activists first and foremost, who believe in the power of knowledge, the power of information."

An Icelandic MP, Birgitta Jónsdóttir, was at the forefront of subsequent moves to draw up a proposal the campaigners called MMI, the Modern Media Initiative, which was endorsed unanimously by the Icelandic parliament. The proposal was stitched together by Assange, his Dutch hacker-businessman friend Rop Gonggrijp, and three Icelanders: Jónsdóttir, McCarthy and Herbert Snorrason. They called for laws to enshrine source protection, free speech and freedom of information. Jónsdóttir, 43, is an anti-capitalist activist, poet and artist – an unexpectedly romantic figure to find in the Reykjavik legislature. "They were presenting this idea they called the 'Switzerland of bytes'," she explains, "which was basically to take the tax haven model and transform it into the transparency haven model."

Assange decided to publish some Icelandic tidbits from his newly acquired secret cache of military material to coincide with the MMI campaign: one was a very recent cable from the US embassy in Reykjavik, dated 13 January 2010, describing Icelandic officials' views about the banking crisis. The deputy chief of mission at the embassy, Sam Watson, had reported that those he met "painted a very gloomy picture for Iceland's future". Assange followed this up with leaked profiles of the Icelandic ambassador to Washington ("prickly but pragmatic ... enjoys the music of Robert Plant, formerly of Led Zeppelin"), the foreign minister ("fond of the US"), and the prime minister, Jóhanna Sigurðardóttir ("although her sexual orientation has been highlighted by the international press, it has barely been noted by the Icelandic public").

The US authorities took no visible action about these leaks. There was nothing apparently to connect Reykjavik, where this stuff was coming out, with an obscure military base in the Mesopotamian desert, thousands of miles away.

So at the end of March, Assange returned to Iceland from his triumphant conference appearance in Norway, and, bankrolled by an advance of €10,000 ($13,000) from Gonggrijp, set about renting a house and editing his Apache helicopter film. Leigh, back in London, tried hard to get back into contact to propose a deal under which the *Guardian* would publicise the helicopter video. Assange said he would get back to him, but never did. It was only later that it seemed Assange might have struck a more attractive journalistic deal with the *New Yorker*, whose writer Raffi Khatchadourian was following Assange about for a major profile. (It appeared in June under the title "No Secrets: Julian Assange's mission for total transparency". Assange assured friends later that it was "too flattering".)

Khatchadourian was present to record Jónsdóttir, the feisty feminist MP for Reykjavik South, rather unwillingly trimming Assange's hair while he sat hunched over his laptop, engaged in important messaging. The profile writer was also taking notes when the message came back from Baghdad:

> The journalists who had gone to Baghdad ... had found the two children in the van. The children had lived a block from the location of the attack, and were being driven to school by their father that morning. "They remember the bombardment,

felt great pain, they said, and lost consciousness," one of the
journalists wrote …

Jónsdóttir turned to Gonggrijp, whose eyes had welled
up. "Are you crying?" she asked.

"I am," he said. "OK, OK, it is just the kids. It hurts."
Gonggrijp gathered himself. "Fuck!" he said … Jónsdóttir
was now in tears, too, and wiping her nose.

Assange premiered the Apache helicopter video at the National
Press Club in Washington on 5 April. He chose to title it "Collateral Murder". Although the video caused a stir, something went
wrong. It did not generate the universal outrage and pressure for
reform of, say, Seymour Hersh's earlier exposé of leaked photos in
the *New Yorker* showing Iraqi prisoners being humiliated and
tortured in Abu Ghraib prison.

One of the reasons why the video caused less of a storm than he
had hoped was that Reuters, whose own employees had been killed,
chose not to go on the attack over the leaked information. They
had, it transpired, been shown privately a partial clip of the two
men's deaths, within days of it happening, although subsequent
freedom of information requests for the actual video had been
repeatedly blocked. Reuters' editor-in-chief, David Schlesinger,
wrote a muted, more-in-sorrow column for the *Guardian*:

"Reuters editors were shown only one portion of the video. We
immediately changed our operating procedures. The first portion of
the video made clear that anyone walking with a group of armed
people could be considered a target. We immediately made it a
rule that our journalists could not even walk near armed groups.
However, we were not shown the second part of the video, where
the helicopter fired on a van trying to evacuate the wounded. Had
we seen it, we could have adjusted our procedures further."

Another reason for the limited response was the tendentious
title: "Collateral Murder". Readers and viewers often hate the

feeling they are being bulldozed into a particular point of view. What went on in the video could be interpreted as a much more nuanced event, to eyes not entirely blinded by rage or sorrow.

For the soldiers had clearly made a mistake. Some of the group they fired on were indeed armed, and the Reuters cameraman's long lens did look like a weapon pointed furtively at "our brothers on the ground" as one of the pilots put it. The cruel decision to treat the Baghdad streets as a battle-space on which all were fair game was made not by individual sadists or war criminals, but by the US military at a much higher level. The pilots were doing the murderous things they had been trained to do – as some soldiers in the ground unit concerned were later to publicly say. Clearly there was far more to be debated than could be encompassed in the crude legend "Collateral Murder".

Nevertheless, it was a debate that might never have been held at all, had not one young US soldier somewhere decided the video ought to be seen, and had not Assange boldly put it on public display. From now on, the civilian death that American soldiers so often rained down from the sky would be treated a little less casually by the US public. This was surely what free speech was meant to be all about. In many people's eyes, Assange deserved to be seen as a hero.

CHAPTER 6
The Lamo dialogues

Contingency Operating Station Hammer, Iraq
21 May 2010

"I can't believe what I'm telling you"
BRADASS87

At his sweltering army base in the Iraqi desert, specialist Bradley Manning showed signs of considerable stress in the weeks following Assange's release of the Apache helicopter video. In web chats, he confided that he had had "about three breakdowns" as a result of his emotional insecurity, and was "self-medicating like crazy". He added: "I've been isolated for so long ... I've totally lost my mind ... I'm a wreck." On 5 May, Manning posted on Facebook that he was "left with the sinking feeling that he doesn't have anything left".

Part of this emotional turmoil was probably related to the break-up of Manning's relationship with Tyler Watkins back in Boston, and part to his feeling he was in the wrong gender. But he was also feeling scared about the possible fall-out from his "hacktivist" activities with WikiLeaks. At one point he boasted that "No one suspected a thing ... Odds are, they never will." But at others he contemplated going to prison for the rest of his life, or even the death penalty.

"I've made a huge mess ... I think I'm in more potential heat than you ever were," he would confide online to Adrian Lamo, a hacker in the US who himself had been sentenced to two years' probation for having hacked into computers in a range of enterprises including the *New York Times*. The combination of losing Watkins and feeling under threat of discovery by the authorities had clearly left Manning feeling rattled. Days before he began unburdening to Lamo over the internet, he was demoted from the rank of specialist to that of private first class, after he punched another soldier in the face.

Julian Assange had recently publicised, in rapid succession, four leaked classified files he had laid his hands on, all of different types, but all accessible to a member of the US army in Manning's position. At some point between mid-January and mid-February, Assange received a copy of the cable from the Reykjavik embassy, which he published to good effect during his Iceland media campaign. Posted on 18 February, it was later described by Manning as a "test".

On 15 March, Assange next posted a lengthy report about WikiLeaks itself, written by an army "cyber counter intelligence analyst" and headlined by Assange "US intelligence planned to destroy WikiLeaks". The "special report" dated from 2008 and its author was exercised about lists of military equipment WikiLeaks had managed to obtain. Despite its 32 pages, the report was really a statement of the obvious: that a good way to deter WikiLeaks would be to track down and punish the leakers. But Assange's bold headline was a sound journalistic method of advertising and attracting donations.

Two weeks later, on 29 March, Assange caused more turbulence in Iceland by posting the series of US state department profiles of top local politicians: they appeared to have been taken from a separate biographical intelligence folder, rather than from a cabled dispatch. Icelandic officials called in the US charge d'affaires, Sam Watson, to make a complaint.

Just one week on, Assange flew from Reykjavik to Washington to publicise the Apache video. It appeared from what Manning said subsequently that he had done detective work on the video and leaked it in February after finding it in a legal dossier, a Judge-Advocate-General (JAG) file, presumably because the Reuters employees' deaths led to a formal investigation at the time.

These four leaks were, of course, only hors d'oeuvres. Assange had also acquired a whole banquet of data: a file on Guantánamo inmates; a huge batch of US army "significant activities" reports detailing the ongoing Afghan war; a similar set of logs from the occupation of Iraq; and – most sensational of all – following the successful "test" with the Reykjavik cable leak, Manning had, it was later alleged, managed to supply Assange with a second entire trove of all 250,000 cables to be found in the "Net-Centric Diplomacy" database to which his security clearance gave the young soldier access.

Although the precautions practised by Manning and Assange had apparently worked well to date, it was perhaps no wonder that Manning felt exposed.

The process in which he first reached out to, and gained confidence in, Assange had been slow and painstaking, according to the later published extracts from what were said to be his chat logs. Neither he nor his lawyers have disputed their authenticity. The geeky young soldier seems to have first contacted the "crazy white-haired dude" in late November 2009, but tentatively so. He needed to be certain that WikiLeaks could be trusted to receive dynamite material without his own identity becoming known.

For a while he remained uncertain even about the person with whom he was communicating. He was in contact with a computer user claiming to be Assange, but was it really him? Sitting at his workstation in the Iraqi desert, how could Manning be sure? It took him four months to acquire that certainty. In his exchanges with Assange, he asked the Australian for details about how he was being followed by US state department officials. He then checked that information against what Assange was quoted as saying in the press, and the two precisely correlated. He also used his own security clearance to check up on the activities of the Northern Europe Diplomatic Security Team, the intelligence body that was most likely to have been doing the surveillance, and found that, too, correlated with Assange's description.

Manning's test with the Reykjavik cable dummy run would have confirmed not only that they could communicate safely, but also Assange's ability to publish what he sent. With mounting confidence, Manning could press ahead with the big stuff.

What precisely were the transactions between the two men? By his own admission to Lamo, Manning "developed a relationship with Assange ... but I don't know much more than what he tells me, which is very little". In interviews, Lamo has gone further, claiming that Manning told him he used an encrypted internet conferencing service to communicate directly with Assange, and that though they never met in person Assange actively "coached" Manning as to what kind of data he should transmit and how. Those claims have only come from Lamo, and have never been substantiated by supporting evidence.

What seems more certain is that some form of secure connection was created chiefly, or perhaps exclusively, for Manning, allowing him to pipe secret documents and videos directly to WikiLeaks. In his exchanges with Lamo, Manning described his technique. He would take a file of material, having scraped it out of the military system somehow, and encrypt it using the AES-256 (Advanced Encryption Standard, with a key size of 256 bits) cipher, considered one of the most secure methods.

He would then send the encrypted material via a secure FTP (file transfer protocol) to a server at a particular internet address. Finally, the encryption passcode that Manning devised would be sent separately, via Tor, making it very hard for any surveillance authorities to know where the information began its journey.

Matt Blaze, an associate professor in computer science at the University of Pennsylvania and an expert in cryptology, says the system believed to have been constructed by Manning was a pretty straightforward technique for secure transmission. "From a computer security point of view straightforward ways are usually pretty good. Complex ways are liable to go wrong."

Kevin Poulsen, the senior editor at *Wired* who published a partial version of the Lamo web chat – and himself a notorious former hacker – points out that the passage in the conversation in which Manning describes the transmission technique is hypothetical. Manning's response is to a hypothetical question from Lamo: "how would I transmit something if I had damning data?" But if Manning was indeed describing the way he passed documents to WikiLeaks then it was very significant. "It goes way, way beyond the usual WikiLeaks method of uploading material to its website," Poulsen says. "If it was the way he transmitted to WikiLeaks then it shows there must have been some degree of contact with WikiLeaks that went beyond the normal procedures."

By 21 May, it can be assumed that Assange and any of their mutual links in the Boston hacker scene were strictly avoiding all contact with Bradley Manning – for his sake as much as theirs. It was unfortunate for them that Manning then started sending messages to Adrian Lamo instead. He made contact with him the day a piece appeared in *Wired* magazine sympathetically quoting Lamo on his own recent diagnosis of Asperger's syndrome, his depressions, and his experience of psychiatric hospitalisation.

According to Lamo's version, published in *Wired*, in that first chat, Manning, who was using the pseudonym Bradass87, volunteered enough information to be easily traced. (The logs have been further edited here, for clarity).

"I'm an army intelligence analyst, deployed to eastern Baghdad, pending discharge for 'adjustment disorder' ... I'm sure you're pretty busy. If you had unprecedented access to classified networks 14 hours a day, seven days a week for eight-plus months, what would you do?"

The next day, he started to blurt out confessions. The statements this tormented 22-year-old made about what was at the time the biggest leak in US official history – some intimate, some desperate, some intelligent and principled – served, in the end, as Bradley Manning's own testament. They make it clear that he was not a thief, not venal, not mad, and not a traitor. He believed that, somehow, he was doing a good thing.

"Hypothetical question: if you had free rein over classified networks for long periods of time, say, 8-9 months, and you saw incredible things, awful things, things that belonged in the public domain, and not on some server stored in a dark room in Washington DC, what would you do? (or Guantánamo, Bagram, Bucca, Taji, VBC [Victory Base Complex] for that matter) Things that would have an impact on 6.7 billion people, say, a database of half a million events during the Iraq war from 2004 to 2009, with reports, date time groups, lat[itude]-lon[gitude] locations, casualty figures? Or 260,000 state department cables from embassies and consulates all over the world, explaining how the first world exploits the third, in detail, from an internal perspective?"

Manning confessed: "The air gap has been penetrated." The air gap is computer jargon, in this context, for the way the military internet is kept physically separate, for security reasons, from civilian servers, on which the ordinary commercial internet runs.

Lamo prompted him: "How so?"

"Let's just say 'someone' I know intimately well has been penetrating US classified networks, mining data like the ones described, and been transferring that data from the classified networks over the 'air gap' onto a commercial network computer: sorting the data, compressing it, encrypting it, and uploading it to a crazy white-haired Aussie who can't seem to stay in one country very long."

He went on: "Crazy white-haired dude = Julian Assange. In other words, I've made a huge mess. (I'm sorry. I'm just emotionally fractured. I'm a total mess. I think I'm in more potential heat than you ever were.)"

Lamo continued to press him: "How long have you helped WikiLeaks?"

"Since they released the 9/11 pager messages. I immediately recognised that they were from an NSA [National Security Agency] database, and I felt comfortable enough to come forward."

"So, right after Thanksgiving timeframe of 2009?"

"Hillary Clinton and several thousand diplomats around the world are going to have a heart attack when they wake up one morning, and find an entire repository of classified foreign policy is available, in searchable format, to the public."

"What sort of content?"

"Uhm ... crazy, almost criminal, political back-dealings. The non-PR versions of world events and crises. Uhm ... All kinds of stuff, like everything from the buildup to the Iraq war ... to what the actual content of 'aid packages' is. For instance, PR that the US is sending aid to Pakistan includes funding for water/food/clothing. That much is true, it includes that, but the other 85% of it is for F-16 fighters and munitions to aid in the Afghanistan effort, so the US can call in Pakistanis to do aerial bombing, instead of Americans potentially killing civilians and creating a PR crisis. There's so much. It affects everybody on earth.

"Everywhere there's a US post, there's a diplomatic scandal that will be revealed. Iceland, the Vatican, Spain, Brazil, Madagascar: if it's a country, and it's recognised by the US as a country, it's got dirt on it. It's open diplomacy, world-wide anarchy in CSV format [a simple text format]. It's Climategate with a global scope, and breathtaking depth. It's beautiful, and horrifying, and it's important that it gets out. I feel for some bizarre reason it might actually change something. I just don't wish to be a part of it, at least not now … I'm not ready. I wouldn't mind going to prison for the rest of my life, or being executed so much, if it wasn't for the possibility of having pictures of me plastered all over the world press *as a boy*. I've totally lost my mind. I make no sense. The CPU [central processing unit of a computer] is not made for this mother-board … >sigh< … I just wanted enough time to figure myself out, to be myself … and not be running around all the time, trying to meet someone else's expectations.

"I'm just kind of drifting now, waiting to redeploy to the US, be discharged and figure out how on earth I'm going to transition – all while witnessing the world freak out, as its most intimate secrets are revealed. It's such an awkward place to be in, emotionally and psychologically.

"I can't believe what I'm confessing to you … I've been so isolated so long. I just wanted to be nice, and live a normal life but events kept forcing me to figure out ways to survive. Smart enough to know what's going on, but helpless to do anything … No one took any notice of me … I'm self-medicating like crazy, when I'm not toiling in the supply office (my new location, since I'm being discharged, I'm not offically intel anymore)."

"What kind of scandal?"

"Hundreds of them."

"Like what? I'm genuinely curious about details."

"I don't know. There's so many. I don't have the original material any more … uhmm … the Holy See and its position on the Vatican sex scandals."

"Play it by ear."

"The broiling one in Germany … I'm sorry, there's so many. It's impossible for any one human to read all quarter-million and not feel overwhelmed, and possibly desensitised. The scope is so broad, and yet the depth so rich."

"Give me some bona fides ... Yanno? Any specifics."

"This one was a test: Classified cable from US Embassy Reykjavik on Icesave dated 13 Jan 2010. The result of that one was that the Icelandic ambassador to the US was recalled, and fired. That's just one cable."

"Anything unreleased?"

"I'd have to ask Assange. I zerofilled [deleted] the original."

"Why do you answer to him?"

"I don't. I just want the material out there. I don't want to be a part of it."

"I've been considering helping WikiLeaks with Opsec [operational security]."

"They have decent Opsec. I'm obviously violating it. I'm a wreck. I'm a total fucking wreck right now."

The transcript edited by Lamo resumes a little while later, with some more confessions:

"I'm a source, not quite a volunteer. I mean, I'm a high profile source, and I've developed a relationship with Assange, but I don't know much more than what he tells me, which is very little. It took me four months to confirm that the person I was communicating was in fact Assange."

"How'd you do that?"

"I gathered more info when I questioned him, whenever he was being tailed in Sweden by state department officials. I was trying to figure out who was following him, and why – and he was telling me stories of other times he's been followed, and they matched up with the ones he's said publicly."

"Did that bear out? The surveillance?"

"Based on the description he gave me, I assessed it was the Northern Europe Diplomatic Security Team, trying to figure out how he got the Reykjavik cable. They also caught wind that he had a video of the Garani airstrike in Afghanistan, which he has, but hasn't decrypted yet. The production team was actually working on the Baghdad strike, though, which was never really encrypted. He's got the whole 15-6 [investigation report] for that incident, so it won't just be video with no context. But it's not nearly as damning: it was an awful incident, but nothing like the Baghdad one. The investigating officers left the material unprotected, sitting in a directory on a centcom.smil.mil server but they did zip up the files, AES-256, with an excellent password, so afaik [as far as I know] it hasn't been broken yet ... 14+ char[acter]s. I can't believe what I'm telling you."

On 23 May, Lamo took the initiative in contacting Manning again. He did not tell the young soldier that he had already turned him in to the US military. Lamo subsequently said he thought it was his patriotic duty: "I wouldn't have done this, if lives weren't in danger. He was in a war zone, and basically trying to vacuum up as much classified information as he could, and just throwing it up into the air." Lamo set out to pump his new friend for yet more details:

"Anything new & exciting?"

"No, was outside in the sun all day, 110 degrees F, doing various details for a visiting band and some college team's cheerleaders. Ran a barbecue, but no one showed up. Threw a lot of food away. Yes, football cheerleaders, visiting on off-season – a part of Morale Welfare and Recreation (MWR) projects. I'm sunburned, and smell like charcoal, sweat, and sunscreen. That's about all that's new."

"Does Assange use AIM [AOL instant messaging] or other messaging services? I'd like to chat with him one of these days about Opsec. My only credentials beyond intrusion are that the FBI never got my data or found me, before my negotiated surrender, but that's something. And my data was never recovered."

"No he does not use AIM."

"How would I get hold of him?"

"He would come to you ... he does use OTR [Off The Record encryption for instant messaging] ... but discusses nothing Opsec ... He *might* use the ccc.de jabber server [the German Chaos Computer Club confidential messaging service] ... but you didn't hear that from me."

"Gotcha."

"I'm going to grab some dinner, ttyl [talk to you later]."

They do resume the talk later, with Lamo asking: "Are you Baptist by any chance?"

"Raised Catholic. Never believed a word of it. I'm godless. I guess I follow humanist values though. Have custom dog-tags that say 'Humanist' ... I was the only non-religous person in town – more pews than people. I understand them, though, I'm not mean to them. They *really* don't know. I politely disagree, but they are the ones who get uncomfortable when I make, very politely, good leading points ... *New Yorker* is running 10k word article on wl.org on 30 May, btw [by the way]."

The next day, on 25 May, Manning reflected that he felt connected to army specialist Ethan McCord, who was pictured in the Apache video carrying wounded children from a van. Manning added McCord as a friend on Facebook after the video came out. McCord left the US army and denounced the helicopter attack.

"Amazing how the world works – takes six degrees of separation to a whole new level. It's almost bookworthy in itself, how this played: event occurs in 2007, I watch video in 2009 with no context, do research, forward information to group of FOI [freedom of information] activists, more research occurs, video is released in 2010, those involved come forward to discuss event, I witness those involved coming forward to discuss publicly, even add them as friends on FB – without them knowing who I am. They touch my life, I touch their life, they touch my life again. Full circle."

"Are you concerned about CI/CID [counter-intelligence/ criminal investigation division] looking into your Wiki stuff? I was always paranoid."

"CID has no open investigation. State department will be uber-pissed ... but I don't think they're capable of tracing everything."

"What about CI?"

"Might be a congressional investigation, and a joint effort to figure out what happened. CI probably took note, but it had no effect on operations. So, it was publicly damaging, but didn't increase attacks or rhetoric. Joint effort will be purely political, 'fact finding' – 'how can we stop this from happening again' regarding state dept cables ..."

"Why does your job afford you access?"

"Because I had a workstation. I had two computers, one connected to SIPRNet the other to JWICS. They're government laptops. They've been zerofilled because of the pullout. Evidence was destroyed by the system itself."

"So how would you deploy the cables? If at all ... Stored locally, or retrievable?"

"I don't have a copy any more. They were stored on a centralised server. It was vulnerable as fuck."

"What's your endgame plan, then?"

"Well, it was forwarded to WL, and God knows what happens now: hopefully worldwide discussion, debates, and reforms. If not, then we're doomed as a species. I will officially give up on the society we have, if nothing happens. The reaction to the video gave me immense hope ... CNN's *iReport* was overwhelmed; Twitter exploded. People who saw knew there was something wrong. I want people to see the truth, regardless of who they are, because without information you cannot make informed decisions as a public. If I knew then what I knew now, kind of thing. Or maybe I'm just young, naive, and stupid."

Manning elaborated his growing disillusionment with the army and US foreign policy:

"I don't believe in good guys versus bad guys any more – only see a plethora of states acting in self-interest, with varying ethics and moral standards of course, but self-interest nonetheless. I mean, we're better in some respects: we're much more subtle, use a lot more words and legal techniques to legitimise everything. It's better than disappearing in the middle of the night, but just because something is more subtle, doesn't make it right. I guess I'm too idealistic.

"I think the thing that got me the most ... that made me rethink the world more than anything was watching 15 detainees taken by the Iraqi Federal Police for printing 'anti-Iraqi literature'. The Iraqi Federal Police wouldn't co-operate with US forces, so I was instructed to investigate the matter, find out who the 'bad guys' were, and how significant this was for the FPs. It turned out they had printed a scholarly critique against PM Maliki [Iraqi prime minister Nouri al-Maliki] ... I had an interpreter read it for me, and when I found out that it was a benign political critique titled *Where Did the Money Go?* and following the corruption trail within the PM's cabinet, I immediately took that information and *ran* to the officer to explain what was going on. He didn't want to hear any of it. He told me to shut up, and explain how we could assist the FPs in finding MORE detainees.

"Everything started slipping after that. I saw things differently. I had always questioned the [way] things worked, and investigated to find the truth, but that was a point where I was a *part* of something. I was actively involved in something that I was completely against."

"That could happen in Colombia. Different cultures, dude. Life is cheaper."

"Oh, I'm quite aware, but I was a part of it, and completely helpless."

"What would you do if your role w/ WikiLeaks seemed in danger of being blown?"

"Try and figure out how I could get my side of the story out before everything was twisted around to make me look like Nidal Hassan [the US army major charged with multiple murder for Fort Hood shooting]. I don't think it's going to happen. I mean, I was never noticed ... Also, there's godawful accountability of IP addresses. The network was upgraded, and patched up so many times ... and systems would go down, logs would be lost ... and when moved or upgraded, hard drives were zeroed. It's impossible to trace much on these field networks, and who would honestly expect so much information to be exfiltrated from a field network?"

"I'd be one paranoid boy in your shoes."

"The video came from a server in our domain! And not a single person noticed ..."

"How long between the leak and the publication?"

"Some time in February it was uploaded."

"Uploaded where? How would I transmit something if I had similarly damning data?

"Uhm ... preferably OpenSSL the file with AES-256 ... then use SFTP at prearranged drop IP addresses, keeping the key separate ... and uploading via a different means ... The HTTPS submission should suffice legally, though I'd use Tor on top of it ... Long term sources do get preference ... Veracity ... The material is easy to verify because they know a little bit more about the source than a purely anonymous one, and confirmation publicly from earlier material, would make them more likely to publish, I guess. If two of the largest public relations 'coups' have come from a single source, for instance. Purely *submitting* material is more likely to get overlooked without contacting them by other means, and saying, 'Hey, check your submissions for *x*.'"

Manning went on to talk about his discovery of the helicopter video:

"I recognised the value of some things. I watched that video cold, for instance. At first glance, it was just a bunch of guys getting shot up by a helicopter, no big deal. About two dozen more where that came from, right? But something struck me as odd, with the van thing, and also the fact it was being stored in a JAG officer's directory. So I looked into it, eventually tracked down the date, and then the exact GPS co-ord[inates] and I was like, 'OK, so that's what happened. Cool ... Then I went to the regular internet, and it was still on my mind ... So I typed into Google the date, and the location, and then I see this [a *New York Times* report on the death of the Reuters journalists] ... I kept that in my mind for weeks, probably a month and a half, before I forwarded it to [WikiLeaks]."

Manning went on to detail the security laxity that made it easy for him, or anyone else, to siphon data from classified networks without raising suspicion.

"Funny thing is, we transferred so much data on unmarked CDs. Everyone did... videos, movies, music, all out in the open. Bringing CDs to and from the networks was/is a common phenomenon. I would come in with music on a CD-RW labelled with something like 'Lady Gaga', erase the music, then write a compressed split file. No-one suspected a thing. Kind of sad. I didn't even have to hide anything ... The culture fed opportunities. Hardest part is arguably internet access – uploading any sensitive data over the open internet is a bad idea, since networks are monitored for any insurgent/terrorist/militia/criminal types."

"Tor?"

"Tor + SSL + SFTP... I even asked the NSA guy if he could

find any suspicious activity coming out of local networks. He shrugged and said, 'It's not a priority,' went back to watching *Eagle's Eye*. So, it was a massive data spillage, facilitated by numerous factors, both physically, technically, and culturally. Perfect example of how not to do Infosec ... Listened and lip-synched to Lady Gaga's 'Telephone' while exfiltrating possibly the largest data spillage in American history ... Weak servers, weak logging, weak physical security, weak counter-intelligence, inattentive signal analysis – a perfect storm. >sigh< Sounds pretty bad huh? ... Well, it SHOULD be better! It's sad. I mean what if I were someone more malicious? I could've sold to Russia or China, and made bank!"

"Why didn't you?"

"Because it's public data. It belongs in the public domain. Information should be free. Because another state would just take advantage of the information, try and get some edge. If it's out in the open, it should be a public good, rather than some slimy intel collector. I'm crazy like that. I'm not a bad person, I keep track of everything. I watch the whole thing unfold from a distance. I read what everyone says, look at pictures, keep tabs, and feel for them since I'm basically playing a vital role in their life without ever meeting them. I was like that as an intelligence analyst as well. Most didn't care, but I knew I was playing a role in the lives of hundreds of people, without them knowing me. But I cared, and kept track of some of the details, made sure everybody was OK. I don't think of myself as playing 'god' or anything, because I'm not: I'm just playing my role for the moment. I don't control the way they react. There are far more people who do what I do, in state interest, on daily basis, and don't give a fuck – that's how I try to separate myself from my (former) colleagues ... I'm not sure whether I'd be considered a type of 'hacker', 'cracker', 'hacktivist', 'leaker', or what. I'm just me, really ... I couldn't be a spy. Spies don't post things up for the world to see."

*

Right after Lamo denounced him, Manning was arrested, and flown out of Iraq to a military jail at Camp Arifjan in Kuwait. A few weeks later, he was charged with "transferring classified data on to his personal computer and adding unauthorised software to a classified computer system in connection with the leaking of a video of a helicopter attack in Iraq in 2007", and "communicating, transmitting and delivering national defence information to an unauthorised source and disclosing classified information concerning the national defence with reason to believe that the information could cause injury to the United States." Later, he was flown back to the US and imprisoned at the Quantico Marine Corps Base in Virginia, 30 miles south-west of Washington DC. Although he had not yet been tried or convicted, he was made to suffer under harsh conditions. He spent 23 hours a day alone in a 6ft by 12 ft cell, with one hour's exercise in which he walked figures-of-eight in an empty room. According to his lawyer, Manning was not allowed to sleep after being wakened at 5am. If he ever tried to do so, he was immediately made to sit or stand up by the guards, who were not allowed to converse with him. Any attempt to do press-ups or other exercise in his cell was forcibly prevented.

"The guards are required to check on PFC Manning every five minutes by asking him if he is OK. PFC Manning is required to respond in some affirmative manner. At night, if the guards cannot see PFC Manning clearly, because he has a blanket over his head or is curled up towards the wall, they will wake him in order to ensure he is OK. He receives each of his meals in his cell. He is not allowed to have a pillow or sheets. However, he is given access to two blankets and has recently been given a new mattress that has a built-in pillow. He is not allowed to have any personal items."

Manning's friends say he was being subject to near-torture in an effort to break him and have him implicate Assange in a conspiracy charge. David House, one of only two people allowed to visit Manning, says he witnessed the soldier's deterioration, both mental and physical, over the months of incarceration. House says that every time he saw Manning in the brig the prisoner was a little less fluid in his speech, a little less able to express complex ideas and put them eloquently. "Each time I go, there seems to have been a remarkable decline. That's physical, too. When I first saw him he was bright-eyed and strong like he was in early photographs, but now he looks weak, he has huge bags under his eyes and his muscles have turned to fat. It's hard watching someone over the months sicken like that."

The US army says that it prodded him every five minutes for Manning's own welfare. Because he was potentially suicidal, they say he was placed under a prevention of injury order. Manning himself may well have recalled what he told his interlocutor in the chat logs: "We're much more subtle, use a lot more words and legal techniques to legitimise everything. It's better than disappearing in the middle of the night, but just because something is more subtle, doesn't make it right." He was allowed books, and late in 2010 asked to be sent in Kant's *Critique of Pure Reason*.

CHAPTER 7
The deal

Hotel Leopold, Rue Luxembourg, Brussels
9.30pm, 21 June 2010

"I felt this was the biggest story on the planet"
Nick Davies

Three men were in the Belgian hotel courtyard café, ordering coffee after coffee. They had been arguing for hours through the summer afternoon, with a break to eat a little pasta, and evening had fallen. Eventually, the tallest of the three picked up a cheap yellow napkin, laid it on the flimsy modern café table and started to scribble. One of those present was Ian Traynor, the *Guardian*'s Europe correspondent. He recalls:

"Julian whipped out this mini-laptop, opened it up and did something on his computer. He picked up a napkin and said, 'OK you've got it.'

"We said: 'Got what?'

"He said: 'You've got the whole file. The password is this napkin.'"

Traynor went on: "I was stunned. We were expecting further very long negotiations and conditions. This was instant. It was an act of faith."

Assange had insouciantly circled several words and the hotel's logo on the Hotel Leopold napkin, adding the phrase "no spaces". This was the password. In the corner he scrawled three simple letters: GPG. GPG was a reference to the encryption system he was using for a temporary website. The napkin was a perfect touch, worthy of a John le Carré thriller. The two *Guardian* journalists were amazed. Nick Davies stuffed the napkin in his case together with his dirty shirts. Back in England, the yellow square was reverently lodged in his study, next to a pile of reporters' notepads and a jumble of books. "I'm thinking of framing it," he says.

Just a few days earlier, Davies had been sitting peacefully in that study, glancing up from his morning paper to his garden and the Sussex landscape. Davies is one of the *Guardian*'s best-known investigative journalists. In a career spanning more than three decades, he has worked on many stories exposing the dark abuses of power. His book *Flat Earth News* was an acclaimed account of how the newspaper industry had gone badly wrong, abandoning real reporting for what he memorably dubbed "churnalism".

Davies was currently embroiled in a long-term investigation into a phone-hacking scandal at the *News of the World* during the editorship of Andy Coulson. Coulson – who was as a result forced to resign in January 2011 as the public relations boss for Conservative prime minister David Cameron – denied all knowledge of his staff illegally hacking the phones of celebrities and members of the royal family.

Today, however, Davies's attention was caught by the *Guardian*'s foreign pages: "American officials are searching for Julian Assange, the founder of WikiLeaks, in an attempt to pressure him not to publish thousands of confidential and potentially hugely embarrassing diplomatic cables that offer unfiltered assessments of Middle East governments and leaders."

The story continued: "The *Daily Beast*, a US news reporting and opinion website, reported that Pentagon investigators are trying to track down Assange – an Australian citizen who moves frequently between countries – after the arrest of a US soldier last week who is alleged to have given the whistleblower website a classified video of American troops killing civilians in Baghdad. The soldier, Bradley Manning, also claimed to have given WikiLeaks 260,000 pages of confidential diplomatic cables and intelligence assessments. The US authorities fear their release could 'do serious damage to national security'."

Davies was thunderstruck. An unknown 22-year-old private had apparently downloaded the entire contents of a US classified military database. Manning was held in prison in Kuwait. But was there any way the *Guardian* could lay its hands on the cables? "I felt this was the biggest story on the planet," says Davies. He searched online for "Bradley Manning", and found the transcripts published by *Wired.com*. These detailed the conversations with former hacker Adrian Lamo, in which Manning apparently confirmed he had illicitly downloaded more than a quarter of a million classified documents, talked of "almost criminal political back-dealings" by the US, and said: "Hillary Clinton and several thousand diplomats around the world are going to have a heart attack."

If only a fraction of what Manning said was true, WikiLeaks was now sitting on hundreds of thousands of cables detailing dubious diplomatic operations, war crimes in Afghanistan and Iraq, and God knows what else. It was a goldmine. "There was clearly a bigger story here. It wasn't hard to see," Davies says. His reporter's radar was bleeping with excitement. But amazingly, nobody else on what used to be known as Fleet Street seemed to have yet worked out the massive potential dimensions.

The key to accessing the cables – and to the stories they contained – had to be Julian Assange. Davies himself had never met him but was aware of Assange's website: he had come across

WikiLeaks during the *Guardian*'s 2009 investigation into tax evasion and Swiss banks. He wanted to get to Assange fast, before the Pentagon investigators or anyone else. But where was he? The *Daily Beast* reported that Assange had cancelled a US public appearance in Las Vegas due to "security concerns"; a group of former US intelligence officers had warned publicly that Assange's physical safety was at risk. There were few clues.

Davies sent a series of exploratory emails to Assange. He offered to assist on Manning, and to publicise the 22-year-old's plight. On 16 June, he wrote: "Hi Julian, I spent yesterday in the *Guardian* office arguing that Bradley Manning is currently the most important story on the planet. There is much to be done, and it will take a little time. But right now, I think the crucial thing is to track and expose the effort by the US government to suppress Bradley, you, WikiLeaks, and anything that either of you may want to put in the public domain." The email went on: "Can you communicate with me about that; or hook me up with somebody who can? Maybe one possibility might be for me to talk to any lawyer who has been helping Bradley. Good luck, Nick."

This tentative pitch elicited a reply from Assange – but not a very helpful one. Assange merely sent back a press release describing how WikiLeaks had persuaded Icelandic parliamentarians to build a "new media haven" in Iceland.

Davies went up to the *Guardian* office in London to consult David Leigh, a colleague and old friend. Leigh had met Assange earlier in the year and, having failed to reach a deal over the Apache helicopter video, was sceptical. He warned Davies that the Australian was unpredictable. He doubted Assange would be willing to co-operate. But, Leigh added, "You're welcome to try."

Davies persevered. He sent Assange another email offering "to travel anywhere to meet you or anybody else, to take any of this forward". This time Assange was more forthcoming. He sent

back the contact name of Birgitta Jónsdóttir, the Icelandic parlia-
mentarian who had co-produced the Apache video, and whose
tweets the US department of justice would later attempt to
subpoena. He also mentioned Kristinn Hrafnsson, his loyal
deputy. Assange signed off: "I'm a bit hard to interview presently
for security reasons, but send me ALL your contacts." Davies sent
further emails to Jónsdóttir, Hrafnsson and other WikiLeaks play-
ers, and spoke to several of them on the phone. He felt he was
beginning to make progress. But he was also painfully aware that
if he simply demanded that WikiLeaks share its information,
Assange would see him as yet another representative of the
greedy, duplicitous mainstream media – or MSM, as it is deri-
sively described on much of the internet. Something more subtle
was called for – something that ultimately gave the *Guardian*
access to the cables, but perhaps also offered Assange a way to
resolve his own problems.

On the evening of Sunday 19 June, Davies received a phone
call. His informant said, "Don't tell Julian I told you, but he's
flying to Brussels to give a press conference tomorrow at the European parliament." Excited, Davies called Leigh, who was at home
in London. Leigh was absorbed in a television detective serial, and
seemed far from impressed by the development. Davies promptly
dialled the editor of the *Guardian*, Alan Rusbridger. The pair had
started on the paper together in 1979 as junior reporters, and had
lived in neighbouring flats in London's Clerkenwell. Rusbridger
trusted Davies completely, and had given him free rein to pursue
investigative projects, believing he would always bring back something of value.

This unusual arrangement had seen Davies launch long-term
investigations into a range of areas, including poverty in the UK,
Britain's education system, and police corruption. Davies's challenging, in-depth journalism had made political waves and proved
popular with readers.

"Alan, what do you know of this guy Bradley Manning?" Davies asked.

"Not much," Rusbridger replied.

"Well, it's the biggest story on the planet ..."

Yes, Rusbridger agreed, "Go to Brussels."

There was no transport to get Davies to Brussels in time for the press conference, however, so the editor suggested that Traynor, who was highly experienced and who was based in the city, should try to buttonhole Assange. Davies emailed Traynor that night:

"Bradley Manning, aged 22, is an American intelligence analyst who has been working at a US base outside Baghdad, where he had access to two closed communication networks. One carried traffic from US embassies all over the world, classified 'secret'; the other carried traffic from US intelligence agencies, classified 'top secret'. Manning decided he didn't like what he saw and copied masses of it on to CDs."

Davies explained his view that Manning then made a "good move and a bad move". The good decision was to approach Assange; the bad one was apparently to blurt out what he had done to Lamo, "a lonesome American computer hacker".

Davies asked Traynor to get to Assange's lunchtime panel debate in the parliament building. "Longer term, it's a question of trying to forge some kind of alliance so that, if and when Assange releases any of the material which Manning claims to have leaked, we are involved."

Traynor successfully made contact with Assange's colleague Birgitta Jónsdóttir, the next day in Brussels. He spotted her in a café with two male companions, including "a guy wearing a large Icelandic woolly jumper". This turned out to be Assange, but Traynor – having never seen him before – failed to recognise him. "Otherwise I would have grabbed him!" Traynor only caught up with Assange himself at the European parliament event. The only other British reporter there was a junior hack from BBC radio. But the room was full, and there were a number of foreign journalists – among them an Austrian television journalist who Traynor knew had a good nose for a story – so the *Guardian* correspondent acted swiftly to get Assange away from the crowd as the meeting ended.

They set off together into a warren of parliament corridors and talked privately for half an hour. Traynor thought Assange quiet, cautious and inscrutable. He was impressed by his intellect and quick wit – and though he sometimes found his gnomic answers evasive and hard to follow, "I liked him and I think he liked me." Traynor was pleased to hear that the WikiLeaks founder presented himself as a big fan of the *Guardian*. He seemed keen to engage in a collaborative project with a newspaper which had progressive credentials. Assange revealed, significantly, that WikiLeaks was planning to dump "two million pages" of raw material on its website. Traynor asked what it was about. Assange replied simply: "It concerns war." Assange gave Traynor his local Brussels cellphone number; they agreed to meet again the next day.

Davies was meanwhile anxiously lunching with Rusbridger at the ground-floor restaurant in Kings Place, the *Guardian*'s London headquarters, overlooking the moored houseboats on the Regent's Canal. In the middle of their lunch, Traynor's email arrived. It confirmed that Assange was willing to meet. That night Davies didn't sleep: "I was too excited." First thing next morning he was on the high-speed train from London St Pancras station, through the Channel tunnel and on to Brussels.

As his Eurostar carriage shot through the green Kent countryside, he formulated and reformulated his pitch. As he saw it, Assange was facing four separate lines of attack. The first was physical – that someone would beat him up or worse. The second was legal – that Washington would attempt to crush WikiLeaks in the courts. The third was technological – that the US or its proxies would bring down the WikiLeaks website. The fourth and perhaps most worrisome possibility was a PR attack – that a sinister propaganda campaign would be launched, accusing Assange of collaborating with terrorists.

Davies also knew that Assange was disappointed at the reception of his original Apache video, single-handedly released in Washington. The story should have set off a global scandal; instead the narrative had flipped, with attention focused not on the murder of innocent Iraqis but on WikiLeaks itself.

There was another important concern. If the *Guardian* alone were to obtain and publish the diplomatic cables, the US embassy in London might seek to injunct the paper. The UK is home to some of the world's most hostile media laws; it is regarded as something of a haven for dodgy oligarchs and other dubious "libel tourists". What was needed, Davies felt, was a multi-jurisdictional alliance between traditional media outlets and WikiLeaks, possibly encompassing non-governmental organisations and others. If the material from the cables were published simultaneously in several countries, would this get round the threat of a British injunction? Davies opened his notebook. He wrote: "*New York Times/Washington Post/Le Monde*." He added: "Politicians? NGOs? Other interested parties?" Maybe the *Guardian* could preview the leaked cables and select the best story angles. The *Guardian* and WikiLeaks would then pass these "media missiles" to other friendly publications. He liked that plan. But would Assange buy it?

Over in Brussels, Traynor was discovering, as many others had, that having Assange's mobile number and actually being able to get in touch with him were two very different things. Fearing that the Australian had gone awol, Traynor headed for the Hotel Leopold on the Place Luxembourg, where Assange was staying, next to the European parliament. Traynor went up to his room and banged on the door. Assange eventually emerged and invited Traynor in. The room resembled that of a modern monk:

Assange's worldly possessions apparently comprised a couple of rucksacks stuffed full of gadgets, three laptops, and a jumble of mobile phones and Sim cards. His wardrobe seemed to be a T-shirt, a jumper and a pair of jeans.

Assange was in mischievous good spirits. The former hacker told Traynor: "You guys at the *Guardian*, you have got to do something about your security. You have got to get your email secure and encrypted."

"He knew the contents of the email I had sent to London," Traynor said, somewhat amazed. "He was showing off, but also expressing concern."

When Davies arrived in town, the two *Guardian* reporters repaired again to the Leopold. They dialled upstairs. Assange – apparently still on Australian time – had crashed out again. He finally appeared 15 minutes later. The three sat in the hotel's covered courtyard café. It was 3.30pm; nobody else was around.

What followed was a six-hour conversation. It would result in an extraordinary, if sometimes strained, partnership between a mainstream newspaper and WikiLeaks – a new model of co-operation aimed at publishing the world's biggest leak. A *Vanity Fair* feature subsequently called it a courtship between "one of the oldest newspapers in the world, with strict and established journalistic standards" and "one of the newest in a breed of online muckrakers". The article's American author, Sarah Ellison, wrote: "The *Guardian*, like other media outlets, would come to see Assange as someone to be handled with kid gloves, or perhaps latex ones – too alluring to ignore, too tainted to unequivocally embrace."

The hopes of an accord risked derailment from the outset, however. Assange had already positioned himself as an ideological enemy of Davies, whose high-profile campaign to force Rupert Murdoch's tabloid the *News of the World* to confront and stop its phone-hacking had previously been denounced by Assange as a contemptible attempt by "sanctimonious handwringing ... politicians and social elites" to claim a right to privacy. Assange had accused Davies of "a lack of journalistic solidarity" for criticising the *News of the World* – calling it merely "an opportunity to attack a journalistic and class rival". Assange now failed to disguise a faint contempt for the MSM in general.

Assange nevertheless struck Davies as "very young, boyish, rather shy – and perfectly easy to deal with". He drank orange juice. Delicately, Davies began setting out the options. He told Assange it was improbable anybody would attack him physically; that would be a global embarrassment for the US. Rather, Davies predicted, the US would launch a dirty information war, and accuse him of helping terrorists and endangering innocent lives. WikiLeaks' response had to be that the world was entitled to know the truth about the murky US led wars in Iraq and Afghanistan.

"We are going to put you on the moral high ground – so high that you'll need an oxygen mask. You'll be up there with Nelson Mandela and Mother Teresa," Davies told Assange. "They won't be able to arrest you. Nor can they shut down your website."

Assange was receptive. This wasn't the first time WikiLeaks had worked with traditional news media, and Assange had decided it might be a good idea on this occasion to do so again. Then Assange revealed the scale of his cache. WikiLeaks had in fact obtained, he confided, logs detailing every single US military incident in the Afghanistan war. "Holy Moly!" remarked Davies. Not only that, Assange added, the website also had similar war logs from Iraq from March 2003. "Fuck!" exclaimed Davies.

But that wasn't all. WikiLeaks was indeed in possession of the secret US state department cables from American diplomatic missions around the world. Fourthly and finally, he had files from enemy combatant review tribunals held in Guantánamo Bay, the US's notorious penal colony in Cuba. In all, jaw-droppingly, there were more than a million documents.

This was stunning stuff. Davies proposed that the *Guardian* should be allowed to preview all the material, bringing context to what would otherwise be an incomprehensible mass data dump.

Assange said that WikiLeaks had been ready to post all the data for the past two weeks, but he was hesitating because, although he would never reveal whether Manning was a source, he was worried about the legal implications for the young soldier. The Army had still not charged Manning; Manning would have been trained to resist interrogation, he believed, and Lamo's allegations were evidentially "not credible"; but Assange was concerned that publishing the leaked material might give Pentagon investigators further evidence to work on.

Davies and Assange discussed adding the *New York Times* as a partner. There was no way, Davies argued, that the Obama administration would attack the most powerful Democrat-leaning newspaper in the US. Any WikiLeaks stories in the paper would enjoy the protection of the free speech provisions of the first amendment to the US constitution; furthermore, there was the precedent of the *New York Times*'s historic battle to gain the right to publish the Pentagon papers. The paper's domestic US status would also make it harder for the authorities to press espionage charges against Manning, which might follow from purely foreign publication. Assange agreed with this.

Ian Traynor recalls: "Assange knew people at the *New York Times*. He was concerned that the stuff should be published in the US and not only abroad. He felt he would be more vulnerable if it was only published abroad."

Assange also insisted that, in any deal, the *Times* in New York should publish five minutes ahead of the *Guardian* in London. He theorised that this would reduce the risk of Manning being indicted for breaking the Espionage Act. Traynor suggested the possibility of additionally bringing on board *Der Spiegel* in Hamburg. The

German news magazine had lots of money, and Germany was itself embroiled militarily in Afghanistan, he pointed out.

Assange said that if the Big Leak were to go ahead, he would want to control the *Guardian*'s timing: he didn't want to publish too soon if this would damage Manning, but he was also prepared to post everything immediately if there was any kind of attack on WikiLeaks.

At one point, the would-be partners went out to refuel at an Italian restaurant. As he ate, Assange scanned nervously over his shoulder to see if he was being watched. (There were no US agents there, as far as anyone could tell – only the European Green leader and former student rebel Daniel Cohn-Bendit sitting just behind them.) Assange cautioned that, if the deal were to go ahead, the *Guardian* would have to raise its game on security and adopt stringent measures. The paper had to assume phones were bugged, emails read, computers compromised, he said. "He was very, very hot on security," Davies recalled. And he seemed media-savvy, too. "He suggested that we find a suitable story to give to Fox News, so that they would be brought on side rather than becoming attack dogs. Another good idea. We were motoring."

Assange popped back to his room, returning with a small black laptop. He showed Davies actual samples from the Afghan database. The WikiLeaks team had examined the data, he said, encouragingly. They had discovered that the killing had gone on at a much higher rate in Iraq than in Afghanistan. But the database samples themselves seemed vast, confusing and impossible to navigate – an impenetrable forest of military jargon. Davies, by this point exhausted after a long day, began to wonder whether they in fact included anything journalistically of value.

And there was another problem. How was Davies to get the Afghan material back to the *Guardian* in London? He could, of course, save it on a memory stick, but this ran the risk that British officials might confiscate it at customs control. Assange, the hacking prodigy, offered the answer: he would transfer the material in encrypted form to a special website. The website would only exist for a short period before disappearing.

Reopening his netbook, Assange typed away and then circled words on the Hotel Leopold napkin. They were the password to decrypt data downloadable from the temporary website he would set up, encrypted in GPG (also known by its generic name, Pretty Good Privacy or PGP). Without the password, the website would be virtually uncrackable unless an opponent happened to stumble on the two large prime numbers which generated the encryption. Armed with the password, *Guardian* staff would soon be able to access the first tranche of data – the Afghan war logs. The three other promised "packages" were to follow.

The two men agreed on other precautions: Davies would send Assange an email saying that no deal had been agreed. (Written on 23 June, it read: "I'm safely back at base. Thanks for spending time with me – no need to apologise for not being able to give me what I'm after.") The idea was to throw dust in the eyes of the Americans. Assange and Davies parted.

Davies grabbed a pastry and a cup of railway station coffee the following dawn and took the first train back to London. In the office he bumped into Rusbridger. "I'm going to tell you a secret," he said. According to Davies, the owlish Rusbridger's reaction was, as ever, understated. But he clearly appreciated the implications. By 9.30am he had agreed to ring Bill Keller, his *New York Times* counterpart, as soon as he woke across the Atlantic.

Heading back to his home in Sussex, Davies waited for news from Assange. Mid-morning on 24 June an email arrived directing Davies to the website. He downloaded the huge file, but was unable to disentangle the procedure required for GPG decryption. He phoned his local computer specialist, who was unable to help. Frustrated, Davies put the still-encrypted data on to a memory stick, and deleted Assange's email. Soon afterwards the website ceased to exist. Davies traveled back up to London and handed the stick to Harold Frayman, systems editor at the Guardian Media Group. Frayman easily downloaded the contents as a decrypted spreadsheet. "It wasn't actually a terribly difficult thing to do at all. We knew what the password was," Frayman said calmly.

So by that evening the *Guardian* had the Afghan database – an unprecedented hour-by-hour portrait of the real, harsh war being fought in the mountains and dusty streets of the Hindu Kush. But it didn't look like it at the time: for the first five or six days the Afghan record proved almost impossible to read. "It was a fucker," Davies said. "The spreadsheet was terribly difficult to extract information from, slow and difficult." Nonetheless, he sent a triumphant email back to Assange. It read: "The good guys have got the girls."

CHAPTER 8
In the bunker

Fourth floor, the *Guardian*, Kings Place, London
July 2010

"It felt like being a kid in a candy shop"
DECLAN WALSH, THE *GUARDIAN*

In the small, glass-walled office on the *Guardian*'s fourth floor, maps of Afghan and Iraqi military districts were stuck with magnets on to a whiteboard. Alongside them, the journalists were scrawling constantly updated lists of hitherto unknown US military abbreviations. "What's EOF?" a reporter would shout? "Escalation of force!" someone would answer. HET? Human Exploitation Team. LN? Local national. EKIA was the body count: enemy killed in action. There were literally hundreds of other jargon terms: eventually the paper had to publish a lengthy glossary alongside its stories.

The discreet office, well away from the daily news operation, had become a multinational war room, with reporters flown in from Islamabad, New York, and eventually Berlin to analyse hundreds of thousands of leaked military field reports. They jostled with London-based computer experts and website specialists. A shredder was installed alongside the bank of six computer screens, and the air of security was intensified by the stern notice stuck on the door: "Project Room. Private & Confidential. No Unauthorised Access."

Nick Davies was so fixated by secrecy that he initially even refused to tell the *Guardian*'s head of news, deputy editor Ian Katz, about the project. He was dismayed to discover how quickly word spread that he was involved in a top-secret story. Another colleague, Richard Norton-Taylor, the *Guardian*'s veteran security editor, soon asked Davies about his "scoop". Davies refused to tell him. A couple of hours later Norton-Taylor encountered Davies again, and teased him gleefully: "I know all your secrets!" A newspaper office is a bad place in which to try and keep the lid on things for very long.

The paper's staff did do their best, however. Declan Walsh, the *Guardian*'s Pakistan-based correspondent, was recalled in conditions of great secrecy. Meeting round a table in the editor's office, the *Guardian*'s team chewed over the technical difficulties. David Leigh was cantankerous: "It's like panning for tiny grains of gold in a mountain of data," he complained. "How are we ever going to find if there are any stories in it?" The answer to that question set the *Guardian*'s old hands on a steep learning curve as they got to grips with modern methods.

First they discovered, embarrassingly, that their first download, the Afghan spreadsheet, did not contain 60,000 entries, as they had spent several days believing. It contained far more. But the paper's early version of Excel software had simply stopped reading after recording 60,000 rows. The real total of hour-by-hour field reports – the war logs – amounted to 92,201 rows of data. The next problem was greater still. It transpired that a spreadsheet of such enormous size was impossibly slow to manipulate, although it could theoretically be sorted and filtered to yield reams of statistics and different types of military event. The Iraq war logs release dumped another 391,000 records into their laps, which quadrupled the data problems.

Harold Frayman, the technical expert, solved those problems: he improvised at speed a full-scale database. Like Google, or sophisticated news search engines such as LexisNexis, the Frayman database could be searched by date, by key word, or by any phrase put between quotation marks. Declan Walsh recalls: "When I first got access to the database, it felt like being a kid in a candy shop. My first impulse was to search for 'Osama bin Laden', the man who had started the war. Several of us furiously inputted the name to see what it would produce (not much, as it turned out)." Leigh, too, began to cheer up: "Now this data is beginning to speak to me!" he said.

Leigh was introduced to another *Guardian* specialist, Alastair Dant: "Alastair's our data visualiser," he was told. Leigh: "I didn't know such a job existed." He was soon brought up to speed. The WikiLeaks project was producing new types of data. Now they needed to be mined with new kinds of journalism. Dant explained that he could convert the statistics of the thousands of bomb explosions recorded in the Afghan war logs into a bespoke moving graphic display. He could use the same basic template with which the *Guardian* had formerly developed a popular interactive map of the Glastonbury festival. That had been a nice bit of fun for music fans. The viewer had been able to move a pointer over a map of the festival field, and up came the artists playing at that spot, at that particular time.

Now, with Afghanistan, the viewer would be able similarly to press a button, but this time a much more chilling display would start to run. It would reveal, day by day and year by year, the failure of the US army to contain the insurgents in Afghanistan, as literally thousands of "improvised explosive devices" blossomed all around the country's road system. The viewer could see how the vast majority of the roadside bombs were slaughtering ordinary civilians rather than military opponents, and how the assaults ebbed and flowed with changes in political developments. It was a rendering that made at least something comprehensible, in an otherwise scrappy and ill-reported war.

The key online expert proved to be Simon Rogers, the *Guardian*'s data editor. "You're good with spreadsheets, aren't you?" he was asked. "This is one hell of a spreadsheet," he said. After working on those spreadsheets, he concluded: "Sometimes people talk about the internet killing journalism. The WikiLeaks story was a combination of the two: traditional journalistic skills and the power of the technology, harnessed to tell an amazing story. In future, data journalism may not seem amazing and new; for now it is. The world has changed and it is data that has changed it."

One obvious opportunity was to obtain genuine statistics of casualties for the first time. The US military had asserted, disingenuously, that at least as far as civilians and "enemies" were concerned, there were no figures available. In fact, the journalists could now see that the war logs contained highly detailed categories that were supposed to be filled in for every military event, breaking them down into US and allies, local Iraqi and Afghan forces, civilians and enemy combatants, and classing them in each case as either killed or wounded. But it wasn't so simple. Rogers and his reporter colleagues had to grapple with the realities on the military ground: those realities made apparently enticing data sets into dirty and unreliable statistics.

At its simplest, a person listed as "wounded" at the time might have actually died later. More sweepingly, the casualty boxes were sometimes not filled in at all. The reporters felt sympathy with exhausted soldiers, after a day of fighting, being confronted with forms to input that required the filling in of no fewer than 30 fields of bureaucratic information. Some units were more meticulous than others. Early years of the wars saw sketchier information gathering than later, when systems were better organised. When there was heavy urban fighting, or when bodies were carried away, casualties were hard to count. Some units had a penchant for writing down improbably large numbers of purported "enemy killed in action". Sometimes, more sinisterly, civilians who were killed were recorded as "enemy". That avoided awkward questions for the troops. All the figures were in any event too low, because some months and years were missing. So were details from the special forces, who operated outside the normal army chains of command. And many of the clashes involving British, German and other "allies" were apparently not recorded on the US army database.

So it was a tricky task to produce statistics that could be claimed to have real value. That highlighted once again the inescapable limitations of the purist WikiLeaks ideology. The material that resided in leaked documents, no matter how voluminous, was not "the truth". It was often just a signpost pointing to some of the truth, requiring careful interpretation.

Assange himself eventually flew into London from Stockholm late one night in July 2010. He arrived in the *Guardian* office with nothing but his backpack and a shy smile, like one of the Lost Boys out of *Peter Pan*. "Have you anywhere to stay?" asked Leigh. "No," he said. "Have you had anything to eat?" Again the answer was no. Leigh walked him down the road to the brasserie which was still open at St Pancras station and presented him with the menu. Assange ate 12 oysters and a piece of cheese, and then went to stay the night at Leigh's flat in nearby Bloomsbury.

He spent several days there, sleeping in the day and working on his laptop through the night. Then he moved to a nearby hotel, spent the World Cup final weekend at Nick Davies' Sussex home (but, says Davies, "He wasn't the slightest bit interested in football") and settled for a while at the Pimlico townhouse of Gavin MacFadyen, the City University professor and journalist. Assange brought with him only three pairs of socks. But he swiftly charmed the MacFadyen household, borrowed poetry books from the shelves, and patiently explained the Big Bang, complete with mathematical formulae, to some wide-eyed visiting children. The only uncomfortable moment came over a meal of risotto, cooked by Sarah Saunders, a gourmet caterer and the daughter of MacFadyen's wife, Susan. Typically, Assange would tap at his laptop throughout meals; other WikiLeaks volunteers who came and went did the same thing. On this occasion Saunders told him to turn his laptop off. Assange, to his credit, instantly complied.

A month later, he was provided with a bigger base for his growing organisation at the journalists' Frontline Club in west London. Something about the wandering Assange made a succession of people he encountered want to look after him and protect him – even if that sentiment was not always enduring.

The team flowing in and out of the *Guardian* war room was also growing in size. The *Guardian*'s two distinguished veterans of the Iraq conflict, Jonathan Steele and James Meek, were co-opted. The executive editor of the *New York Times*, Bill Keller, sent over Eric Schmitt, his highly experienced war correspondent. Schmitt, whose knowledge of the military background was helpful, was able to report back that the war logs seemed authentic. He put them on a memory stick and flew home to start the process of building a database in New York.

The German contingent, too, were able to make a crucial contribution to the verification process. As the broker of the original deal with the *Guardian* and the *New York Times*, Nick Davies had not at first been entirely pleased with the arrival of *Der Spiegel* – a prospect that had only been tentatively mentioned at the Brussels meeting by his colleague Ian Traynor. Assange told him that lunch with *Der Spiegel* was taking place in Berlin. Then, in a phone call from a man calling himself Daniel Schmitt – actually Assange's then No 2, Daniel Domscheit-Berg – he was told not only *Der Spiegel* but also a German radio station would be full "media partners" on the war logs. "I felt very confused. My first instinct was to say no," Davies recalled. "A deal is a deal. Security is very important.

I felt: 'You can't come in.'" Davies eventually agreed that while German radio was out, *Der Spiegel* could be in. Their reporters John Goetz and Marcel Rosenbach flew over to the war room.

"They fitted in very well. We liked them as people. They had lots of background expertise on Afghanistan," Davies says. Crucially, *Der Spiegel* sources had access to the German federal parliament's own investigation into the war in Afghanistan, including secret US military material. This proved vital in confirming that the details in the database the *Guardian* had been given were authentic.

The papers had another headache. Normally, with a story of this magnitude, the practical thing to do was to run it over several days. This maintained reader interest and helped sell more copies. In a previous campaign, on corporate tax avoidance, the *Guardian* had run a story a day non-stop for two weeks. This time, such a strategy was going to be impossible. For one thing, the two dailies in London and New York were now yoked to a weekly magazine in Germany. With only one shot at it, *Der Spiegel* would want to get all its stories out on Day One.

Secondly, and more gravely, none of the editors knew whether they would be allowed a Day Two at all. The US government's response might be so explosive that they sent their lawyers in with a gag order. So it was decided that, in the *Guardian*'s case, the paper would run everything they had over 14 pages, on the day of launch. There was, of course, a downside to the approach: although the launch of the Afghan war logs was to cause an immense uproar, it was difficult to find anyone in London the next day who had actually ploughed through all 14 pages. It was simply too much to read. For the Iraq logs, by which time it was clear the US government was not going to seek court injunctions and gag orders against the media, publication was to be more comfortably spread over a few days.

The knottiest problem surrounded redactions. The papers planned only to publish a relatively small number of significant stories, and with them the text of the handful of relevant logs. WikiLeaks, on the other hand, intended simultaneously to unleash the lot. But many of the entries, particularly the "threat reports" derived from intelligence, mentioned the names of informants or those who had collaborated with US troops. In the vicious internecine politics of Afghanistan, such people could be in danger. Declan Walsh was among the first to realise this:

"I told David Leigh I was worried about the repercussions of publishing these names, who could easily be killed by the Taliban or other militant groups if identified. David agreed it was a concern and said he'd raised the issue with Julian, but he didn't seem concerned. That night, we went out to a Moorish restaurant, Moro, with the two German reporters. David broached the problem again with Julian. The response floored me. 'Well, they're informants,' he said. 'So, if they get killed, they've got it coming to them. They deserve it.' There was, for a moment, silence around the table. I think everyone was struck by what a callous thing that was to say.

"I thought about the American bases I'd visited, the Afghan characters I'd met in little villages and towns, the complex local politics that coloured everything, and the dilemmas faced by individuals during a bloody war. There was no way I'd like to put them at risk on the basis of a document prepared by some wet-behind-the-ears American GI, who may or may not have correctly understood the information they were receiving. The other thing that little exchange suggested to me was just how naive – or arrogant – Julian was when it came to the media. Apart from any moral considerations, he didn't seem to appreciate how the issue of naming informants was likely to rebound on the entire project."

Davies, too, was dismayed by the difficulty of persuading Assange to make redactions. "At first, he simply didn't get it, that it's not OK to publish stuff that will get people killed," Davies said. The *Guardian* reporter had been studying Task Force 373, a shadowy special operations group whose job was to capture or kill high-ranking Taliban. One war log was especially troubling: it described how an unnamed informant had a close relative who lived an exact distance south-east of the named target's house and "will have eyes on target". Clearly it was possible to work out these identities with the help of some local knowledge, and to publish the log might lead to the Taliban executing both Afghans. But Assange, according to Davies, was unbothered. For all his personal liking of the WikiLeaks founder, says Davies: "The problem is he's basically a computer hacker. He comes from a simplistic ideology, or at that stage he did, that all information has to be published, that all information is good."

In fairness to Assange, he eventually revisited his view, despite the technical difficulties it posed for WikiLeaks. And by the time the US state department cables were published, five months later, Assange had entirely embraced the logic of redaction, with his role almost that of a mainstream publisher. Short of time before the Afghan launch, he removed wholesale the 15,000 intelligence files, listed as "threat reports", which were most likely to contain identifying details. This left some identities still discoverable in the main body of the cables, a fact which Rupert Murdoch's London *Times* published prominently. Despite their supposed disapproval of WikiLeaks, the paper had pointed to information that could have helped the Taliban to murder people. By the time the Iraq logs were launched, Assange had time to construct a more sophisticated editing programme, which redacted a vast number of names. And when it came to publishing the diplomatic cables, on the face of it at least, Assange had abandoned his original ambition to dump out everything. He contented himself during the course of 2010 with only publishing a small fraction of the cables – those whose text had already been individually redacted by journalists from the five print media partners.

In the end, then, all these anxieties about the fate of informants remained purely theoretical. By the end of the year in which WikiLeaks published its huge dump of information, no concrete evidence whatever had surfaced that any informant had suffered actual reprisals. The only reports were of defence secretary Robert Gates telling a sailor aboard a US warship in San Diego, "We don't have specific information of an Afghan being killed yet." CNN reported on 17 October that, according to a senior Nato official in Kabul, "There has not been a single case of Afghans needing protection or to be moved because of the leak."

As Walsh had predicted, the enemies of WikiLeaks nevertheless did their worst. Admiral Mike Mullen, chairman of the joint chiefs of staff, was among the first. "The truth is they might already have on their hands the blood of some young soldier or that of an Afghan family," Mullen told a Pentagon news conference four days after the leak. This slogan – "blood on their hands" – was in turn perverted from a speculation into a fact, endlessly repeated, and used as a justification for bloodlust on the part of some US politicians, who seemingly thought they might profit in votes by calling for Assange himself to be murdered. Particularly repellent was hearing the phrase being used by US generals who, as the WikiLeaks documents revealed, had gallons of genuine civilian blood on their own hands.

Assange was starting to prove a volatile partner in several respects. Nick Davies was his chief contact, and the man who had reeled him in for the *Guardian*. So it was a jolt when the pair fell out. Davies believed he and Assange had developed a rapport, cemented over dinners, jokes, late-night philosophical debates and al fresco dinners in Stockholm's island old town. "I thought he was clever and interesting and fun to hang around with. The two of us were involved in this rather exciting, very important adventure." But the day before the Afghan war logs launch, Davies' phone rang. On the other line was Stephen Grey, a freelance reporter. Grey began: "Guess what? I've just been with Julian Assange." Grey explained that Assange had given him an exclusive TV interview about the blockbusting Afghan war logs. He had also provided material for Channel 4's website. And there was more bad news: Grey said that Assange had approached CNN and Al Jazeera offering them an interview as well. Davies was fuming. Assange, however, insisted: "It was always part of our agreement that I was going to do this."

This quarrel did not bode well for the future. Nor did Assange's growing friction with the *New York Times*. The *NYT* were refusing to link directly to the WikiLeaks cable dump from their own website. Bill Keller played it differently to the *Guardian* and *Der Spiegel*, who, after some debate internally, both decided to post a link to the WikiLeaks site in the normal way. The *New York Times* took the equally defensible view that readers – and indeed their own hostile US government – would not see the paper's staff as detached reporters if they directed readers to WikiLeaks in such a purposeful manner. Keller says: "We feared – rightly, as it turned out – that their trove would contain the names of low-level informants and make them Taliban targets." Assange was angered at what he saw as pusillanimity by the Americans. He went about declaring in his Australian twang, "They must be punished!" The editor of the *New York Times*, in turn, came to see Assange as "a self-important quasi-anarchist" Keller recalls. "I talked to Assange by phone a few times, and heard out his complaints. 'Where's the respect?' he demanded. 'Where's the respect?' Another time he called to tell me how much he disliked a profile we had written of Bradley Manning ... Assange complained that we had 'psychologicalised' Manning and given short shrift to his 'political awakening'."

Beneath the surface, all these tensions simmered. But to the public, the launch of the first tranche of war logs about Afghanistan represented a smooth and well-orchestrated media coup. It gave the three papers massive exposure, and turned Julian Assange, for a time, into the world's most famous man. It was the biggest leak in history – until it was followed by an even bolder set of disclosures about Iraq. These were the two immensely controversial wars which the United States had inflicted on the world, and now, at last, it seemed possible to lift the lid on them.

CHAPTER 9
The Afghanistan war logs

Cyberspace
25 July 2010

*"We are saddened by the innocent lives that were lost
as a result of militants' cowardice"*
US ARMY MAJOR CHRIS BELCHER, AFGHANISTAN

One night in Afghanistan, five heavy rockets, fired from a new type of weapon, came shrieking out of the darkness on to a religious school, a madrassa, completely reducing it to rubble. When the assault helicopters landed and US special forces came tumbling out, they discovered they had killed seven children. Their real target, a top al-Qaida fighter, escaped. This event, one of many during the benighted Afghan war, took place on 17 June 2007, and was described in the following way by the US army's special operations command news service:

Airstrike in Paktika
BAGRAM AIRFIELD, Afghanistan.
Afghan and Coalition forces conducted an operation in Paktika Province's Zarghun Shah District late Sunday, which resulted in several militants and seven civilians killed and

two militants detained. Credible intelligence named the compound, which contained a mosque and a madrassa, as a suspected safehouse for al-Qaida fighters.

Coalition forces confirmed the presence of nefarious activity occurring at the site before getting approval to conduct an airstrike on the location. Following the strike, residents of the compound confirmed that al-Qaida fighters had been present all day.

Early reporting [suggests] seven children at the madrassa died as a result of the strike. "This is another example of al-Qaida using the protective status of a mosque, as well as innocent civilians, to shield themselves," said Army Maj Chris Belcher, a Combined Joint Task Force-82 spokesman. "We are saddened by the innocent lives that were lost as a result of militants' cowardice."

The real story only emerged from the text of a leaked military log obtained by WikiLeaks three years later, and published worldwide by the *Guardian* and its partners the *New York Times* and *Der Spiegel*. The field report was among the 92,000 allegedly turned over to WikiLeaks founder Julian Assange by US soldier Bradley Manning.

The log disclosed that there had actually been no "airstrike" (whose reconnaissance cameras might indeed have been less inaccurate). Instead, what had happened was a trial of a powerful, if potentially indiscriminate, new missile system – a GPS-guided rocket volley that could be fired from the back of a truck up to 40 miles away, known as HIMARS (high mobility artillery rocket system). The assault was not launched by ordinary "Afghan and Coalition forces" but by a shadowy troop of US killers known as Task Force 373, whose targets were written on a special list. And the rocket attack was not prompted by general "nefarious activity", but by the hope that a top listed target, Commander Al Libi, was on the premises.

The leaked war log gave the following account (abbreviations have been expanded):

Date 2007-06-17 21:00:00
Type Friendly Action
Title 172100Z[ulu time] T[ask] F[orce] 373 OBJ[ective] Lane

Summary
NOTE: The following information (TF-373 and HIMARS) is Classified Secret / NOFORN. The knowledge that TF-373 conducted a HIMARS strike must be kept protected. All other information below is classified Secret / REL[ease] ISAF. [International Security Assistance Force]

Mission
S[pecial] O[perations] T[ask] F[orce] conducts kinetic strike followed with H[elicopter] A[ssault] Force raid to kill/ capture ABU LAYTH AL LIBI on N[amed] A[rea of] I[nterest] 2.

Target
Abu Layth Al Libi is a senior al-Qaida military commander, Libyan Islamic Fighting Group (LIFG) leader. He is based in Mir Ali, Pakistan and runs training camps throughout North Waziristan. Collection over the past week indicates a concentration of Arabs I[n] V[icinity] O[f] objective area.

Result
6 x E[nemy] K[illed] I[n] A[ction]; 7 x N[on] C[ombatant] KIA 7 x detainees

Summary

H[elicopter] A[ssault] F[orce] departed for Orgun-E [base] to conduct link-up and posture to the objective immediately after pre-assault fires. On order, 5 rockets were launched and destroyed structures on the objective (NAI 2). The HAF quickly inserted the assault force into the H[elicopter] L[anding] Zone. I[intelligence] S[urveillance] R[econnaissance] reported multiple U[n]I[dentified] M[ale]s leaving the objective area. The assault force quickly conducted dismounted movement to the target area and established containment on the south side of the objective. During the initial assault, dedicated air assets engaged multiple M[ilitary] A[ge] M[ale]s squirting off the objective area. G[round] F[orce] C[ommander] assessed 3 x EKIA squirters north and 3 x EKIA squirters south of the compound were neutralised from air asset fires. The assault force quickly manoeuvred with a SQ[ua]D[ron] element on the remaining squirters. The squirter element detained 12 x MAMs and returned to the objective area. GFC passed initial assessment of 7 x NC KIA (children). During initial questioning, it was assessed that the children were not allowed out of the building, due to UIMs presence within the compound. The assault force was able to uncover 1 x NC child from the rubble. The MED[ical] T[ea]M immediately cleared debris from the mouth and performed CPR to revive the child for 20 minutes. Due to time restrictions, TF C[omman]D[e]R launched Q[uick] R[eaction] F[orce] element to action a follow-on target (NAI 5). They quickly contained the objective and initiated the assault. The objective was secured and the assault force initially detained 6 x MAMs. The GFC recommended that 7 MAMs be detained for additional questioning. The TF CDR assessed that the assault force will continue SSE. The local governor was notified of the current situation and requests for assistance were made to cordon the A[rea of] O[perations] with support from A[fghan] N[ational] Police and local coalition forces in search of H[igh] V[alue] I[ndividual]. A P[rovincial] R[econstruction] T[eam] is enroute to AO.

1) Target was an A[l] Q[aida] Senior Leader

2) Patterns of life were conducted on 18 June from 0800z 1815z (strike time) with no indications of women or children on the objective

3) The mosque was not targeted nor was it struck initial reports state there is no damage to the mosque

4) An elder who was at the mosque stated that the children were held against their will and were intentionally kept inside

UPDATE: 18 0850Z June 07

– Governor Khapalwak has had no success yet in reaching President Karzai (due to the President's busy schedule today) but expects to reach him within the hour (P[resident] o[f] A[fghanistan] reached later in the afternoon ~ 1400Z)

– The governor conducted a Shura [consultation] this morning, in attendance were locals from both the Yahya Yosof & Khail Districts

– He pressed the Talking Points given to him and added a few of his own that followed in line with our current story

- The atmospherics of the local populous [sic] is that they are in shock, but understand it was caused ultimately by the presence of hoodlums

- The people think it is good that bad men were killed

- The people regret the loss of life among the children

- The governor echoed the tragedy of children being killed, but stressed this could've been prevented had the people exposed the presence of insurgents in the area

- The governor promised another Shura in a few days and that the families would be compensated for their loss

- The governor was asked what the mood of the people was and he stated that "the operation was a good thing, and the people believe what we have told them"

There is less clipped military jargon than usual in this war log entry. The report is untypically loquacious, and in relatively plain English, because the slaughter of the seven children turned into quite a scandal, and because President Karzai was making ever louder protests about the civilian death toll from US operations in Afghanistan. But otherwise the report is representative of the kind of documents that surfaced when the Afghan war logs were first published on 25 July 2010. On that day, *Der Spiegel* made the activities of the killer squad Task Force 373 its cover story, headlining it "America's secret war". In the *Guardian*, Nick Davies unearthed much detail about TF 373's 2,000-strong target-list for "kill or capture". The hit-list appeared as yet another cryptic acronym in the war logs, JPel – the "joint priority effects list".

Davies wrote: "The United Nations' special rapporteur for human rights, Professor Philip Alston, went to Afghanistan in May 2008 to investigate rumours of extrajudicial killings. He warned that international forces were neither transparent nor accountable and that Afghans who attempted to find out who had killed their loved ones 'often come away empty-handed, frustrated and bitter'. Now, for the first time, the leaked war logs reveal details of deadly missions by TF 373 and other units hunting down JPel targets that were previously hidden behind a screen of misinformation. They raise fundamental questions about the legality of the killings and of the long-term imprisonment without trial, and also pragmatically about the impact of a tactic which is inherently likely to kill, injure and alienate the innocent bystanders whose support the coalition craves."

The *Guardian*/WikiLeaks publication smoked out profound divisions about these tactics among the occupying coalition. "The war logs confirm the impression that this is a military campaign without a clear strategic direction, under generals struggling to cope with the political, economic and social realities of Afghanistan," says Sir Sherard Cowper-Coles, until June 2010 the UK government's special representative to Afghanistan and from 2007 to 2009 its ambassador to Kabul. "The truth is that the military campaign in Afghanistan is not under proper political supervision or control … Nato's Joint Priority Effects List [the so-called kill or capture list] is not subject to genuine political oversight. It is driven by the military. The situation has deteriorated further since the war logs came out. General Petraeus has stepped up the campaign of slaughtering Taliban commanders, without a clear strategy for harvesting that politically, and in defiance of his own field manual's assertion that countering insurgency is 80% politics."

*

A hitherto veiled face of the Afghan war was thus revealed in the story of TF 373 and the hit-lists. Another veil was lifted to reveal the relentless toll taken on perfectly innocent civilians by the jittery troops riding in convoys. The foreign troops – not just Americans, but also British, Germans and Poles – were understandably terrified of roadside bombs, or of suicide bombers driving up to them in cars or on motorbikes. In theory there are strict regulations about the graded series of warning steps that soldiers have to take in Afghanistan before firing to kill. These are the procedures governing EOF – "Escalation of Force". In reality, as log entries repeatedly implied, some soldiers tended to shoot first and ask questions later.

The field reports almost never contained any direct admissions of misbehaviour: these entries are written by comrades, and designed to be viewed by more senior officers. But the Americans were a little less inhibited when giving accounts of the conduct of their allies than they were when writing up their own behaviour. As a result, David Leigh and his colleague Rob Evans were able to tease out clusters of what looked like excessive use of force against civilians on the part of certain British units. They identified a detachment of the Coldstream Guards which had recently taken up position at Camp Soutar in Kabul. The Coldstream Guards' unofficial blog described their mood at the time: "The overriding threat is that of suicide bombers, of which there have been a number in the recent past."

Four times in as many weeks, this unit appears to have shot civilians in the town in order to protect its own members. The worst was on 21 October 2007, when the US soldiers reported a case of "blue-on-white" friendly fire in downtown Kabul, noting that some unknown troops had shot up a civilian vehicle containing three private security company interpreters and a driver. The troops had been in "a military-type vehicle that was brown with a gunner on top ... There were no US forces located in the vicinity of the event that may have been involved. More to follow!" They updated a short while later, saying "INVESTIGATION IS CONTROLLED BY THE BRITISH. WE NOT ABLE TO GET THE COMPLETE STORY. THIS EVENT BELONGS TO THE BRITISH ISAF FORCES."

It took another three months' stalling, after the WikiLeaks logs went public, before the Ministry of Defence in London admitted these Kabul shootings had indeed taken place. They confirmed the British patrol had shot dead one civilian and wounded two others in a silver minibus. It was claimed the minibus failed to stop when the soldiers signalled for it to do so.

A few days after the minibus shooting, on 6 November, the British reported around midday that they had wounded another civilian in Kabul in broad daylight with what was at first claimed to be a "warning shot". At the end of the afternoon, the Americans heard the man had died, and there might be trouble: "There could be some demonstration, the civilian was a son of an Afghan aviation general, his wedding was planned for this evening with numerous people." They later updated: "It was not the wedding of the dead person. The wedding for this evening was planned for his brother but now it is cancelled. The family will get the dead body tomorrow morning." Again the British army eventually confirmed this WikiLeaks disclosure after a long delay: the official British version is that the general's son had "accelerated" his Toyota towards a patrol, leaving the soldiers only time for a shouted warning before firing at the car. The car then skidded to a halt and a man fell out, they say.

These events, and hundreds like them, together constitute the hidden history of the war in Afghanistan, in which innocent people were repeatedly killed by foreign soldiers. The remarkable level of detail provided by the war logs made it accessible for the first time.

*

However, while the European media focused on the sufferings of civilians, the *New York Times* tended to take a more strategic approach to the Afghan war. One of their major interests was to study the large – and often surprising – quantity of evidence in the war logs that US efforts to suppress the Taliban were being hampered by Pakistan. There were repeated detailed entries telling of clashes or intelligence reports in which Pakistan's intelligence service, the ISI, appeared to be the villain, covertly backing the Taliban for reasons of its own.

The Obama administration had a relatively sophisticated response to this information, which it was aware the papers had discovered. It used the situation to project a message. As the logs were published at 10pm GMT on Sunday evening, a White House spokesman emailed newspapers' Washington correspondents a note not intended for publication under the subject line: "Thoughts on WikiLeaks". They even attached some handy quotes from senior officials highlighting concerns about the ISI and safe havens in Afghanistan. "This is now out in the open," a senior administration official told the *New York Times*. "It's reality now. In some ways, it makes it easier for us to tell the Pakistanis that they have to help us." A spokesman stated in public: "The safe havens for violent extremist groups within Pakistan continue to pose an intolerable threat to the United States, to Afghanistan, and to the Pakistani people."

The British prime minister, David Cameron, on a two-day trip to India, chimed in, in what seemed a synchronised way. Speaking to a business audience in Bangalore two days after the war logs were released, he signalled the same hard line. "We cannot tolerate in any sense the idea that this country [Pakistan] is allowed to look both ways and is able to promote the export of terror, whether to India or Afghanistan or anywhere else in the world," he said. "That is why this relationship is important. But it should be a relationship based on a very clear message: that it is not right to have any relationship with groups that are promoting terror. Democratic states that want to be part of the developed world cannot do that. The message to Pakistan from the US and from the UK is very clear on that point."

It was a surprising turn of events, confirming what most investigative journalists know instinctively, that full disclosure of hitherto secret information can stimulate all kinds of unexpected outcomes. The *Guardian* summed up in an editorial the purpose of its co-operation with WikiLeaks:

> The fog of war is unusually dense in Afghanistan. When it lifts, as it does today … a very different landscape is revealed from the one with which we have become familiar. These war logs – written in the heat of engagement – show a conflict that is brutally messy, confused and immediate. It is in some contrast with the tidied-up and sanitised "public" war, as glimpsed through official communiqués as well as the necessarily limited snapshots of embedded reporting … The *Guardian* has spent weeks sifting through this ocean of data, which has gradually yielded the hidden texture and human horror stories inflicted day to day during an often clumsily prosecuted war. It is important to treat the material for what it is: a contemporaneous catalogue of conflict. Some of the more lurid intelligence reports are of doubtful provenance: some aspects of the coalition's recording of civilian deaths appear unreliable. The war logs – classified as secret – are encyclopedic but incomplete. We have removed any material which threatens the safety of troops, local informants and collaborators.
>
> With these caveats, the collective picture that emerges is a very disturbing one. We today learn of nearly 150 incidents in which coalition forces, including British troops, have killed or injured civilians, most of which have never been reported;

of hundreds of border clashes between Afghan and Pakistani troops, two armies which are supposed to be allies; of the existence of a special forces unit whose tasks include killing Taliban and al-Qaida leaders; of the slaughter of civilians caught by the Taliban's improvised explosive devices; and of a catalogue of incidents where coalition troops have fired on and killed each other or fellow Afghans under arms ...

In these documents, Iran's and Pakistan's intelligence agencies run riot. Pakistan's Inter-Services Intelligence is linked to some of the war's most notorious commanders. The ISI is alleged to have sent 1,000 motorbikes to the warlord Jalaluddin Haqqani for suicide attacks in Khost and Logar provinces, and to have been implicated in a sensational range of plots, from attempting to assassinate President Hamid Karzai to poisoning the beer supply of western troops. These reports are unverifiable and could be part of a barrage of false information provided by Afghan intelligence. But yesterday's White House response to the claims that elements of the Pakistan army had been so specifically linked to the militants made it plain that the status quo is unacceptable. It said that safe havens for militants within Pakistan continued to pose "an intolerable threat" to US forces. However you cut it, this is not an Afghanistan that either the US or Britain is about to hand over gift-wrapped with pink ribbons to a sovereign national government in Kabul. Quite the contrary. After nine years of warfare, the chaos threatens to overwhelm. A war fought ostensibly for the hearts and minds of Afghans cannot be won like this.

What the paper did not dare advertise, for security reasons, was that the world would shortly be presented with a far bigger trove of leaked documents, detailing similar truths about the bloodbath in Iraq.

CHAPTER 10
The Iraq war logs

Cyberspace
22 October 2010

"You know we don't do body counts"
GENERAL TOMMY FRANKS

The Iraq war logs were all about numbers. Both the US administration and the British prime minister refused to admit how many
ordinary Iraqis had been killed since the mixed blessing of their
being "liberated" by US and UK troops. General Tommy Franks
had notoriously been quoted in 2002 saying, "We don't do body
counts" – a year before he led the US military invasion of Iraq. He
may have really meant that he was not going to fall into the over-
optimistic trap of the Vietnam war in the 1960s, when US generals
had claimed to have slaughtered virtually the entire military
manpower of North Vietnam several times over, before admitting
eventual defeat.

But because the invasion and occupation of Iraq in 2003
turned into an unplanned bloodbath, "We don't do body
counts" became the unspoken mantra of Bush and Blair as well.
Authorities meticulously recorded that 4,748 US and allied
troops lost their lives up to Christmas Day 2010. But western

governments claimed for years that no other official casualty statistics existed.

The publication of the huge leaked database of Iraqi field reports in October 2010 gave the lie to that. The logs disclosed a detailed incident-by-incident record of at least 66,081 violent deaths of civilians in Iraq since the invasion. This figure, dismaying in itself, was nevertheless only a statistical starting-point. It is far too low. The database begins a year late in 2004, omitting the high casualties of the direct 2003 invasion period itself, and ends on 31 December 2009. Furthermore, the US figures are plainly unreliable in respect of the most sensitive issue – civilian deaths directly caused by their own military activities.

For example, the town of Falluja was the site of two major urban battles in 2004, which reduced the place to near-rubble. Yet no civilian deaths whatever are recorded by the army loggers, apparently on the grounds that they had previously ordered all the inhabitants to leave. Monitors from the unofficial Iraq Body Count group, on the other hand, managed to identify more than 1,200 civilians who died during the Falluja fighting.

In other cases, the US army killed civilians, but wrongly recorded them in the database as enemy combatants. It was as enemy combatants, for example, that the two hapless Reuters employees shot in Baghdad in 2007 by an Apache helicopter gunship – the episode captured on a gun-camera video, and subsequently discovered and leaked to WikiLeaks – were registered.

As so often, further journalistic investigation was needed to improve these raw and statistically dirty figures. Iraq Body Count, an NGO offshoot of the Oxford Research Group and co-founded by a psychology professor, John Sloboda, had dedicated itself for years to counting up otherwise unregarded corpses. They were able to cross-check with the leaked military data. The group says: "The release and publication by WikiLeaks of the 'Iraq War Logs' provided IBC with the first large-scale database we could compare and cross-reference with our own. For most of its incidents this military database is as detailed as IBC's, and quite often more so. Its release in such a highly detailed form enabled us to carry out some preliminary research into the number of casualties that the logs might contain, that have not been reported elsewhere. IBC was consequently able to provide an initial, but fairly robust, estimate that, once fully analysed, the logs would reveal another 15,000 civilian deaths (including 3,000 ordinary police) beyond the previously known death toll."

The numbers contained in the war logs proved not only to generate that extra 15,000 casualties, but also to be broadly comparable with the IBC's own unofficial figures. At the end of 2010, IBC concluded that the full total of documented civilian deaths from violence in Iraq since 2003 now ranged between 99,383 and 108,501. The increased confidence that the public can have in these numbers can be presumed to be directly due to the whistleblowing of Manning and Assange, along with the dedication of IBC researchers, and the hard work of journalists from three news organisations. Future historians may be able to assess whether that work might make future American and British military adventures any less reckless and bloody.

Another aspect of the war logs statistics which is likely to be exceptionally reliable – because the US army had no reason to play down the figures – is the appalling total of civilians, local troops and coalition forces whose deaths were caused either by insurgent landmines or by internecine fighting. No fewer than 31,780 deaths were attributed to improvised roadside bombs (IEDs) planted by insurgents. Sectarian killings (recorded as "murders") claimed another 34,814 victims. Overall, the war logs detailed 109,032 deaths.

This total of dead broke down into the 66,081 civilians detailed above, plus 15,196 members of the Iraqi security forces, and 23,984 people classed as "enemy". At 31 December 2009, when the leaked database stops, the total was arrived at by the addition of 3,771 dead US and allied soldiers. Every one of those westerners who died had a name, a family and probably often a photograph published in their local newspaper along with grieving tributes. But these files showed they represented less than 3.5% of the real death toll in Iraq.

Such appalling bloodshed was justified by the US, the UK and their occupying partners on the grounds that they had at any rate rescued Iraqis from the brutal police state run by Saddam Hussein. It was therefore doubly disturbing when an analysis of the data by the *Guardian*'s Nick Davies revealed that Iraq was still a torture chamber. The legacy being left behind by western troops was of an Iraqi army and police force which would continue to arrest, mistreat and murder its own citizens, almost as if Saddam had never been overthrown.

It was Bradley Manning's revulsion at the behaviour of the Iraqi police, and US military collusion with it, which had led him, according to statements in his chat logs, to think in 2009 about becoming a whistleblower in the first place. After being rebuffed in an effort to exculpate a group of improperly detained Iraqis, "everything started slipping ... I saw things differently ... I was actively involved in something that I was completely against."

Davies reported in the *Guardian* on 23 October:

US authorities failed to investigate hundreds of reports of abuse, torture, rape and even murder by Iraqi police and soldiers whose conduct appears to be systematic and normally unpunished ... The numerous reports of detainee abuse, often supported by medical evidence, describe prisoners shackled, blindfolded and hung by wrists or ankles, and subjected to whipping, punching, kicking or electric shocks. Six reports end with a detainee's apparent death.

As recently as December 2009 the Americans were passed a video apparently showing Iraqi army officers executing a prisoner in Tal Afar, northern Iraq. The log states: "The footage shows approximately 12 Iraqi army soldiers. Ten IA soldiers were talking to one another while two soldiers held the detainee. The detainee had his hands bound ... The footage shows the IA soldiers moving the detainee into the street, pushing him to the ground, punching him and shooting him." The report named at least one perpetrator and was passed to coalition forces.

In two Iraqi cases postmortems revealed evidence of death by torture. On 27 August 2009 a US medical officer found "bruises and burns as well as visible injuries to the head, arm, torso, legs and neck" on the body of one man claimed by police to have killed himself. On 3 December 2008 another detainee, said by police to have died of "bad kidneys", was found to have "evidence of some type of unknown surgical procedure on [his] abdomen".

But the logs reveal that the coalition has a formal policy of ignoring torture allegations. They record "no investigation is necessary" and simply pass reports to the same Iraqi units implicated in the violence. By contrast all allegations involving coalition forces are subject to formal inquiries.

Even when torture like this was not being alleged, vignette after vignette emerged from the Iraq logs of killings which must have been deeply degrading and damaging to their military perpetrators.

On 22 February 2007, for example, an Apache helicopter gunship crew – from the same unit that killed the Reuters employees, call sign Crazyhorse 18 – radioed back to base for advice about their aerial man-hunt. They were chasing down a pair of insurgents who had been lobbing mortar shells at a US base, and then attempted to make off in a van. Crazyhorse 18 shot up the van. The two men jumped out and tried to escape in a dumper truck. Crazyhorse 18 shot that up, too. "They came out wanting to surrender," the helicopter crew signalled back to base, asking for advice. What were they to do? It is a sign of US respect for legal forms that the base lawyer was immediately on hand, ready to be consulted. The controller signalled back: "Lawyer states they cannot surrender to aircraft and are still valid targets." So the helicopter crew killed the men, as they were attempting to surrender.

Those two dead men were enemy combatants. The same could probably not be said of a car which drove too close to a supply convoy outside Baghdad. The marines in the rear Humvee claimed afterwards that they had made hand signals and fired warning shots to the engine-block "to warn the vehicle to slow down and not approach the convoy". When it had closed to within 20 yards of the Humvee, the marines started putting shots into its windscreen.

The spare uppercase prose of the leaked field report takes up the story.

THE VEHICLE SWERVED OFF THE ROAD INTO A CANAL 1.5KM NORTH OF SAQLAWIYAH (38S LB 768 976) AND SANK. (1) ADULT MALE EXITED THE VEHICLE AND WAS RECOVERED FROM THE CANAL; ALL OTHER PASSENGERS SANK WITH THE VEHICLE. THE ADULT MALE WAS TREATED BY THE CORPSMAN ON THE SCENE AND WAS TRANSPORTED TO THE SAQLAWIYAH JCC AND SUBSEQUENTLY TRANSPORTED TO THE JORDAN-IAN HOSPITAL. SAQLAWIYAH I[RAQI] P[OLICE] S[ERVICE] RESPONDED TO THE SCENE AND RECOVERED (2) ADULT FEMALES, (3) CHILDREN AGES 5 TO 8, AND (1) INFANT FROM THE VEHICLE.

ALL (6) HAD DROWNED. THE SAQLAWIYAH IPS ARE
TAKING ALL RECOVERED BODIES TO RAMADI.

These were not the hi-tech military heroics so frequently put out
by the US army's press releases, but acts of cruelty more worthy
perhaps of a place in a modern version of Goya's dark etchings
from early 19th-century Spain, "The Disasters of War".

Assange had launched the publication of the Iraq logs in the
grandiose ballroom of the Park Plaza hotel on the Thames, with
Iraq Body Count, Phil Shiner of Public Interest Lawyers, and a
TV documentary team all in attendance. Shortly before 10am,
the teams lined up in the corridor behind Assange, who was
wearing a sharp suit and tie, and led them out into a blizzard of
flashbulbs and camera lights. He was mobbed. It was as if the
Australian were a rock star with his entourage. About 300 journalists had turned out to watch his performance, five times more
than at the launch of the Afghan logs. When the packed room
was called to order, Assange intoned: "This disclosure is about
the truth."

He had now delivered two of his controversial leaked "packages" to the newspapers, with striking results. But the question in
the *Guardian* and *New York Times* journalists' minds, as they
watched the adulation, was would Assange be prepared to honour
his undertaking, and hand over "package three" for publication?
That might prove even more sensational.

CHAPTER 11
The cables

Near Lochnagar, Scotland
August 2010

*"ACollectionOfDiplomaticHistorySince_1966_
ToThe_PresentDay#"*
ASSANGE'S 58-CHARACTER PASSWORD

David Leigh had listened patiently to Assange, who had instructed him that he must never allow his memory stick to be connected to any computer that was exposed to the internet, for fear of electronic eavesdropping by US intelligence. But there was currently no danger of that at all. Leigh's rented cottage way up in the Scottish Highlands was unable even to receive a TV signal, never mind a broadband connection. The *Guardian*'s investigations editor had originally planned to spend his annual summer vacation with his wife, hill-walking in the Grampians. But the summits of Dreish, Mayar, Lochnagar and Cat Law went unclimbed. He sat transfixed at his desk instead, while the sun rose and set daily on the heather-covered hills outside. On the tiny silver Hewlett Packard thumb-drive plugged into his MacBook were the full texts of more than 250,000 diplomatic cables. To search through them was maddening, tiring – and utterly compelling.

It had been a struggle to prise these documents out of Assange back in London. There were repeated pilgrimages to the mews house belonging to Vaughan Smith's Frontline Club near Paddington station before Assange reluctantly turned them over. "We have to able to work on them, Julian," Leigh had argued. "None of the partners have any real idea what's there, except their contents are supposed to give Hillary Clinton a heart attack!" Assange was keeping the three news organisations dangling, despite his original agreement to deliver all the material for publication. He willingly passed on the less important war logs from Afghanistan and Iraq, but talked of how he would use his power to withhold the cables in order to "discipline" the mainstream media.

The atmosphere had become even more problematic since Nick Davies personally broke off relations in the summer, after Assange breached the original compact, as Davies saw it, by going behind his back to the *Guardian*'s TV rivals at Channel 4, taking with him all the knowledge acquired by privileged visits to the *Guardian*'s research room. Davies at the time said he felt betrayed: Assange simply insisted there had never been a deal.

The other *Guardian* journalists tightened their lips and held their peace. There was still a long road to travel if all the leaks were ever to come out. But after the publication of the Afghan war logs, Assange proposed to change the terms of the deal once again, before the planned launch of the much bigger tranche of Iraq logs. He wanted more television, in order to provide "emotional impact". He had by now made some new friends in London – Ahmad Ibrahim, from the Qatari-funded Al Jazeera, and Gavin MacFadyen from City University in London. MacFadyen, a veteran of *World in Action*, one of Britain's most distinguished investigative TV series in the 1970s, had recently helped set up an independent production company based at the university. Called the Bureau of Investigative Journalism, it was funded by the David and Elaine Potter Foundation. Elaine had been a reporter during the great days of London's *Sunday Times*, and her husband David had made millions from the development of the Psion computer. There was a distinct prospect that the wealthy Potter Foundation might become patrons of WikiLeaks: the Florentine Medicis, as it were, to Assange's Michelangelo. Rapidly, the "Bureau" was drawn into Assange's new plans.

He demanded that print publication of the Iraq war logs be postponed for at least another six weeks. This would enable the Bureau, under Assange's guidance, to sell a TV documentary to Channel 4's well-regarded *Dispatches* series. The Bureau would also make and sell a second documentary, of a more wide-ranging nature, to be aired on both Al Jazeera's Arabic and English-language channels, which could be guaranteed to cause uproar in the Middle East. Both documentaries eventually got made, and Assange sensibly hired a respected NGO, Iraq Body Count, to analyse the casualty figures for the TV productions.

The fledgling Bureau, headed by former TV journalist Iain Overton, unsuccessfully attempted to make further lucrative sales to TV channels in the US. Overton then exasperated his unenthusiastic print partners by giving an on-the-record interview to Mark Hosenball of *Newsweek*, betraying in advance the entire top-secret plan to publish the Iraq war logs.

"Exclusive: WikiLeaks Collaborating With Media Outlets on Release of Iraq Documents", ran the headline above the article, which opened: "A London-based journalism nonprofit is working with the WikiLeaks website and TV and print media in several countries on programmes and stories based on what is described as a massive cache of classified US military field reports related to the Iraq war ... The material is the 'biggest leak of military intelligence' that has ever occurred, Overton says."

Assange's side deal with the Qataris also angered the original partners. Al Jazeera English was to break the agreed embargo for simultaneous publication by almost an hour, leaving the other media organisations scrambling to catch up on their websites. Leigh found it hard to disagree with Eric Schmitt of the *New York Times* when he protested that Assange seemed to be doing media deals with "riff-raff". The founder of WikiLeaks had been rocketed to the status of a huge celebrity, in large part thanks to the credibility bestowed on him by three of the world's major news organisations. But was he going out of control?

Leigh tried his best not to fall out with this Australian impresario, who was prone to criticise what he called the "snaky Brits". Instead, Leigh used his ever-shifting demands as a negotiating lever. "You want us to postpone the Iraq logs' publication so you can get some TV," he said. "We could refuse, and simply go ahead with publication as planned. If you want us to do something for you, then you've got to do something for us as well." He asked Assange to stop procrastinating, and hand over the biggest trove of all: the cables. Assange said, "I could give you half of them, covering the first 50% of the period."

Leigh refused. All or nothing, he said. "What happens if you end up in an orange jump-suit en route to Guantánamo before you can release the full files?" In return he would give Assange a promise to keep the cables secure, and not to publish them until the time came. Assange had always been vague about timing: he generally indicated, however, that October would be a suitable date. He believed the US army's charges against the imprisoned soldier Bradley Manning would have crystallised by then, and publication could not make his fate any worse. He also said, echoing Leigh's gallows humour: "I'm going to need to be safe in Cuba first!"

Eventually, Assange capitulated. Late at night, after a two-hour debate, he started the process on one of his little netbooks that would enable Leigh to download the entire tranche of cables. The *Guardian* journalist had to set up the PGP encryption system on his laptop at home across the other side of London. Then he could feed in a password. Assange wrote down on a scrap of paper:

A Collection Of History Since_1966_To The_Present Day#. "That's the password," he said. "But you have to add one extra word when you type it in. You have to put in the word 'Diplomatic' before the word 'History'. Can you remember that?"

"I can remember that."

Leigh set off home, and successfully installed the PGP software. He typed in the lengthy password, and was gratified to be able to download a huge file from Assange's temporary website. Then he realized it was zipped up – compressed using a format called 7z which he had never heard of, and couldn't understand. He got back in his car and drove through the deserted London streets in the small hours, to Assange's headquarters in Southwick Mews. Assange smiled a little pityingly, and unzipped it for him.

Now, isolated up in the Highlands, with hares and buzzards for company, Leigh felt safe enough to work steadily through the dangerous contents of the memory stick. Obviously, there was no way he, or any other human, could read through a quarter of a million cables. Cut off from the *Guardian*'s own network, he was unable to have the material turned into a searchable database. Nor could he call up such a monolithic file on his laptop and search through it in the normal simple-minded journalistic way, as a word processor document or something similar: it was just too big.

Harold Frayman, the *Guardian*'s technical expert, was there to rescue him. Before Leigh left town, he sawed the material into 87 chunks, each just about small enough to call up and read separately. Then he explained how Leigh could use a simple program called TextWrangler to search for key words or phrases through all the separate files simultaneously, and present the results in a user-friendly form.

Leigh was in business. He quickly learned that although the cables often contained discursive free-text essays on local politics, their headers were always assembled in a rigid format. In fact, the state department posted on its own website an unclassified telecommunications handbook which instructed its cipher clerks exactly what to do and how to do it, every time.

So, to type in, for example, "FM AMEMBASSY TUNIS" could be guaranteed to fetch up a list of each dispatch sent back to Washington from the American embassy in the capital of Tunisia. Similarly, the dispatches always signed off with the upper-case surname of the ambassador in post at the time. So the legend TUTTLE would fetch every cable during the ambassadorship of Robert Tuttle, George W Bush's London envoy.

There were limits to the dossier's contents. There was very little material prior to 2006 and the "Net-Centric Diplomacy" system had clearly been built up from some restricted pilot proj-ects. So only a few embassies contributed material at first. Even the more up-to-date and voluminous dispatches were only a partial selection: many cables or sections that the state depart-ment could not bring themselves to share with other parts of the Washington military and bureaucratic forest were missing. Never-theless, what the cables contained was an astonishing mountain of words, cataloguing the recent diplomacy of the world's sole superpower in ways that no one in earlier decades could have even imagined.

Its sheer bulk was overwhelming. If the tiny memory stick containing the cables had been a set of printed texts, it would have made up a library containing more than 2,000 sizeable books. No human diplomats would have attempted to write so much down before the coming of the digital age: if written down, no human spy would have been able to purloin copies of that much paper without using a lorry, and no human mind would have been able subsequently to analyse it without spending half a lifetime at the task.

To be confronted with this set of data therefore represented a severe journalistic problem.

*

Leigh began his experiments by typing in the word "Megrahi". He thought the name of the Libyan intelligence officer imprisoned for his part in the notorious 1988 Lockerbie plane bombing might be unusual enough to throw up relevant results. The Megrahi case was an ongoing diplomatic altercation involving the Americans, the Libyans, the British, the Scottish and – as it transpired – even the Qataris. Against US wishes, Megrahi had been released from a UK prison in August 2009, supposedly on compassionate grounds because he was on the brink of death from prostate cancer. A year later, he was still alive, after receiving a hero's welcome back in Tripoli. That much was known to the outside world, and conspiracy theories abounded. Was there now a way of uncovering the insider truth?

The TextWrangler software took barely two minutes to throw up and itemise no fewer than 451 appearances of the word Megrahi in US dispatches. Taken together, the picture they painted was certainly different from the one officially fed to the British public at the time. The first cable up on the screen was from Richard LeBaron, the charge d'affaires in London, dated 24 October 2008. Marked "PRIORITY" for both the secretary of state in Washington and also the department of justice, the cable was classified "CONFIDENTIAL//NOFORN". It began, "Convicted Pam Am 103 bomber Abdelbasset al-Megrahi has inoperable, incurable cancer, but it is not clear how long he has to live."

A succession of cables then charted growing pressure – described as "thuggish" – heaped on the British by Libya. Viewed sidelong from a US perspective, the dilemma for their junior ally in London was clear, and even evoked some sympathy. The American public was going to be furious if the ailing Megrahi was let out too soon: many US citizens had died on the bombed plane, and Megrahi was the only Libyan who had ever received any kind of punishment for the atrocity.

On the other hand, if Megrahi was allowed to die in a Scottish prison (the fragments of the plane had fallen on a Scottish town, and Scotland had its own legal system) then Muammar Gaddafi, the megalomaniac ruler of Libya, was threatening dire commercial reprisals. The British ambassador was privately warning that UK interests could be "cut off at the knees". It was the crucial truth no British politician wanted to come clean about in public.

The British administration in London managed to push the decision for Megrahi's release – and the subsequent blame for it – on to the autonomous government in Scotland. The Scottish nationalist politicians complained bitterly to the US that they had got nothing out of the deal. The US diplomats recorded privately that it served the Scot Nats right for getting out of their depth. The Americans also noted their own suspicions that the Scots might have been in effect bribed with the offer of Qatari trade loans to let Megrahi out (both parties vociferously denied it) and that Tony Blair, when prime minister, might have cynically promised leniency for Megrahi in return for lucrative British oil deals. (The British equally vociferously denied that accusation.)

The cables left the British looking ineffectual: they failed to prevent Gaddafi's son Saif from arranging an embarrassing hero's welcome for Megrahi, although celebrations were somewhat toned down. And UK intelligence was so weak that diplomats were wringing their hands over the prospect of a public Megrahi funeral the following year – but on the basis of false information, duly passed on to the US, that he was now due to die any minute.

The cables also disclosed that the Americans spoke with forked tongues. While it was left to US domestic politicians to huff angrily about Libyan perfidy, the state department signalled that Gaddafi might be co-opted to help hunt down al-Qaida fundamentalists. And the Libyan ruler was continuing to dismantle his would-be nuclear arsenal, even if Hillary Clinton had to personally sign a grovelling letter to mollify one of his massive sulks.

This particular sulk came about, the cables revealed, when Gaddafi, who appeared at the UN accompanied everywhere by a "voluptuous blonde Ukrainian nurse", flew into a rage at the derisive reception accorded to his lengthy general assembly speech. His pique was compounded by US refusal to let him pitch his iconic Bedouin-style tent in New York. Gaddaffi vented his ire, it transpired, by suddenly refusing to allow a "hot" shipment of highly enriched uranium be loaded on a transport plane and shipped back to Russia, as part of his nuclear-dismantling agreement. US diplomats and experts warned in terrified tones of a radioactive calamity, as the uranium container sat for a month, unguarded and in danger of heating up and cracking open.

This picture that emerged of US diplomatic dealings with Libya was thus richly textured and fascinating. It showed a superpower at work: cajoling, fixing, eavesdropping, manoeuvring and sometimes bullying. It also showed the dismayingly crazed attitudes of a foreign ruler possessing both nuclear ambitions and a lucrative reservoir of the world's oil – a truth which his own subjects would rarely be allowed to see. And, from the point of view of a domestic British reporter, it showed how limited the options open to the UK seemed to be despite its pretensions to punch above its weight in the world.

These documents had to be treated carefully, Leigh realised. Some of the informants who described Gaddafi's idiosyncrasies would clearly have to have their identities protected. Although the cables themselves were obviously genuine, it did not mean that the analysis and gossip reported therein were also always correct. And one had to bear in mind that the authors of these dispatches to Washington also had their own agendas. They wanted to impress. They wanted to promote their own views. Sometimes they simply wanted to demonstrate that they knew what was going on: diplomats, like journalists, were all too capable of turning a shallow lunch with a "contact" into a hot story, for career-enhancing reasons.

Nevertheless, with all these caveats, it was clear that America's secret diplomatic dealings over Libya were immensely revelatory. They were not only newsworthy, but also important. This was a picture of the world seen through a much less scrambled prism than usual. And there were more than another 100 countries to go! Leigh was plunging once more into the database bran-tub when his landline suddenly rang, breaking into the silence of the surrounding Highland hills. It was his London colleague Nick Davies, with a bewildering message. It was one that threatened to derail the entire WikiLeaks enterprise. "Julian's about to be arrested in Sweden!" he said "He's being accused of rape."

CHAPTER 12

The world's most famous man

Sonja Braun's flat, Stockholm
Friday 13 August 2010

*"Sonja tried a number of times to reach for a condom, but
Assange stopped her by holding her arms and pinning her legs"*
Braun testimony, Swedish police dossier

The revelation that Julian Assange had been accused of rape came
as a bombshell. In a series of frantic overseas phone calls, Leigh
and Davies attempted to piece together a history of the disastrous
sexual collisions that occurred in that Nordic high summer, which
would eventually lead to Swedish prosecutors pursuing extradition of Assange from Britain to face questioning over allegations
of sexual misconduct. No one had anticipated this.

One thing is clear: on present evidence Julian Assange is
absolutely not a rapist as the term is understood by many – that
is, he does not practise, nor is he accused of, the premeditated
and brutal sexual violence that the word "rapist" evokes in tabloid
headlines.

But during his time in London, Assange did often seem to
have a restlessly predatory attitude towards women. It contrasted
with his otherwise cool demeanour. Assange's behaviour once

even caused his own blonde lawyer, Jennifer Robinson from the firm of Finers Stephens Innocent, to blush brick-red. Gathered at the head of the stairs inside the *Guardian* building, a group of hungry reporters, with Assange and a number of his legal team, were debating plans to go out and eat. "Shall we take the lawyers with us?" a journalist asked. Assange leered at Robinson and said, "Let's just take the pretty one."

A WikiLeaks staffer confided later: "We've simply had to tell Julian he must stop making sexually inappropriate remarks." Icelandic MP Birgitta Jónsdóttir, one of several exasperated women, said, charitably, that it was important to bear in mind the culture Assange came from. She told the online *Daily Beast*: "Julian is brilliant in many ways, but he doesn't have very good social skills … and he's a classic Aussie in the sense that he's a bit of a male chauvinist."

Men like Assange, who refer to women as "hotties", hail from the land of coarse jokes about the one-eyed trouser snake – a considerable contrast to sober Swedes, who are well-advanced in their understanding of women's sexual rights.

The stage was thus set in Sweden for an ambiguous – and, as it proved, highly controversial – encounter.

On Wednesday 11 August Assange flew in from London. That evening he dined out at the Beirut Café, a Lebanese restaurant in north Stockholm, one of a party of five. Present were 56-year-old Donald Böstrom, the Swedish journalist who was WikiLeaks' local connection, and his wife. The other pair round the table were Russ Baker, a US reporter with cropped grey hair who last year published a controversial book about the Bush family, and a woman friend with whom Baker was travelling. Assange made such a brazen, though unsuccessful, play for this latter woman, according to those present, that a row broke out. "Assange and

Baker actually ended up squaring up to each other outside the restaurant," says one of those closely involved.

Böstrom says he felt uneasy for his celebrity friend. He warned Assange that his behaviour was a security risk, for "he would not be the first great man to be brought down by a woman in a short skirt". Böstrom says that he could see that Assange's notoriety and evident courage were proving remarkably attractive to women: "There's a bit of the rock star phenomenon about it. The world's most famous man, in some people's eyes. Really intelligent – and that's attractive – and he takes on the Pentagon. That's impressive to many. I could say the majority of women who come in contact with him fall completely. They become bewitched."

Friday the 13th lived up to its reputation, at least as far as Assange was concerned. When his trip began, the celebrity leaker was staying in the suburb of Sodermalm, in an unoccupied Stockholm flat belonging to Sonja Braun (not her real name), a politically active 31-year-old official of the Brotherhood movement, a Christian group affiliated to the large Social Democrat party. Braun is a slim, dark-haired feminist who speaks English and was previously an equality officer at a top Swedish university. It was Braun who invited Assange to come to Sweden and give a seminar, and indeed she seems to have specifically arranged that Assange should sleep at her flat. Significantly, that flat has only one room and only one bed, say Assange's lawyers.

Before Assange's arrival, Braun called Böstrom, the journalist recalls. "We had never met before, and she says: 'Hello, my name is Sonja Braun and I'm planning this seminar and I'll be away on a business trip and my flat will be empty and Julian could stay there. Would you suggest it?' It would be cheaper for the Brotherhood movement, who wouldn't need to pay hotel bills, and Julian would rather live in a flat than in a hotel, so I suggest it and he jumps at it. So I put the two of them together. I'm the middleman, so to speak. The idea was that Julian would live there up to the Friday, I think. The seminar was on Saturday. Sonja was supposed to return on the Saturday."

Braun decided to come back a day early, however. At this point, accounts begin to diverge. Assange's lawyers supplied a brisk chronology to a later London court hearing, saying: "Braun arrives without explanation, takes him to dinner and invites him to bed. She supplies a condom and they have intercourse several times." The lawyers add tartly: "Early morning: Braun takes photograph of Julian asleep in her bed (unauthorised), later posted on the internet."

A rather different version was later given to police by Braun herself. According to her, it was a tale of a night of bad sex, with one peculiar twist. The police document recorded:

"As they sat drinking tea, Assange stroked Sonja's leg. Sonja has stated that at no point earlier in the evening had Assange attempted to press any physical attentions on her, which Sonja initially welcomed. Then, according to Sonja it all went very quickly. Assange was heavy-handed and impatient. He pulled off her clothes and at the same time snapped her necklace. Sonja tried to put on some articles of clothing as it was going too quickly and uncomfortably but Assange ripped them off again. Sonja says that she didn't want to go any further but that it was too late to stop Assange as she had gone along with it so far. She says that she felt she only had herself to blame, and so she allowed Assange to take off her clothes."

This vigorous wooing does not sound out of character. Another woman in London who got involved with Assange around the same time told the authors: "I kissed him. Then he started trying to rip my dress off. That was his approach."

Braun's complaints went further, however. According to the statement, she realised he was trying to have unprotected sex with her. "She tried to wriggle her hips and cross her legs to stop penetration. Braun tried a number of times to reach for a condom but

Assange stopped her by holding her arms and pinning her legs and continued to try and enter her without a condom. Braun says that she was on the verge of tears and couldn't get hold of a condom and thought, 'This is going to end badly.'

"After a while, Assange asked Sonja what it was she was reaching out for and why she was crossing her legs and she said she wanted him to put a condom on ... Assange had by now released her arms and put on a condom that Sonja gave him. Sonja says she felt there was an unspoken resistance from Assange which gave her the idea that he didn't like being told to do things."

Braun told the police that at some stage Assange had "done something" with the condom that resulted in it becoming ripped, and ejaculated without withdrawing.

When he was later interviewed by police in Stockholm, Assange agreed that he had had sex with Braun but said he did not tear the condom. He told police that he had continued to sleep in her bed for the following week and she had never mentioned a torn condom.

At 9.30 the following morning, according to the Assange camp, a journalist called to collect Assange for the lecture. "He is amazed to find Braun there." She herself seemed embarrassed, and actually denied having had sex with him. Böstrom told police: "When someone asked, she joked that Julian was living in her flat and was sleeping in her bed, but that they hadn't had sex. She said that he tried, but she refused." Much later, according to Böstrom, she sheepishly confessed that she did in fact have sex with Assange. Her explanation: "I was really proud of having the world's most famous man in my bed, and living in my flat."

At Assange's 11am seminar, on the WikiLeaks theme that "Truth is the first casualty of war", Sonja Braun can be seen onstage in video footage. She appeared businesslike, if somewhat subdued.

Böstrom himself was beginning to wonder. At lunch after the seminar, he noted that Braun and Assange were chatting in intimate tones: "She told me, laughing, that he was a strange guy who got up in the middle of the night to work on his laptop, and she's quite jokey about this. But then at the party she's sitting next to Julian and takes it up again ... 'Were you awake last night?' she says. And she says, 'I woke up and you had got out of bed, and I felt abandoned.' And it was just that word that caught my attention. Why did she feel abandoned if they weren't ..." His account tails off and changes direction. "Peter Weiderud [a Brotherhood official] says it's crayfish time in Sweden and Julian is here from abroad, so he should try Swedish crayfish." Braun then dutifully tweeted, at 2pm, "Julian wants to go to a crayfish party. Anyone have a couple of available seats tonight or tomorrow?" The party was eventually arranged at her own flat at 7pm.

But Assange had, it seems, found other fish to fry. Promising to show up later for the crayfish party, he left the lunch not with Braun but with another admirer in a bright pink sweater. With long blonde hair halfway down her back, 25-year-old Katrin Weiss (not her real name) is a worker at a local museum, or "some random woman" as Braun is later alleged to have described her.

In Weiss's witness statement, she explained that some weeks earlier she had seen Assange on television and had followed the WikiLeaks news avidly thereafter. She thought Assange "interesting, brave and admirable", had been Googling his name, and excitedly discovered he was actually coming to speak in Sweden. She was one of the first to sign up for his talk. "Sonja came up to Katrin and asked if she could help out by getting hold of a cable for Julian's computer. She then went and bought two cables just to make sure she had the right one. When she returned, he didn't even thank her."

However, Katrin did manage to parlay this into a chance to get closer to her hero. "She ... overheard that they were all going out to eat and asked if she could come too because she had been helping out. She then went with Sonja, Julian and some others to a restaurant." According to the statement, she sent excited texts to two friends from the restaurant to say she was with the Australian. "He looked at me!" she wrote in one. She took the opportunity to speak to him. "At one point when he had some cheese on a piece of flatbread, she asked if it was nice, and he reached over and fed it to her. Later he mentioned that he needed a charger for his laptop and she offered to help, as she had fixed him up with a cable earlier on. He took her round the waist and said, 'Yes, you got me a cable.' Katrin thought this was flattering and felt that he was now flirting with her."

Assange's lawyers argue, however, that it was Katrin who "flirted with Julian". Böstrom says: "After all the journalists have disappeared we're left with this woman who I've never seen before. I get the impression that this is one of those, you know, groupies … who are attracted by his stardust. I actually don't think she said much apart from when I asked her about how she got into contact with Sonja so I didn't give her much thought other than that she seemed interesting. She and Julian sat across from each other and spoke a bit … I got the impression of a person who was fascinated by Julian."

After lunch, Weiss offered to hook him up to her own work-place computer. Assange eventually tired of surfing the net and searching for tweets about himself on Katrin's computer at the museum , and they went to the cinema. "On the way, Julian stopped to pat some dogs, which Katrin thought was charming." He held her hand, he kissed her, and fondled her in the darkness of the back row. Before he caught a cab to shoot back to Braun's crayfish party, they exchanged phone numbers. He also hugged her, said he didn't want to leave, and, yes, he did want to see her again.

The crayfish party that night at Braun's flat appears to have had its tricky moments. One woman friend told the police she "asked Sonja whether she had slept with Julian … Sonja said,'Yes!' and seemed quite proud of it." Braun then tweeted, apparently enthusiastically, "Sitting outdoors at 2am, hardly freezing, with the world's coolest, smartest people." But meanwhile Assange was discreetly chatting on the phone to Weiss. According to another female friend interviewed by the police, Kajsa, Assange was simultaneously making approaches to her, which Braun did not take particularly well:

"[Kajsa] wondered about the strange tension between Sonja and Julian, [who] was flirting with Kajsa and other girls. Kajsa asked Sonja if she was going to sleep with Julian. Sonja said she already had done and it was the worst sex she's ever had. She told Kajsa that she could have him." Braun allegedly added something else: "Julian had held her hands down when they had sex and it had been unpleasant. Not only had it been the world's worst screw it had also been violent." At 3am, according to Kajsa, Assange actually tried to leave the party with her. Kajsa refused, she says.

The Assange camp has a different take. They say Braun was acting "warmly" towards him. She was asked, they say, whether she wanted Julian to move out, but "insists that he stay ... She says: 'No it's not a problem, he is very welcome to stay here.'"

Donald Böstrom was at the do, but is not much help in shedding further light on events. It seems he was preoccupied with crustacea: "During the crayfish party, I mostly just sat and ate. I'm very fond of eating. There was talk about Julian moving and staying with another couple, but the general impression was that Julian would be staying with Sonja."

Braun shared a bed with Assange again that night, but during the course of the weekend she spoke critically of him to another friend, Petra. She told her on the Sunday "they had not had sex any more because Julian had exceeded the limits of what she felt she could accept ... She didn't feel safe ... Julian had been violent and had snapped her necklace. She thought he had torn [the condom] on purpose." Petra added that her friend had volunteered to her a

lot of other off-putting information "about Julian not taking show-
ers and not flushing the toilet".

The Assange camp tell it differently. They say Sonja hosted
dinner for Assange that Sunday night. She spoke highly of him
and again refused offers to house him elsewhere. The following
day she phoned Böstrom, they claim, and joked ruefully that
Assange has become "their first adopted child" because she has
insisted on washing his clothes, makes sure he eats properly and
she feels like his stepmother. There has been no more sexual intercourse, despite Assange's efforts to win her round.

Meanwhile, Weiss has been vainly trying to get back in contact
with Assange: his mobile is frequently switched off. Among other
things, he has been busy looking at how he might acquire Swedish
residence and journalistic credentials. It is not until late on Tuesday
17 August that they meet up again. Weiss was later to give to police
an account of what turned out to be an unhappy one-night stand.

"She agreed to wait for him, and after she was finished at
work, she hung around town a bit. When she hadn't heard from
him by nine, she called him and he said there was another meeting he had to go to, and that she should come to him there."
When Assange finally emerged, they agree to get the train together
to Enköping, the little town 50 miles away where she lives. He
asked that Katrin pay for the tickets; it was too dangerous for him
to use his credit card, he said. Weiss told the police that, on the
train, he admitted he slept in Braun's bed after the crayfish party
but made the unlikely claim that "Sonja only liked girls – that she
was lesbian".

It was midnight when they at last got home to Weiss's place.
"They took off their shoes, but the relationship between them
seemed to have cooled off. The passion and the excitement had
disappeared ... They brushed their teeth together, which seemed
everyday and boring." Assange pushed her vigorously on to the
bed "to show he was a real man", Weiss told the police, but his

heart plainly wasn't in it. Assange suddenly turned over, went to sleep, and started snoring.

Weiss says she felt "rejected and shocked", and stayed awake, miserably texting her friend Maria. Maria recalls being "woken by a lot of texts from Katrin that were not positive. There had been bad sex and Julian had not been nice. She said she would have to get tested because of his lengthy foreplay." Matters improved somewhat in the course of the night. Julian woke up and had successful sex, grumbling about her insistence on a condom. He "muttered that he preferred her, rather than latex". In the early morning, he started ordering her about, demanding she fetch water and orange juice, and then sending her out to buy breakfast. Weiss testified she didn't much like leaving him alone in her flat. She said, "Be good," as she went out, leaving him sprawled emperor-like and naked on the bed, holding one of his mobile phones. He answered: "I'm always bad!"

While Weiss was at the shops purchasing breakfast, she took the opportunity to call her friend Maria. "Katrin said she was damned if she was going to buy all this stuff and just wait on him hand and foot." But she nevertheless went home, she says, cooked him porridge, climbed back into bed, and they had another go, using a condom. "They slept again and she woke with the realisation that he was inside her. She said, "Are you wearing anything?" and he answered, "You." She said, "You better not have HIV," and he answered, "Of course not." She knew it was too late, she said, as he was already inside her so she let him continue. She had never had unprotected sex before. "She said: what if she got pregnant? And he replied that Sweden was a good place to bring up a child. She looked at him, shocked."

According to her testimony he added, flippantly, that they could call the baby "Afghanistan". The police report adds a strange and disturbing remark from Katrin: "He also said he often carried abortion pills but that they were actually sugar pills."

Whatever did he mean? Assange often seemed curiously proud of his prowess in paternity: he told friends during this time period that he had recently impregnated a Korean woman he met in Paris, and she was about to give birth.

This single night he spent with Katrin is the basis of a rape charge against Assange. To have sex with a sleeping or unconscious woman is a crime, both in Sweden and in the UK. The subsequent investigation collected testimony from Weiss's former boyfriend that she was particularly anxious to avoid the risks from unprotected sex, and never allowed it. After Assange headed back to Stockholm (she had to pay for his train ticket again), Weiss changed the stained sheets, which she thought were "disgusting", and got a morning-after pill from a chemist. "When she spoke to her friends, she realised that she had been the victim of a crime. She went to Danderyd University Hospital and from there to Södersjukhuset (Stockholm South General Hospital) where she was tested with a so-called rape kit."

Katrin's friend Hanna, one of those she said she contacted that morning, takes up the story: "She said it had not been good and she had just wanted him to leave ... Assange's personality had changed when he got home to her flat and Katrin regretted letting him stay there ... What bothered her was that Assange had had unprotected sex with her while she was asleep. He had also tried again and again to have unprotected sex with her during the night. Hanna asked why Katrin hadn't pushed him away when she knew he wasn't wearing a condom and Katrin said she was too shocked and paralysed and didn't really know what was happening. Hanna is sure that she didn't just let it happen because he was famous, although it could have been significant that he was older. Hanna said that Katrin wanted Assange to be tested for sexually transmitted diseases."

The Assange camp's account contradicts Weiss's version of events in at least one important respect. She describes buying the breakfast first, before the alleged rape occurred. They stated to the UK court that the breakfast shopping came not before, but "AFTER she claims that he had entered her without a condom". But Assange does not dispute that he had condomless sex while his partner was, as he puts it, "sleepy".

Once back in Stockholm, having stayed out all night, Assange now had to return to the home of Sonja Braun, where he was still staying. According to Braun, to whom it seemed clear that he had spent the night with another woman, his approach to this delicate situation was unusual. "Assange suddenly took all the clothes off the lower part of his body and rubbed Sonja with his erect penis. Sonja says she thought this was strange and unpleasant behaviour. She no longer wanted Assange to live in her flat, which he ignored."

As a result of this alleged incident, Assange was later accused by the Swedes of "molestation". This would translate into the UK legal canon as "indecent assault" or, as it is now known, "sexual touching". Braun says she slept on a mattress that night, and the next night stayed with friends.

Her friend Petra adds that on that Wednesday "although Sonja wanted Julian to leave her flat, he wouldn't". Braun did not seem frightened, however: "He wasn't aggressive or dangerous, she just wanted him out." Böstrom, meanwhile, recalls: "On the Wednesday, Sonja says, 'I want him to leave.' 'Well, tell him,' I say, and she says, 'I have done, but he won't.' So I confronted him with it. 'Sonja would like you to move out and says she has asked you.' He's surprised and says she hasn't said a word to him about it. So now it's like stereo – one channel says one thing, the other channel says another." Assange's version of events is completely different: "Böstrom remains in contact with Braun, who continues to insist Julian should stay with her, and speaks warmly of him."

Behind all the muffled prose of police testimony, some clumsily translated from Swedish, anyone can see how electric the whole situation had become. All that was needed was for someone to bring the ends of the wires into contact. If Braun and Weiss were to get together, they might start to compare notes. Sparks would fly.

Katrin Weiss the very next day sent Sonja Braun a text message. Worried she might have caught a disease, Weiss was anxiously trying to renew contact with Assange. She says she thought Braun might know where to find him. According to Braun's close friend Kajsa, "Sonja realised what had happened, and they met up." According to this witness: "Sonja said the other girl decided to go to the police and report Julian for rape and that Sonja would go along as support."

Braun's other friend, Petra, testified in similar terms. She said Braun rang her "and said she had met the other girl who had told her she had been raped by Julian. They had found many similarities between hers and Sonja's experience, and Julian wanted to have sex with the other girl without a condom. Sonja said she didn't wish to have Julian charged, she just wanted to support the other girl. Petra said that the whole story was becoming more and more confused."

Böstrom was startled also to receive a phone call from Braun:

"I can hear from her voice that it's something serious and she says, 'It's not true what I said [before], we *did* have sex.' Then she goes on and says that the other woman – Katrin – had called her and told her that Julian had been there and had sex with her. On both occasions it was voluntary ... Katrin told her that the next morning Julian continued to want to have sex with her without a condom. And she won't, and protests, but Julian continues in spite of her protests.

"'OK,' I say, quite dumbfounded at suddenly having this conversation. Sonja goes on: 'And I must tell you that we had sex at an earlier stage at my place and to my surprise during the act, he tears the condom ... He has torn the condom and continues against my wishes.'"

Böstrom adds: "I believe that Sonja is very, very credible, so I won't discount it without speaking to Julian and confronting him with what this is all about – what the hell he thinks he's playing at … They want Julian to take an Aids test otherwise they will report him, as they put it. They don't want to speak to Julian themselves. So she goes off with Katrin and we speak on the phone a few times and text a bit and I call Julian a couple of times."

Böstrom determinedly confronted Assange: "And his reaction is one of shock. He doesn't understand it … [He says,] 'Katrin didn't object at all,' and they had a 'nice time' … And I'm really trying to press him here – 'Did you take the condom off, did you rip the condom?' He doesn't understand any of it … So there are two stories and I can't draw any conclusions … Julian says that he doesn't understand, and that they just had normal sex." Told that Katrin claims to have protested about his lack of a condom, "Julian becomes angry a number of times, saying that they just had normal sex … 'She did not [protest] … It's lies, lies, lies!'" Assange later assures Böstrom that he has talked to Katrin and he thinks this is all an over-reaction. "But I tell Julian that if he takes a test they won't report him – and if he doesn't, they will."

It is common ground that Assange at first refused to take an HIV test. Had he agreed, it seems unlikely that the subsequent legal dramas would have unfolded. Katrin's younger brother says Assange had a conversation with his sister about it: "She asked Julian if he would get tested, and he said he didn't have time." Weiss was allegedly told that she would just have to take his word that he had no diseases. Assange's lawyers dispute that. According to them, he said: "I can do a blood test but I don't want to be blackmailed … I'd prefer to do it out of goodwill."

Böstrom told the *Guardian* subsequently: "I was a kind of middleman – calling her, calling Julian. It went on for hours." Late on the Friday afternoon, Assange finally agreed to take a test. But it was too late. The clinics had closed for the weekend.

Braun phoned Böstrom to say that they have been to the police, who say they cannot simply tell Assange to take a test. The police insist that their statements must be passed to the duty prosecutor, and a call was put out for the arrest of an accused foreigner, Julian Assange.

That night, the story about the allegations made against the man behind WikiLeaks leaked to the Swedish tabloid newspaper *Expressen*. Who leaked it? We don't know. The prosecutor, who later got into trouble for confirming the allegation, says it was put to her by the newspaper, which had apparently been tipped off.

As a result of this hectic Friday, when the following morning dawned, Saturday 21 August, allegations that Assange was wanted by police for "rape" had begun to be sprayed all over the world. In the electronic global village, anyone can become famous within 15 minutes. Assange was in an unexpected predicament and his conviction that he had not "raped" anyone is perhaps understandable. But Assange's new status as an international celebrity, as "the world's most famous man", was proving to be a cruelly double-edged sword. Journalists were demanding a reaction.

At 9.15am, he tweeted under the WikiLeaks name: "We were warned to expect 'dirty tricks'. Now we have the first one." The following morning, he tweeted: "Reminder: US intelligence planned to destroy WikiLeaks as far back as 2008." In an interview, the Swedish tabloid *Aftonbladet* asked if he had had sex with his two accusers. He replied: "Their identities have been made anonymous so even I have no idea who they are." He added: "We have been warned that the Pentagon, for example, is thinking of deploying dirty tricks to ruin us." Yet Assange must have realised which two women had been threatening to report him to the police.

This line of attack proved unwise. He must have known his statements were, at best, highly misleading. His conspiracy theory of a Pentagon "honeytrap" gave a hostage to fortune and it also appears to have infuriated the two women. The Assange interview in *Aftonbladet* was published on 22 August. When it appeared, Weiss's friend Maria told police, "Katrin was upset by the fuss, and very angry with Julian." Sonja, too, seemed exasperated, telling *Aftonbladet*: "The charges are of course not orchestrated either by the Pentagon or anyone else. The responsibility for what happened to me and the other girl lies with a man who has a warped attitude to women, and a problem with taking 'no' for an answer." She added: "He is not violent and I do not feel threatened by him."

It took four months of stonewalling before Assange would accept in public that there was no evidence of a "honeytrap". His lawyer, Mark Stephens, who had been using the phrase, had been misquoted, Assange would finally explain to the BBC's *Today* programme on 21 December, and "that type of classic Russian, Moscow thing … is not probable". While still claiming that "powerful interests" could have pushed along the smears, he did at last concede: "That doesn't mean they got in there at the very beginning and fabricated them."

What appeared to be Plan B came next: depict the women's complaints as driven, if not by the CIA, then at least by a fit of man-hating. Once ensconced back in London, Assange spoke dolefully to contacts about the strong approach Swedish officialdom took to sex allegations: "Sweden is the Saudi Arabia of fundamentalist feminism," he complained to friends. "One of the women has written many articles on taking revenge against men for infidelity, and is a notorious radical feminist," he told the London *Times*. His lawyers stirred into this conspiracy mix some unsubstantiated hints of financial greed: "Text messages from them … speak of revenge and of the opportunity to make lots of money."

Assange's money allegations link significantly to the contents of one official witness statement from Weiss's friend Maria, which may offer a more innocent explanation: "She remembered them talking about going to [the rival tabloid] *Expressen*, because Julian had spoken to *Aftonbladet* himself. But this was just something they said, and had no intention of doing. Maria said Katrin had been contacted by an American newspaper and they had joked that she should get well paid." None of them ever did, apparently, sell their story to anyone. In any case, these conversations came after the women had already been to the police.

Assange then shifted to what appeared to be Plan C. This was to characterise the complaining women as feather-brained types who "got into a tizzy" and were "bamboozled": "The suggestion is they went to the police for advice and they did not want to make a complaint. What they say is that they found out they were mutual lovers of mine, and they had unprotected sex, and they got into a tizzy about whether there was a possibility of sexually transmitted diseases, and they went to the police to have a test ... A ridiculous thing to go to the police about," he told *Today*. "One of the witnesses, one of the friends of one of those women, she says that one of the women states that she was bamboozled into this by police and others. These women may be victims in this process."

Swedish prosecutors were later to be criticised for a clumsy, or even sinister, handling of the case. A duty prosecutor ordered an arrest that same Friday night. Over the weekend, senior prosecutor Eva Finne, in Stockholm, withdrew the "rape" accusations involving both women, to be replaced on 24 August with an investigation into a less serious and non-arrestable charge equivalent to "sexual harassment", confined solely to the case of Sonja Braun. On 30 August, therefore, 10 days after the storm broke, Assange voluntarily turned up for a formal interview with the police, to relive his short and ultimately calamitous spell as Braun's house-guest.

Present were a detective, Mats Gehlin from the Klara police station family violence unit, and a lawyer.

Assange: Between the 13th and 14th August, I, as you put
it, deliberately tore a condom during intercourse?
Police: How do you react to that?
Assange: It's not true.

He agreed that something had been said at the time, the police
account notes. "Sonja looked at the sheet and saw that it was wet
and said, 'Look at that,' and Julian answered, 'It must be you' …
Julian just thought she was pointing to it as an indication of how
loving the sex had been although she spoke as if it came from him
… Then they didn't discuss it any more." He accepted there was
no more intercourse all week after that event "but there were
other sexual acts".

He told the interrogators that Braun only challenged him at
the very end of the week he spent at her flat: "She accused me of
various things… many of which were false … That I took the
condom off during sex. It was the first I had heard of it." Her
friend Klara (not her real name) had also been in contact and
Assange had been arranging to meet her on the following day to
discuss what he had heard were "incredible lies" being told about
him. He did not consider that Braun was planning to make any
formal complaint and was "really surprised" to find she had been
to a hospital and there was talk of DNA and the police. "I expected
the whole thing to be over until I heard the news from *Expressen*."

That might have been the end of the story. But the two
aggrieved women appointed a high-profile lawyer on their own
behalf, Claes Borgström, former Swedish equal opportunities
ombudsman and prominent Social Democrat politician. He got
both cases reopened, as law allowed, by appealing to a chief prosecutor (*överåklagare*), the sex crimes specialist Marianne Ny. He
told a news agency the women didn't even know it was possible
to appeal a prosecutor's decision until he so advised them. "I had
read the police reports. I had seen my clients and heard their

stories," Borgström said. "In my opinion, it was rape and attempted rape or sexual molestation." He added: "We have better knowledge than other countries in the field of gender equality ... That also means women don't accept certain things in the same way they do in other countries."

Not surprisingly, Assange was much dismayed. Facing a further interrogation about his unhappy one-night stand with the second woman, Katrin Weiss, he decided to leave town. He told friends he feared being arrested and paraded in front of a media circus. Subsequently, he circulated the idea that the resultant demand for his extradition was the result of covert pressure from the US government, who wanted to get their hands on him for the WikiLeaks exploits. No concrete evidence has yet surfaced to support this theory, although the US has threatened repeatedly that it will seek to bring its own indictment against Assange for information crimes. The claim certainly muddied the WikiLeaks waters, as conspiracy theories began to rage up and down the internet.

That summer, contemplating the imbroglio in Sweden from afar, the *Guardian*'s reporters in London were also dismayed. Leigh and Davies took a decision that it was nevertheless their duty to ensure the *Guardian* was steadfast – and indeed first – in reporting the facts. What happened in Stockholm may have been complex and equivocal, but some questionable sexual encounters had certainly occurred, and there was no evidence to support the claims of dirty tricks and honeytraps. The journalists were acutely aware that to ignore the fresh controversy that had erupted around their new collaborator could only increase the risk that it might taint the WikiLeaks enterprise as a whole.

CHAPTER 13

Uneasy partners

Editor's office, the *Guardian*, Kings Place, London
1 November 2010

"I'm a combative person"
JULIAN ASSANGE, TED CONFERENCE, OXFORD, 2010

The three partner papers decided it was time for a meeting with Julian Assange. Everything was threatening to get rather messy. The embattled WikiLeaks founder now wanted the Americans frozen out of the much-delayed deal to publish the diplomatic cables jointly – a punishment, so it was said, for a recent profile of him, by the *New York Times* veteran London correspondent John F Burns. Assange had intensely disliked it.

The British were anxious about the fact that another copy of the cables had apparently fallen into the hands of Heather Brooke, a London-based American journalist and freedom of information activist. And the Germans were worried that things could get acrimonious all round unless the editors held a clear-the-air meeting with what was left of WikiLeaks.

There were at least three loose copies of the cables believed to be circulating now: with Brooke in the UK, Daniel Ellsberg – of Pentagon papers fame – in the US, and Smári McCarthy, an

Icelandic former WikiLeaks programmer who had, according to Assange, let a copy pass to Brooke. David Leigh had signalled to the *New York Times* he was willing personally to hand them a copy if Assange would not co-operate. But none of the huge secret cache of state department dispatches had yet actually been analysed and published to the world as originally planned. Would the whole audacious project end in tears?

The conference was arranged for 1 November, at the *Guardian*'s London offices near King's Cross station, with an initial meeting to go through the material in detail, trying to reach agreement on a possible day-by-day running order. Assange was supposed to join around 6pm – but a series of text messages to deputy editor Ian Katz indicated he was running late. Around 7pm, Rusbridger's phone rang. It was Mark Stephens, a British libel lawyer he'd known for years. He said he had something to tell him: could he come straight round? Twenty minutes later Stephens burst through the door of the editor's office, followed by Assange himself, along with his dour Icelandic lieutenant Kristinn Hrafnsson, and a young woman lawyer, later introduced as a junior solicitor in Stephens' office, Jennifer Robinson. It looked, and felt, like an ambush.

Assange had barely sat down before he started angrily denouncing the *Guardian*. Did the *New York Times* have the cables? How did they have them? Who had given them to them? This was a breach of trust. His voice was raised and angry. Every time Rusbridger tried to respond, he pitched in with another question. When he finally paused for breath Rusbridger pointed out that the *Spiegel* people and other *Guardian* executives were waiting. Why didn't we tell them to come in to continue the discussion? But Assange's fury returned: this matter had to be settled first. He needed to know the truth about the *New York Times*. "We are getting the feeling that a large organisation is trying to find ways to step around a gentlemen's agreement. We're feeling a bit unhappy."

Rusbridger responded that things had changed. WikiLeaks had sprung a leak itself. The cables had fallen into the hands of Heather Brooke. Things would soon move out of our control unless they decided to act more quickly. Assange didn't look well. He was pale and sweating and had a racking cough. Rusbridger stuck to the line that he hadn't given anyone the cables – which was perfectly true – and eventually persuaded Assange that it was better to deal with the larger group.

David Leigh immediately objected, however, to the presence of Stephens and Robinson. This was an editorial meeting, he protested. If Assange was going to have lawyers there, the *Guardian* needed lawyers. Rusbridger went off to try and raise a lawyer. The *Guardian*'s head of legal was cycling home and could not hear her BlackBerry ringing, so Geraldine Proudler, from the legal firm Olswang, who had fought many battles on behalf of the *Guardian* in the past, was interrupted at her gym and jumped in a taxi.

The argument – for the moment without lawyers – began again with the *Spiegel* team of editor-in-chief Georg Mascolo, Holger Stark and Marcel Rosenbach. Assange seemed obsessed with the *New York Times*, however, and launched into repeated denunciations of the paper.

"They ran a front-page story – the front page! – a front-page story which was just a sleazy hit job against me personally, and other parts of the organisation, and based upon falsehoods. It wasn't even an assemblage of genuine criticism, assembling criticism without any balance. Their aim is to make themselves look impartial. It is not enough to simply *be* impartial. It is not enough to simply go: 'That's the story' and put it through – they actually have to be actively hostile towards us, and demonstrate that on the front page, lest they be accused of being some kind of sympathiser."

The Burns profile had dwelt, among other things, on the continuing police investigation into the Swedish sex allegations.

Assange was quoted saying: "They called me the James Bond of journalism. It got me a lot of fans, and some of them ended up causing me a bit of trouble."

Burns had written that WikiLeaks staff had turned against Assange in the scandal's wake. They complained, he wrote, that their founder's "growing celebrity has been matched by an increasingly dictatorial, eccentric and capricious style". To one defector, 25-year-old Icelander Herbert Snorrason, Assange messaged: "If you have a problem with me, you can piss off." Assange had announced: "I am the heart and soul of this organisation, its founder, philosopher, spokesperson, original coder, organiser, financier, and all the rest." Snorrason riposted stoutly: "He is not in his right mind."

Burns' piece actually omitted the full facts: Assange's key lieutenant, Daniel Domscheit-Berg, was also privately denouncing Assange's "cult of stardom". The German would write later: "It is not for nothing that many who have quit refer to him as a 'dictator'. He thinks of himself as the autocratic ruler of the project and believes himself accountable to no one. Justified, even internal, criticism – whether about his relations with women or the lack of transparency in his actions – is either dismissed with the statement 'I'm busy, there are two wars I have to end' or attributed to the secret services' smear campaigns."

Round the *Guardian* editor's table, the others now sat silently as Assange fulminated against Burns and the *New York Times* in the strangely old-fashioned declamatory baritone he used when angry. He returned to his questions. Did they have the cables? How?

The problem, interjected Rusbridger, was that the paper now had a second source for the cables. It was negotiating with Heather Brooke for her to join the *Guardian* team. Otherwise she would be free to take them to any paper – which would mean the *Guardian* losing all access, control and exclusivity. Assange turned on Rusbridger. This wasn't a second source. Brooke had stolen the cables. It had been done "by theft, by deception ... certainly unethical means". He knew enough about the way she had operated to "destroy" her. The climax came when Assange (the underground leaker of illegal secrets) threatened that his lawyers could sue for the loss of WikiLeaks' "financial assets".

"I'd look forward to such a court case," said the *Guardian*'s editor with a smile. None of this tirade made sense to Rusbridger. Brooke was a professional journalist: she had stolen nothing. More to the point, either the *Guardian* had a second source – in which case it no longer had to rely on Assange's copy – or it all originated, as Assange claimed, from a single source, WikiLeaks, in which case WikiLeaks had broken its agreement to make a copy only for the *Guardian*, and Assange was in a poor position to be ranting at others.

Katz asked what other copies of the database existed: for instance, was it correct that Ellsberg had one? Assange shot back: "Daniel Ellsberg's is an encrypted back-up copy of the database which he was to give the *New York Times* in a piece of political theatre."

Assange returned to his favourite theme of how a gentleman leaker would behave: "People who aren't behaving like gentlemen should start behaving like one. On the basis that the *Guardian* has given this to the *New York Times*, why should we collaborate with the *Guardian*?"

Assange began suggesting deals with other American papers. The *Washington Post* was hungry for this stuff. Under questioning, he elaborated a little, admitting that he had already been in discussion both with the *Post* and the US McClatchy newspaper group about possible co-operation.

Assange launched into the *NYT* again: "The strategy that the *New York Times* engaged in was ... not very gentlemanly ... They wrote a terrible piece about Bradley Manning and this terrible, terrible piece about me on the front page by John F Burns. He says that he has received the most criticism of anything that he has ever written in his entire journalistic career over that piece, from senior people, and there's a reason for that.

"We're willing to engage in *realpolitik* if necessary, but that's an organisation whose modus operandi is to protect itself, by destroying us. I do advise you to read it. It is obvious to anyone who reads it that it is designed to be a smear. It uses unnamed sources to quote some random person who has never had anything to do with our organisation except running some chat room, saying that I'm mad, etcetera, etcetera. It really is bad journalism. I'm not asking much. We are asking for the *Times* to follow its own standards. The standards that it follows for other people, because those standards apply, and the *Times* should not go out of its way to produce a negative, sleazy hit-piece and place it on the front page."

Katz asked him directly how far he had got in negotiation with the *Washington Post*. "I haven't made an agreement. Though I think we'll probably go with the *Post* unless we get a very good counter-offer, because the *Times* has defiled the relationship."

Rusbridger suggested a short break. When they reassembled, still without lawyers (Stephens and Robinson were sitting outside the room, Proudler down the corridor) the temperature had lowered a bit. Rusbridger suggested they look at some of the issues around the sequencing of stories. Ian Katz led Assange through the work they had done earlier in the day on which items should run in which order. Assange listened calmly. Gone was the aggression and finger-pointing. In its place there was a new engagement – as though his brain had flicked a switch to channel the rational, highly strategic zones which had been missing in the early confrontation.

He was, however, now insisting on yet further delay. The journalists asked how WikiLeaks would ideally release the cables. He replied, "Our ideal situation is not till next year. Anything before one month is semi-lethal even under emergency conditions. We have woken a giant by wounding one of its legs [the US defence department] and the release of this material will cause the other leg [the state department] to stand up. We are taking as much fire as we can but we can't take any more." He stressed that he wanted the cables to be released in an orderly way and not in a "big dump". Ideally, a "gradual release played out over two months". But he was willing to see the launch in as soon as a month's time: "We can gear up to attempt to be in a position such that we can survive, in a month."

Assange had already spoken, only half-jokingly, of his need to have a safe refuge in Cuba before the cables came out. Now he said the ordering had to be arranged so that it didn't appear anti-American. He didn't want WikiLeaks to seem obsessed with America. The stories in the cables had far wider significance – so it was important to establish a running order which would make people realise that this wasn't simply about the US.

"There are security exposés and abuses by other countries, these bad Arab countries, or Russia," he said. "That will set the initial flavour of this material. We shouldn't go exposing, for example, Israel during the initial phase, the initial couple of weeks. Let the overall framework be set first. The exposure of these other bad countries will set the tone of American public opinion. In the initial couple of weeks the frame is set that will colour the rest of it."

Assange then made another startling announcement. He wanted to involve other newspapers from the "Romance languages", to broaden the geopolitical impact. He mentioned *El País* and *Le Monde*. The others in the room looked at each other. This was going to double the complexities of an arrangement that was difficult enough to co-ordinate. How could they possibly do a deal between an American daily on a different time zone, with a French afternoon paper, a Spanish morning paper and a German weekly?

But by now there was at least a negotiation about the means to go forward. It was nearly 10pm. The discussions had been going relentlessly for nearly three hours. Rusbridger produced a couple of bottles of Chablis. The mood eased. Everyone readily agreed it could all be settled over some food at the Rotunda restaurant downstairs at Kings Place. The journalists moved, meeting Mark Stephens, Geraldine Proudler and Jennifer Robinson still sitting patiently outside the editor's office.

Dinner was more relaxed, though Assange was still obsessed with the *New York Times* and its behaviour. Asked under what conditions he would now collaborate with the Americans, he said he would only consider it if the paper agreed to run no more negative material about him and offered him a right to reply to the Burns piece with equal prominence. "Good relationships extend to good people, they don't extend to bad people. Unless we see a very serious counter-offer [from the *New York Times*] they have lost their exclusivity … Is the *NYT* a lost cause or is it a credible media outlet? Have things got that bad?"

The others decided to ignore that for the time being. They talked in more detail about how they could draw up a publication schedule, with agreed themes for each day. Assange was keen for the period of exclusivity to continue beyond the new year, or "the Christian calendar", as he put it. He said WikiLeaks had already redacted the cables "and if there is a critical attack against us we will publish them all".

By midnight the restaurant was empty and closing. It was decided that Rusbridger would go and ring Bill Keller in New York while the others relocated – taking the wine with them – to another meeting room back upstairs in the *Guardian*. Rusbridger had known Keller for about 10 years, which helped shortcut what was bound to be a slightly surreal conversation. "I'm going to tell you what Assange is demanding," said Rusbridger. "I know what you're going to say, but I have to go back and say I've put this to you."

"Go ahead," said Keller.

"OK, he wants a front-page rejoinder for the Burns piece and he also wants a guarantee that you're not going to publish any more sleazy hit pieces on him."

Keller let out a little snort. "He can write a letter," he said curtly. "Strictly speaking, that's not my department, but I'd certainly use any influence I had to suggest that it's published. And – what was the second one? – er, you can certainly assure him we are not planning any sleazy hit pieces."

Rusbridger returned to the room and conveyed Keller's message. As he feared, Assange reacted furiously, saying this was not sufficient and, in terms, all bets were off. He announced that both the *New York Times* and *Guardian* themselves were now to be thrown out of the deal.

It was Georg Mascolo's turn to speak – deliberately and firmly. The three papers were tied together. If Assange was cutting out the other two papers then *Der Spiegel* was out, too.

It was now nearly 1.30am. The discussion was going nowhere, so Rusbridger turned to Assange and summarised the position.

"As I see it you have three options. One, we reach no deal; two, you try and substitute the *Washington Post* for the *New York Times*; three, you do a deal with us three.

"One and Two don't work because you've lost control of the material. That's just going to result in chaos. So I can't see that you have any option but Three. You're going to have to continue with us. And that's good. We have been good partners. We have treated the material responsibly. We've thrown huge resources at it. We're good at working together, we like each other. We've communicated well with your lot. It's gone well. Why on earth throw it away?"

If Assange was convinced, he wasn't going to show it. Not that night, anyway. Rusbridger could see that doing it Assange's way he would still be up for another few rounds before dawn. As the WikiLeaks *capo di tutti capi* headed off coughing into the night, he shook hands with David Leigh, with whom he had previously worked so closely. Assange shot him a meaningful look and said in low, distinct tones: "Be careful."

The next day Rusbridger sent Mark Stephens 10 bullet points to put to Assange:

- Publish on Nov 29 in a staggered form.
- Run over two weeks or more up to just before Xmas.
- Exclusive to G, NYT, DS (plus El Pais and ? Le Monde).
- Subject matter to be co-ordinated between partners and to stay off certain issues initially. No veto to anyone over subjects covered over whole course of series (post Jan). WL to publish cited documents at same time.
- After Xmas the exclusivity continues for one more week, starting around Jan 3/4.
- Thereafter WL will start to share stories on a regional basis among 40 serious newspapers around the world, who will be given access to "bags" of material relating to their own regions.
- G to hire HB [Heather Brooke] on an exclusive basis.
- If "critical" attack on WL they will release everything immediately.
- If material is leaked to/shared with any other news organisation in breach of this understanding all bets are off.
- If agreed the team will commence work on a grid of stories for the first phase.

Within 24 hours Stephens rang back to say Assange had okayed the deal. Whether or not it met Assange's criteria for "a gentlemen's agreement", it was, anyway, an agreement.

*

Five of the world's most reputable papers were now committed to selecting, redacting and publishing, on an unprecedented scale, the secret leaked diplomatic dispatches of a superpower. It was a project of astonishing boldness, which stood a chance of redefining journalism in the internet age. But while the newspapers laboured to behave responsibly, Assange continued to go his own way.

Disguising himself as an old woman, as detailed in Chapter 1, he moved operations to his rural hideaway at Ellingham Hall, out in the Norfolk countryside. There, his security over the cables, which he had once described as worth at least $5 million to any foreign intelligence agency, seemed less than watertight. Staff say that Assange handed over batches of of them to foreign journalists, including someone who was simply introduced as "Adam". "He seemed like a harmless old man," said one staffer, "apart from his habit of standing too close and peering at what was written on your screen." He was introduced as the father of Assange's Swedish crony, the journalist Johannes Wahlstrom, and took away copies of cables from Russia and post-Soviet states. According to one insider, he also demanded copies of cables about "the Jews".

This WikiLeaks associate was better known as Israel Shamir. Shamir claims to be a renegade Russian Jew, born in Novosibirsk, but currently adhering to the Greek Orthodox church. He is notorious for Holocaust-denying and publishing a string of anti-semitic articles. He caused controversy in the UK in 2005, at a parliamentary book launch hosted by Lord Ahmed, by claiming: "Jews ... own, control and edit a big share of mass media."

Internal WikiLeaks documents, seen by the *Guardian*, show Shamir was not only given cables, but he also invoiced WikiLeaks for €2,000, to be deposited in a Tallinn bank account, in thanks for "services rendered – journalism". What services? He says: "What I did for WikiLeaks was to read and analyse the cables from Moscow."

Shamir's byline is on two previous articles pillorying the Swedish women who complained about Assange. On 27 August, in *Counterpunch*, a small radical US publication, Shamir said Assange was framed by "Langley spies" and "crazy feminists". He alleged there had been a "honeytrap". On 14 September, Shamir then attacked "castrating feminists and secret services", writing that one of the women involved, who he deliberately named, had once discussed the Cuban opposition to Castro in a Swedish academic publication "connected with" someone with "CIA ties".

Subsequently, Shamir appeared in Moscow. According to a reporter on the Russian paper *Kommersant*, he was offering to sell articles based on the cables for $10,000. He had already passed some over to the state-backed publication *Russian Reporter*. He travelled on to Belarus, ruled by the Soviet-style dictator Alexander Lukashenko, where he met regime officials. The Interfax agency reported that Shamir was WikiLeaks' "Russian representative", and had "confirmed the existence of the Belarus dossier". According to him, WikiLeaks had several thousand "interesting" secret documents. Shamir then wrote a piece of grovelling pro-Lukashenko propaganda in *Counterpunch*, claiming "the people were happy, fully employed, and satisfied with their government."

Assange himself subsequently maintained that he had only a "brief interaction" with Shamir: "WikiLeaks works with hundreds of journalists from different regions of the world. All are required to sign non-disclosure agreements and are generally only given limited review access to material relating to their region."

One can only speculate about whose interests Shamir was serving by his various wild publications. Perhaps his own personal interests were always to the fore. But while the newspapers had hammered out a deal to handle the cables in a responsible fashion, Shamir's backstairs antics certainly made WikiLeaks look rather less so.

CHAPTER 14
Before the deluge

El País newspaper, Calle de Miguel Yuste, Madrid
14 November 2010

*"It was a fruit machine. You just had to hold
your hat under there for long enough"*
ALAN RUSBRIDGER, THE *GUARDIAN*

Viewed on screen, the unkempt, silhouetted figures looked like
hostages held in the basement of a terrorist group's safehouse.
One of the stubbly, subterranean figures moved closer to the
camera. He held up a sheet of paper. Written on it was a mysterious six-digit number. A secret Swiss bank account, perhaps? A
telephone number? Something to do with *The Da Vinci Code*?

The shadowy figures had not, in fact, been seized by some radical faction, but were a group of journalists from Spain's *El País*
newspaper. Nor was their note a ransom demand. It was the index
reference of one of more than 250,000 cables. Since being invited
to join the existing British-US-German consortium – or "tripartite
alliance" as the *New York Times*'s Bill Keller dubbed it – *El País* had
wasted no time in setting up its own underground research room.

The paper – and France's *Le Monde* – had joined the WikiLeaks
party late. They had only two weeks to go through the cables

before the D-day publication night. The *Guardian* had been in the luxurious position of having held the same material for several months. *El País*'s editor-in-chief, Javier Moreno, and executive Vicente Jiménez urgently summoned back to Madrid their foreign correspondents; sitting in the paper's bunker, next to endless discarded coffee cups, they ploughed through the database.

The journalists may have been heartened to read that, according to a secret cable from US officials in Madrid dated 12 May 2008, *El País* was Spain's "newspaper of record". It was also, apparently, "normally pro-government". But they also found sensational material: the US embassy in Madrid had tried to influence judges, the government and prosecutors in cases involving US citizens. One involved a detainee at Guantánamo Bay, another covered secret rendition flights in Spain, and another was about the murder of a Spanish journalist by US fire in Baghdad. They also discovered stories from all across Latin America: from Mexico, Argentina, Colombia and Venezuela.

From the beginning, the papers had agreed to work collaboratively. They shared some discoveries from the cables and even circulated lists of possible stories. Assange later claimed in a Swedish TV documentary that it was he personally who was pulling the strings of the old-fashioned MSM. He said: "What is new is us enforcing co-operation between competitive organisations that would otherwise be rivals – to do the best by the story as opposed to simply doing the best by their own organisations."

In reality, this was a co-operative technique that the *Guardian*, along with other international outlets, had long been building. The previous year, for example, the paper had successfully beaten off lawyers for the Trafigura company, who had dumped toxic waste, by working in concert with BBC TV's *Newsnight*, with a Dutch paper, *Volkskrant*, and with the Norwegian TV channel NRK. The British arms giant BAE had also been brought to a $400m corruption settlement with the US department of justice, following a campaign in which the *Guardian* co-operated with other TV and print media in countries from Sweden to Romania to Tanzania.

The most distinguished pioneer of this globalised form of investigation was probably Charles Lewis, founder of the Center for Public Integrity in Washington DC, who, a full decade earlier, organised a massive exposure of the British American Tobacco company's collusion in cigarette smuggling, with simultaneous publication by media in Colombia, London and the US.

So the present five-way media consortium was not a new invention. It was – or would be if it actually worked – the culmination of a growing media trend. What made this trend possible was what also made it necessary: the technological growth of massive, near-instantaneous global communications. If media groups did not learn to work across borders on stories, the stories would leave them behind.

In the run-up to cable D-Day, Ian Katz, the deputy editor managing these complex relationships, held regular Skype chats with the *Guardian*'s multilingual counterparts. "They were hilarious conversations," Katz recalls. The reason the Spaniards were holding up the number of a US state department cable to the Skype camera was security – it had been agreed that no sensitive mentions would be made over the phone or by email.

In Berlin, similarly, Marcel Rosenbach, from *Der Spiegel*, was the first to unearth a cable with the deceptively bland title: "National HUMINT Collection Directive on the United Nations." In fact, it revealed the US state department (on behalf of the CIA) had ordered its diplomats to spy on senior UN officials and collect their "detailed biometric information". They were also told to go after "credit card account numbers; frequent flyer account numbers; work schedules and other relevant biographical information". The cable, number 219058, was geopolitical dynamite. Nobody else had spotted it. "Marcel had written down the number. I could only see half of it. I had to tell him: 'Left a bit, left a bit,'" Katz recalls.

For Julian Assange – like Jason Bourne, the Hollywood secret agent constantly on the run from the CIA – elaborate security precautions may have been second nature. But for journalists used to spilling secrets down at the pub after a gossipy pint or two they were a new and tricky-to-master art form. Katz and Rusbridger borrowed inspiration from *The Wire*, the cult US drama series set amid the high rises and drug dealers of Baltimore. The noir show was popular among some of the *Guardian*'s staff; in it, the dealers typically relied on "burners", or pay-as-you-go phones, to outsmart the cops.

Katz therefore asked his assistant to go out and buy 20 burner phones for key members of the cables team. The *Guardian* now had its own leak-proof network. Unfortunately, nobody could remember their burner number. At one point Alan Rusbridger sent a text from his "burner" to Katz's regular cellphone – an elementary error that in *The Wire* would almost certainly have prompted the cops to swoop. The *Guardian* editor picked up another burner during a five-day trip to Australia. When he got back to London Katz called him on that number. The conversation – routed right round the world – fizzled out after just three minutes when Katz ran out of credit. "We were basically completely useless at any of the spooky stuff," Katz confesses.

Like *El País*, the *Guardian* had deployed a team of experts and foreign correspondents for a thorough final sift through the cables. Some – such as the *Guardian*'s Moscow correspondent Luke Harding – were physically recalled to London for security reasons. Other foreign staff accessed the cables remotely via a VPN (virtual private network) connection. Ian Traynor in Brussels examined cables referring to the European Union, Nato and the Balkans; Declan Walsh, the *Guardian*'s correspondent in Islamabad, looked at Afghanistan and Pakistan; David Smith did Africa and Jason Burke took on India.

Other reporters included Washington correspondent Ewen MacAskill and Latin America correspondent Rory Carroll in Caracas. (Carroll's VPN connection quickly packed up, making it impossible to eyeball the Chávez cables.) Simon Tisdall, Ian Black and Jonathan Steele, all immensely experienced, combed through the cables on the Middle East and Afghanistan. The sheer range of journalistic expertise that five major international papers were throwing at the data would perhaps demonstrate the value of the world's remaining MSM. They could be the genuine information professionals, standing out in an otherwise worthless universe of internet froth.

Sitting in the fourth-floor bunker, Harding and a colleague, reporter Robert Booth, were among those who would spend long hours staring, increasingly dizzy eyed, at the dispatches. It soon became clear that there was an art to interrogating the database. If your search term was too big – say, "Britain", or "corruption" – the result would be unfathomably large. The search engine would announce: "More than 1,000 items returned." The trick was to use a relatively unusual name. Better still was to experiment with something off the wall, or even a bit crazy. Putting in "Batman", for example, yielded just two results. But one was a delightful cable in which a US diplomat noted that "Dmitry Medvedev continues to play Robin to Putin's Batman." The comparison between the Russian president and his prime minister would whizz round the world, and prompt a stung Vladimir Putin to accuse the United States of "arrogance" and unethical behaviour.

Likewise, punching in the search term "vodka" popped the cork on unexpected results: drunken meetings between US ambassadors and central Asian despots; a memorable wedding in Dagestan in which Chechnya's president – the murderous Ramzan Kadyrov – danced with a gold-plated revolver stuck down his trousers; and a Saudi Arabian sex party that spoke volumes about the hypocrisy of the Arab state's princely elite.

In contrast to the staccato jargon of the war logs, the cables were written in the kind of prose one might expect from Harvard or Yale. Harold Frayman had improvised the original search engine used to sift the much smaller Afghan and Iraq war logs. By now he had improved these techniques. "I'm a journalist. I knew what we were going to look for," he explains. "Diplomats were much more verbose than squaddies in the field. They knew longer words."

The data set contained more than 200 million of those words. Frayman had originally used the computer language Perl to design the Afghan and Iraq databases. He describes it as a "very well developed set of bits of software … It did little jobs very tidily." For the cables Frayman added refinements. Journalists were able to search the cables sent out by individual embassies. In the case of Iran, which had not had a US mission since the 1970s, most of the relevant diplomatic chatter actually came out of the US embassy in Ankara. It was therefore helpful to be able to quickly collect up the Ankara embassy output.

Of the files, 40% were classified confidential and 6% secret. Frayman created a search by five detailed categories: secret/noforn (that is, not to be read by non-Americans); secret; confidential/ noforn; confidential; and unclassified. There was no top-secret: such super-sensitive material had been omitted from the original SIPRNet database, along with a substantial number of dispatches that the state department in Washington considered unsuitable for sharing with its colleagues in the military and elsewhere. There were idiosyncrasies in the data: for example, very little material from Israel seemed to be circulated: suggesting that the US embassy there did not play an intimate role in the two-way dealings between Tel Aviv and Washington, and was largely kept out of the loop.

"Secret" was the place for the rummaging journalists to start. Some of these searches produced remarkable scoops. Many, however, did not. The secret category, it soon emerged, tended to cover a limited number of themes: the spread of nuclear material and nuclear facilities; military exports to Iran, Syria and other states considered unsavoury; negotiations involving top-ranking US army personnel. By far the largest number of stories came from lower classified documents.

Like the other reporters, Harding and Booth soon found themselves developing their own quirky search techniques. They discovered it was often useful to start at the bottom, working backwards from a country's most recent cables, written as they were up to 28 February 2010. Such searches became, however, an exercise in stamina; after reading a batch of more than 40 cables, the reporters had to take a break. Adjacent to the secret bunker was a free coffee machine. There was also a relaxation room. "Here, after a long session of cable-bashing, you could at least flick the sign to engaged, grab a cushion and lie groaning on the floor," says Harding. Katz said the company would pay for massages: but none of the *Guardian*'s weary cable slaves had time to spare.

To editor-in-chief Alan Rusbridger, the abundant disclosures pouring out of the US cables at first seemed like a player hitting the jackpot every time in an amusement arcade. He recalled how Leigh – after reading the material for a couple of weeks over the summer, chortling and astonished – had come back with enough stories for 10 splashes, articles that could lead the newspaper front page. "It was a fruit machine. You just had to hold your hat under there for long enough," Rusbridger says.

The analogy is a good one. But it perhaps makes the task sound too easy. To comb properly through the data, teams of *Guardian* staff had to be recruited. The reporters, especially the foreign correspondents, brought much to the table: contextualisation, specialist knowledge and a degree of entrepreneurship in divining what to look for. All these skills were needed to turn the cables into significant newspaper stories.

Leigh sent a memo to Rusbridger:

We've now got to the stage of story selection on project 3. The previous exercises (Iraq and Afghanistan) worked well politically, I thought, because Nick and I were able to focus the coverage [and the resultant global coverage] on elements that it was highly in the public interest to make known.

With Afghanistan, this was civilian casualties. With Iraq, it was torture. This time, I think it's also important that we try and major on stories that ought to be made known in the public interest. That was the compass-needle which helped me when I originally tried to put together the first dozen stories.

So – top stories revealing corruption and crime (Russia, Berlusconi, etc) and improper behaviour (eg unwarranted US pressure on other countries, unwarranted leaking to the US by other country officials). This will then position us where we can be best defended on all fronts??

A herd of publishable articles began to grow in size. The task of readying them for publication fell to Stuart Millar, the *Guardian*'s web news editor, who says he felt like a harried cowboy. "I was trying to lasso them into some kind of shape." This was a far more complicated production problem than the similar exercise with the Iraq and Afghan war logs. At first, it had seemed the cables would yield just a hatful of stories. By the eve of D-day, *Guardian* journalists had produced more than 160 articles, with more coming in all the time. "There was a crazy, enormous heave of copy," Millar recalls.

For Millar, as a web expert, it was clear that the emergence of the vast cables database marked the end of secrecy in the old-fashioned, cold-war-era sense. "The internet has rendered that all history," he reflects. "For us, there was a special responsibility to handle the material carefully, and to bring context to the stories, rather than just dump them out."

There were further concerns. The full text of relevant cables was intended to be posted online alongside individual news stories. This practice – what Assange called "scientific journalism" – was something the *Guardian* and some other papers had now been routinely doing for several years, ever since the technology had made it possible.

Each reporter was now made responsible for "redacting" their own cables – blanking out from the original any sources who might have been put at risk if their names were published. Heads of state, well-known politicians, those in public life generally, were fair game as a rule. In some parts of the world, however – the Middle East, Russia and central Asia, Iraq, Afghanistan and Pakistan – to be seen even talking to the Americans was a risky proposition.

The cables team took a conservative approach. If there was seen to be a risk of someone being compromised, then the name was scrubbed out. This was at times frustrating: long, informative cables might be stripped down to a couple of dull paragraphs. But the alternative was far worse. Redactions were passed on to Jonathan Casson, the paper's apparently miracle-working head of production, and his harassed-looking team, who set up camp in a neighbouring fourth-floor room normally used as a training suite. Rusbridger had suggested early on that each paper nominate a "redactions editor" to ensure a belt and braces approach to protecting sources. Now Casson worked brutally long days comparing the *Guardian*'s editing decisions with those of his counterparts, and considering the representations about particular cables from the US state department that were passed on by the *New York Times*. The task was made vastly more difficult by the journalists' determination not to discuss cables on the phone or in emails; after his daily round of Skype calls with international partners, Casson would meticulously alter the colour of some of the 700 or so cables listed on a vast Google spreadsheet that only he could understand. He looked like a man close to the edge.

And then there were the legal risks. Could the *Guardian* be prosecuted under the British Official Secrets Act or the US Espionage Act? And, if so, would it have to hand over internal documents and emails? Rusbridger had already sought the opinion of Alex Bailin, a QC who specialised in secrecy law, ahead of publication of the Afghan war logs. There had been no prosecution. But this did not mean that the White House would necessarily acquiesce in the far more damaging publication of the secret US state department cables.

Geraldine Proudler, of the *Guardian*'s law firm, Olswang, had been full of forebodings. Ahead of the publication of the Afghanistan and Iraq war logs she suggested it was "entirely possible" the US could bring a prosecution against the *Guardian* under the Espionage Act – though an all-out assault against the international media partners seemed unlikely. It was also possible the Americans could seek to lay hands on Rusbridger. "In a worst case scenario we cannot rule out extradition attempts." At the least, it was "very likely" that the US might serve a subpoena demanding that the *Guardian* hand over material after publication, she had advised.

In addition to worrying about the risks of possible injunctions under the Official Secrets Act and the Espionage Act, Gill Phillips, the *Guardian*'s in-house head of legal, spent many hours weighing up the libel and privacy dangers: both were big problems domestically, because the UK lacked the free speech protections enshrined in the US constitution. The cables were fascinating, and credible as documents. They revealed international skullduggery and double-dealing, among other things. But the fact they had been written by US diplomats didn't make them libel proof. Some of the cables from the former Soviet Union, Pakistan and Afghanistan made eye-popping assertions of top-level corruption, but could they land the *Guardian* with a costly writ? All had to be handled with care.

To a certain degree, Phillips could rely on the Reynolds defence, following a celebrated 1999 ruling that journalists were able to publish important allegations that could not be proved, so long as the material was in the public interest, the paper acted responsibly, and it followed proper journalistic procedures. (The case got its name after Albert Reynolds, the Irish premier, sued the London *Sunday Times*.) But the Reynolds judgment wasn't a Get Out of Jail Free card; in some cases the *Guardian* had still, if necessary, to be able to prove in court the truth of what it had published.

Silvio Berlusconi was a case in point. The cables alleged that the controversial Italian prime minister had profited "personally and handsomely" from a close – the cables said too close – relationship with Vladimir Putin, Russia's prime minister and former president. But might Berlusconi sue the *Guardian* in Rome, Phillips wondered? In the event, the Italian papers beat the *Guardian* to that one, and sprayed the detailed allegations all over the world.

There were further considerations. Responsible journalists normally approach the person they are writing about before publication, giving them the opportunity for comment or even rebuttal. In this case, however, there was a big danger in going too soon. That would reveal the *Guardian* possessed the cables: the other, alerted party could immediately seek an injunction, on the grounds that the paper was in unlawful possession of confidential documents. A sweeping UK gag order could be disastrous for the *Guardian*'s journalism: it might scupper their entire cables project.

Phillips, and Jan Thompson, the *Guardian*'s managing editor, held rambunctious meetings with the battle-scarred Leigh. His objective was to publish the best stories possible. The equally experienced lawyer's task was to keep the paper out of the courts and the editor out of jail. Leigh proposed what he thought were ingenious solutions to libel problems. Sometimes the lawyer agreed. It was a very fine line. "We were incredibly careful legally, and responsible," Phillips says. But "legalling" the *Guardian*'s cable stories was "exhilarating", she adds. "You got completely sucked in. Suddenly you find yourself becoming an expert on all the world's governments." Phillips felt confident in the end. She nevertheless arranged for both a QC and junior barrister to be on stand-by on the evening of the planned cables launch. Legal opponents had been known in the past to wake up British judges, fully prepared to issue gag orders against the *Guardian*, even in their pyjamas.

There was a final grand conference in London of all the parties on Thursday 11 November to fine-tune the elaborate publication grid of day-by-day cable stories. Assange arrived in the *Guardian* offices rigged out this time in chief executive style, with a sharp, well-fitting blue suit. His Australian lawyer Jennifer Robinson was by his side. Representatives from *Der Spiegel*, *El País*, and *Le Monde* had flown in, together with Ian Fisher, a deputy foreign editor with the *New York Times*. In contrast to the difficult atmosphere at the last meeting, Assange was a model of bonhomie and charm; Leigh, with whom he had previously had some angry words, decided to be absent with what some suspected to be a case of diplomatic flu. The meeting went surprisingly smoothly.

Afterwards, the partners again headed for dinner in the Rotunda restaurant beneath the *Guardian* offices. Here, as the journalists sank pints of Pilsner Urquell, Assange confided he was thinking about going to Russia. Russia was an odd choice – especially in the light of soon-to-be-published cables that described it as a "virtual mafia state". He did not disclose, however, details of the relationship he had privately struck up with WikiLeaks' new "Russian representative", the bizarre figure of Israel Shamir.

How much did the US administration know of this planned challenge to their secrets? The journalists assumed the CIA had followed every twist and turn of the project. The US army had certainly been aware that thousands of diplomatic cables had gone astray since the summer, when Private Bradley Manning had been specifically indicted for purloining them. But the Obama administration appeared remarkably unaware of just which cables WikiLeaks and its media partners now had in their possession.

In the week before publication, the state department warned many of its allies about the cables' embarrassing contents. But they appeared not to know that the leaked cables ceased at the end of February, believing some to be more recent. Rumours circulated that Washington had been unimpressed with David Cameron and Britain's new coalition government, which took power in May. The US ambassador in London, Louis B Susman, allegedly said as much in a post-election cable. The Americans, it was gathered, had now sheepishly briefed Downing Street about its contents. They were under the impression the leaked cables went up to June 2010, the month of Manning's arrest.

The *Guardian* didn't have that Cameron cable. As a result Cameron survived the WikiLeaks drama relatively unscathed. "We were amazed about how little the US knew about what we were doing," Katz says. 'They clearly had no idea which data set we had. They massively over-briefed about what was in the cables."

The *New York Times* had decided to forewarn the state department which cables it was intending to use. The *Guardian* – which worked in Britain under a peculiarly oppressive legal regime – was not going to follow the Americans quite that far. The paper was willing to listen, but was already doing all it could, without official prompting, to protect sensitive human contacts from reprisal, and not to publish irresponsibly.

A few days before the cables' release, two senior figures from the US embassy in Grosvenor Square called in to the *Guardian*'s London offices for a chat. This discussion led to a surreal transatlantic telephone call on Friday 26 November – two days before D-Day. Rusbridger had agreed to ring Washington. He made the conference call from the circular table in his office. On the line in Washington was PJ Crowley, the US assistant secretary of state for public affairs. The conversation began:

"OK, here's PJ Crowley. I just want you to know in this phone call we've got secretary of state Clinton's private secretary, we have representatives of the DoD, the intelligence communities, and the National Security Council."

All Rusbridger could offer in reply was, "We have our managing editor here ..."

Crowley then set out how the cable scandal looked from the lofty heights of US power: "Obviously, from our perspective these are stolen documents. They reveal sensitive military secrets and addresses that expose people to security risks."

Crowley made his pitch. He said the US government was "willing to help" the *Guardian* if the newspaper was prepared to "share the documents" it had – in other words, tip off the state department which cables it intended to publish. Rusbridger was non-committal. He said: "I don't think we are going to agree on that now, so why don't we return later to that."

Crowley said some special forces operations and dealings with some countries were sensitive. He then asked for a pause. He came back a couple of minutes later: "Mr Rusbridger, we don't feel this conversation is working for us because at the moment we are just giving a lot of stories, and we are not getting a lot in return."

Clinton's private secretary chipped in. She said: "I've got a very direct question for you, Mr Rusbridger. You journalists like asking direct questions and I know you expect direct answers. So I'm going to ask you a direct question. Are you going to give us the numbers of the cables or not?"

"No, we're not."

"Thank you very much."

Rusbridger did decide to tell the Americans the *Guardian*'s broad publication schedule. Day one, he said was to feature Iran, with North Korea on day two and Pakistan on day three. Then the conversation was over.

In Germany, the editor-in-chief of *Der Spiegel* had taken a call from the US ambassador. He told Georg Mascolo that there was huge concern at the "highest, highest levels" about the security of sources: "Lives could be in jeopardy." Mascolo replied that *Der Spiegel* had done everything it could to protect sources who might be in danger. He invited the state department to share with him their areas of concern.

The *New York Times* had been holding its own sometimes tense negotiations with US government officials. The paper's lawyers were confident that it could report on the secret documents without violating American law. But Bill Keller felt a large moral and ethical responsibility to use the material responsibly: "While we assumed we had little or no ability to influence what WikiLeaks did, let alone what would happen once this material was loosed in the echo chamber of the blogosphere, that did not free us from the obligation to exercise care in our own journalism. From the beginning we determined that in our articles and in any documents we published from the secret archive we would excise material that could put lives at risk," he wrote later.

The *New York Times*'s policy was to err on the side of caution. With the Afghan and Iraq war logs, the paper redacted names of all sources who had spoken to US soldiers and diplomats, and edited out details that might have revealed continuing intelligence-gathering operations or military tactics. But because of the range of the material and the hypersensitivities of diplomacy, the embassy cables were bound to be more explosive than the war logs, Keller considered.

Dean Baquet, the *New York Times*'s Washington bureau chief, gave the White House an early warning on 19 November. Five days later, the day before Thanksgiving, Baquet and three colleagues were invited to a windowless room in the state department, where they encountered an unsmiling crowd: representatives of the White House, the state department, the director of national intelligence, the CIA, the Defence Intelligence Agency, the FBI and the Pentagon, gathered around a conference table. Others, who never identified themselves, lined the walls. A solitary note-taker tapped away on a computer.

The meeting was off the record, but it is fair to say the mood was tense. Scott Shane, one of the reporters who participated in the meeting, described "an undertone of suppressed outrage and frustration". Subsequent meetings and daily conference calls were less prickly and more businesslike, Keller says. The US administration had three areas generally of concern. It wanted to protect individuals who had spoken candidly to US diplomats in oppressive countries – something the *New York Times* was happy to do. It also wanted to remove references to secret American programmes relating to intelligence. Lastly, it did not want the paper to reveal candid remarks by heads of state and other top foreign officials, and feared publication would strain relations with those countries. "We were mostly unpersuaded," Keller recalls.

This was, of course, hardly the first time the *New York Times* had published secrets that discomfited the US government. Before the year of WikiLeaks, nothing the paper had done on Keller's watch had caused quite the agitation of two articles the paper published about tactics employed by the Bush administration after the attacks of 11 September 2001. One article, which was published in 2005 and won a Pulitzer prize, revealed that the National Security Agency was eavesdropping on domestic phone and email conversations without the legal courtesy of a warrant. The other, published in 2006, described a vast treasury department programme to screen international banking records.

The editor had vivid memories of sitting in the Oval Office as President George W Bush tried to persuade him and the *New York Times*'s publisher to withhold the eavesdropping article. Bush told him that if the paper published, it should share the blame for the next terrorist attack. Unconvinced, the paper published anyway, and the reaction from the government and conservative commentators in particular was vociferous.

This time around, the US administration reaction was different. It was, for the most part, sober and professional. The Obama White House, while strongly condemning WikiLeaks for making the documents public, did not seek an injunction to halt publication. There was no Oval Office lecture, no plea to Keller or the publisher not to write about the documents. "On the contrary, in our discussions before the publication of our articles, White House officials, while challenging some of the conclusions we drew from the material, thanked us for handling the documents with care. The secretaries of state and defence and the attorney general resisted the opportunity for a crowd-pleasing orgy of press-bashing," Keller says, adding: "Though the release of these documents was certainly painfully embarrassing, the relevant government agencies actually engaged with us in an attempt to prevent the release of material genuinely damaging to innocent individuals or the national interest."

From his secret hideout back in Ellingham Hall, Assange sought to open his own channel of negotiations, sending a letter on 26 November to the US embassy in London. Headed "Julian Assange, editor-in-chief, WikiLeaks", it began: "Dear Ambassador Susman, I refer to recent public statements by United States government officials expressing concern about the possible publication by WikiLeaks and other media organisations of information allegedly derived from United States government records."

Assange invited the US government to "privately nominate" examples where publication of a cable could put an individual "at significant risk of harm". He promised WikiLeaks would quickly consider any US government submissions ahead of publication. The state department's legal adviser Harold Koh sent an uncompromising letter back. It stated that the cables "were provided in violation of US law and without regard for the grave consequences of this action".

Releasing them "would place at risk the lives of countless individuals", jeopardise ongoing military operations, and threaten co-operation between the US and its allies and partners, the letter said. It would hinder co-operation on "common challenges such as terrorism, pandemic diseases and nuclear proliferation".

The letter ordered WikiLeaks to halt plans to publish the cables, hand back the stolen files, and "destroy all records of this material from WikiLeaks' databases."

Assange wrote to Susman again on 28 November. He made clear that WikiLeaks had no intention of putting anybody at risk, "nor do we wish to harm the national security of the United States". He continued: "I understand that the United States government would prefer not to have the information that will be published in the public domain and is not in favour of openness. That said, either there is a risk or there is not. You have chosen to respond in a manner which leads me to conclude that the risks are entirely fanciful and that you are instead concerned only to suppress evidence of human rights abuses and other criminal behaviour."

The negotiations with the state department – such as they were – thus terminated. All that was left was to prepare for simultaneous publication of the biggest leak in the history. What could possibly go wrong?

CHAPTER 15

Publication day

Basel railway station, Switzerland
28 November 2010

"Launch! Launch! Launch!"

<small>GUARDIAN</small> NEWSROOM

It was Sunday morning at the sleepy Badischer Bahnhof. Few were around. The station sits precisely on the border between Germany and Switzerland. It is a textbook example of European co-operation – with the Germans providing the trains, and the Swiss running the cafés and newspaper kiosks. This morning, however, the station would become briefly notorious for something else: a gigantic foul-up.

Early in the morning, a van rolled in, bearing 40 copies of the German news magazine *Der Spiegel*. The weekly normally starts distributing copies to newsagents over the weekend, with revellers in Berlin able to buy it late on Saturday night on their way home. But on this occasion – as with the publication of the Afghan war logs – *Der Spiegel* was supposed to have held all copies of its edition back. The international release of the US embassy cables had been painstakingly co-ordinated for 21.30 GMT that Sunday evening. The *Guardian*, *New York Times*, *El País* and *Le Monde* were all waiting anxiously to push the button on the world's biggest leak. *Der Spiegel* had agreed to roll its stories out at the same time on its website, with the magazine only published on the following Monday morning. Everyone knew the script.

But the gods of news had decided to do things differently. At around 11.30am Christian Heeb, the editor-in-chief of the local Radio Basel, discovered a copy of *Der Spiegel* at the station. It was dated 29/11/10. It cost €3.80. The front cover was nothing less than sensational: "Revealed: How America Sees the world". The strap-line confirmed: "The secret dispatches of the US foreign ministry". Against a red background was a photo-gallery of world leaders, each accompanied by a demeaning quotation culled from the US cables. Angela Merkel, Germany's increasingly unpopular chancellor, was "risk averse and rarely creative". Guido Wester-welle, Merkel's disastrous foreign minister, was "aggressive". Then there were the others. Vladimir Putin? "Alpha dog". Dmitry Medvedev? "Pale and hesitant". Silvio Berlusconi? "Wild parties". Mahmoud Ahmadinejad? "Hitler". Next to Libya's Muammar Gaddafi were the tantalising words "Luxuriant blonde nurse". More extraordinary revelations were promised inside.

Heeb's station started to broadcast the news, saying a few early copies of *Der Spiegel* had become available at Basel station. It was at this point that an anonymous Twitter user called Freelancer_09 decided to check out the prospect for himself. He tweeted: "*Der Spiegel* zu früh am Badischen Bahnhof Basel! Mal schaun was da steht." (*Der Spiegel* too early at Basel station! Let's see what's there.) Freelancer_09 managed to obtain one of the last two or three copies of the rogue *Spiegel* batch, just as panicked executives at the magazine's Hamburg headquarters were realising something had gone horribly wrong: one of the distribution vans sent to criss-cross Germany had set off for Switzerland 24 hours too early.

Radio Basel in Switzerland received a hasty phone call from Germany. Would they come off the air in return for subsequent help with the story? But it was too late. Freelancer_09 was already at work: within minutes he had begun tweeting the magazine's contents. Merkel had a better relationship with US president George W Bush than with his successor Barack Obama! US diplomats have a low opinion of Germany's regional politicians! The Americans think Westerwelle is a jerk! At the start of the morning Freelancer_09 had a meagre tally of 40 Twitter followers. His own political views seemed pretty clear – alternative, counter-cultural, even anarchist – judging from the leftist Twitter users he followed, and from his own profile photo: a child shouting through a loudhailer above the words: "Police state". Who he was exactly was uncertain. (His identity remained mysterious; some weeks later his Twitter account went dormant.)

Soon, word spread through the blogosphere that an anonymous local journalist in Basel had stumbled on the Holy Grail. Other German journalists started "retweeting" his posts. *Der Spiegel* frantically messaged him to make contact. He ignored them. "His Twitter follows rapidly snowballed. We could see it was becoming a serious problem," admits *Der Spiegel*'s Holger Stark. "While we were closing the hole, he had managed to get a copy of the magazine."

Sitting helplessly in London, Alan Rusbridger realised that the 9.30pm GMT embargo for the release of the cables looked wobbly. "You have five of the most powerful news organisations, and everything was paralysed by a little freelancer. We started having conferences on the hour wondering what to do," Rusbridger says. There was more bad news. Rival German news organisations contacted Freelancer_09 and asked him to start scanning entire pages of Der Spiegel's edition. By about 3pm, he had 150 followers, with more joining every minute. By 4pm he had found a scanner, and was pumping the embargoed articles out onto the internet. His followers jumped to around 600. A French mirror site began translating Freelancer_09's posts. "We realised the story wasn't going to hold. We had sprung a leak ourselves," Rusbridger recalls wryly. It was a great irony. Rusbridger had been an early Twitter proselytiser; he had relentlessly encouraged *Guardian* journalists to sign up to the San Francisco-based micro-blogging site. Now Twitter had turned round and – figuratively speaking – skewered him in the bottom.

The previous day, Saturday, at around 5pm a German technician from *Der Spiegel*'s own online service in Hamburg had made an earlier gaffe: he managed to go live on the website with an extract from the edition of the magazine. It gave a few intriguing early details: that there were 251,287 cables; that one cable dated back to 1966, but most were newer than 2004; that 9,005 documents dated from the first two months of 2010. Stark apologised for the accident and said the German link was erased as soon as it was discovered. The screen shots circulated through the net for some time. Then on Sunday afternoon more material appeared on *Spiegel*'s popular English-language site. The rumours were now sweeping feverishly across Twitter. The anticipation was reaching bursting point.

The *New York Times* soon spotted the *Spiegel* online story. The paper's executives said the embargo was dead – now effectively meaningless. "What was so brilliant was the irony that of all the people to mess up it was the Germans," said Katz – not always the *Guardian*'s most politically correct representative. Until now, it was the Germans – impeccably ethical at all times – who had managed to avoid the recriminations hurled freely by Assange at both the Americans and the British. Janine Gibson, editor of guardian.co.uk, the *Guardian*'s website, compared the pratfall-strewn cables launch to Britain's 1993 Grand National. That shambolic instalment of the historic horse race was infamously cancelled after two false starts.

"It all got terribly untidy," Rusbridger says. "But it was the most complicated thing we have ever done, co-ordinating a

Spanish morning paper with a French afternoon paper with a German weekly with an American [paper] in a different time zone and a bunch of anarchists in a bunker who would only communicate via Jabber [online instant messaging]."

By 6pm the *Guardian* and everyone else agreed just to publish, go with it. As though at Nasa's Mission Control Center in Houston, the *Guardian*'s production staff stood poised at the newspaper's King's Cross office in front of a flickering bank of screens. Production boss Jon Casson asked: "Will we launch?" Katz replied: "LAUNCH!" The word was taken up and spread instantly across the back bench, the newsroom echoing with the words: "Launch! Launch! Launch!" The world's biggest leak had gone live.

The *Guardian*'s front-page splash made the historic dimensions of the story clear. With David Leigh's byline, it appeared on guardian.co.uk at 6.13pm. The headline proclaimed: "US embassy cables leak sparks global diplomatic crisis." It began:

"The United States was catapulted into a worldwide diplomatic crisis today, with the leaking to the *Guardian* and other international media of more than 250,000 classified cables from its embassies, many sent as recently as February this year. At the start of a series of daily extracts from the US embassy cables – many designated 'secret' – the *Guardian* can disclose that Arab leaders are privately urging an air strike on Iran and that US officials have been instructed to spy on the UN leadership."

The story went on: "These two revelations alone would be likely to reverberate around the world. But the secret dispatches, which were obtained by WikiLeaks, the whistleblowers' website, also reveal Washington's evaluation of many other highly sensitive international issues."

At 6.15pm the *Guardian* launched a WikiLeaks live blog, to chart reaction as it came in. More live blogs would follow; they would become an innovative part of the cables coverage. The disclosures in Leigh's story were the first of many over the next four weeks. Despite its scrappy launch, the publication of the US state department cables amounted to the biggest leak since 1971 when Daniel Ellsberg gave the Pentagon papers to the *New York Times*, provoking a historic court case and revealing the White House's dirty secrets in Vietnam. This data spillage was far bigger – an unprecedented release of secret information from the heart of the world's only superpower.

Nobody could think of a bigger story – certainly not one authored by the media themselves. "You could say the World Trade Center was a bigger story, or the Iraq war. But in terms of a newspaper, where by the act of publication you unleash one story that is then talked about in every single corner of the globe, and you are the only people who have got it, and you release it each day, this was unique," Rusbridger says.

The US state department had already assembled a team of 120 people, to burn the midnight oil and sift through those cables likely to be disclosed. The department also issued a condemnatory statement. It said: "We anticipate the release of what are claimed to be several hundred thousand classified state department cables on Sunday night that detail private diplomatic discussions with foreign governments. By its very nature, field reporting to Washington is candid and often incomplete information. It is not an expression of policy, nor does it always shape final policy decisions. Nevertheless, these cables could compromise private discussions with foreign governments and opposition leaders, and when the substance of private conversations is printed on the front pages of newspapers around the world, it can deeply impact not only on US foreign policy interests, but those of our allies and friends around the world." The release of the cables was a "reckless and dangerous action". It had put lives at risk, the White House declared.

The statement was a damage limitation exercise. Even opponents of WikiLeaks had to acknowledge that some of the disclosures – for example, that the US had spied on UN officials and sought to gather their credit card account numbers – were overwhelmingly in the public interest. The White House, moreover, frequently expressed concern when other authoritarian regimes clamped down on freedom of speech. This testy response when the leak came from inside its own large governmental machinery would provoke the Russians, Chinese, and just about everyone else, to accuse Washington of double standards.

The *Guardian* posted its own riposte. It pointed out that the paper had carefully redacted many cables. This was done "in order to protect a number of named sources and so as not to disclose certain details of special operations".

The *New York Times* also vigorously defended its decision to publish: "The cables tell the unvarnished story of how the government makes its biggest decisions, the decisions that cost the country most heavily in lives and money. They shed light on the motivations – and, in some cases, the duplicity – of allies on the receiving end of American courtship and foreign aid. They illuminate the diplomacy surrounding two current wars and several countries, like Pakistan and Yemen, where American military involvement is growing. As daunting as it is to publish such material over official objections, it would be presumptuous to conclude that Americans have no right to know what is being done in their name."

Franco Frattini, Italy's foreign minister, was one of the earliest politicians to grasp that the leak could not be undone, and was game-changing. "It will be the 9/11 of world diplomacy," he exclaimed. For once the comparison didn't look like hyperbole. "It was being discussed in the White House, the Kremlin, the Élysée, by Berlusconi and the UN, by Chávez, in Canberra, in every capital city of the world," Rusbridger said. "The ones where it wasn't being discussed, you knew they were bracing themselves. You just had this sense of mayhem being let loose. All these incredibly powerful people, the most powerful people in the world, were scrambling into emergency board meetings."

At Kings Place, the following day's editorial conference was more crowded than usual. Morning conferences are a *Guardian* ritual: the heads of department – home, foreign, city, sport, as well as features, comment and arts – give a quick run-down of the day's offerings. All staff can attend and anybody can speak. The seating arrangement mirrors the *Guardian*'s unspoken hierarchy: Rusbridger sits in the middle of an elongated yellow sofa; junior staff perch uncomfortably on stools around the glass walls. After the news roundup the editor typically says: "What else?" The words are often hard to hear. It is a brave, or foolish, person who opens the debate; sometimes the silence extends awkwardly for 10 seconds. This morning, however, there was no hesitation. The room was packed; the atmosphere one of excitement, and aston-ishment that the *Guardian* had managed, with a few glitches, to pull the story off.

One of the unfamiliar faces there was Luke Harding, the *Guardian*'s Moscow correspondent, who had mined the cables for a series of hard-hitting stories about Russia and who, having just returned again from Moscow, stood unshaven and jet-lagged next to the door. Ian Katz recalled Sunday's dramatic events and explained the decision to bring forward publication when it became clear that Cablegate itself had sprung a leak. Katz described the *Guardian*'s sitcom-style wranglings with its many Euro-partners: "It was a cross between running a Brussels committee and an episode of *'Allo 'Allo!*" He came up with a characteristically rococo analogy – "like being a kind of air traffic controller, with several small aircraft crashing at Stansted but managing to land a couple of big jets at Heathrow".

The *Guardian*'s website had gone "absolutely tonto", Janine Gibson reported. The story produced remarkable traffic – the

4.1 million unique users clicking on it that day was the highest ever. Record numbers would continue, with 9.4 million browsers viewing WikiLeaks stories between 28 November and 14 December. Some 43% of them came from the US. The *Guardian* team had designed an interactive graphic allowing readers to carry out their own searches of the cable database. This feature became the most popular aspect of the *Guardian*'s coverage. People from around the world looked to see what US officials had privately written about their rulers. "This was really pleasing," says Gibson. "People were looking for themselves and engaging with the cables and not just the Assange-ness."

As the cables rolled out day by day, an ugly, and in many ways deranged, backlash took place in the US. A vengeful chorus came mostly from Republicans. New York congressman Peter King, incoming chair of the homeland security committee, talked of "treason" and proposed WikiLeaks should be designated as "a foreign terrorist organisation". Eschewing any risk of understatement, he said: "WikiLeaks presents a clear and present danger to the national security of the US."

Congressman Pete Hoekstra of Michigan was reported calling for executions. "Clearly the person that leaked the information or hacked into our systems we can go after and we can probably go after them for espionage and maybe treason. If we go after them, and are able to convict them on treason, then the death penalty comes into play."

His Michigan colleague, Mike Rogers, was not to be outdone. He told a local radio station: "I argue the death penalty clearly should be considered here. He clearly aided the enemy to what may result in the death of US soldiers, or those co-operating. If that is not a capital offence, I don't know what is."

Former Alaska governor Sarah Palin, darling of the unhinged right, denounced Assange's "sick, un-American espionage" and came close to inciting his assassination: "Why was he not pursued with the same urgency we pursue al-Qaida and Taliban leaders? … He is an anti-American operative with blood on his hands."

But it was Senator Joe Lieberman, Senate homeland security committee chairman, a foreign policy hawk and maverick Democrat, who was the most practical attack dog. Lieberman described the leak in apocalyptic terms as "an outrageous, reckless and despicable action that will undermine the ability of our government and our partners to keep our people safe and to work together to defend our vital interests". He stopped short of denouncing Assange as a "terrorist" but said: "It's a terrible thing that WikiLeaks did. I hope we are doing everything we can to shut down their website."

On the first day of publication of the cables, Sunday, WikiLeaks came under massive hacker attack. The net traffic heading to WikiLeaks leapt from 13 gigabits (thousand million bits) per second to around 17Gbps. It peaked at 18Gbps. WikiLeaks was no stranger to DDOS or "distributed denial of service" attacks. Someone controlling a "botnet" of tens of thousands of compromised Windows PCs was apparently orchestrating them in an attempt to bring wikileaks.org crashing down.

In a usual DDOS attack, the PCs try to communicate with the targeted site. A typical method is to send a "ping" request with a few packets of data. It's a bit like ringing the site's front doorbell. The site generally responds by acknowledging that the data reached it. On its own, a ping request is easy for a site to deal with. But when a blizzard of them arrives from all over the world and continues and continues, it becomes impossible for the site to do anything useful: it's too busy answering the ping requests to deliver any useful data.

The DDOS attack that hit WikiLeaks that afternoon was eight times as large as any previous ones. The hacker behind it appeared to be a curious right-wing patriot called "The Jester" – or, in the argot he used, "th3j35t3r". The Jester described himself as a "hacktivist for good". His goal, as stated on his Twitter account, was to obstruct "the lines of communication for terrorists, sympathisers, fixers, facilitators, oppressive regimes and general bad guys". As the attacks continued to pummel WikiLeaks, he tweeted excitedly: "www.wikileaks.org – TANGO DOWN – for attempting to endanger the lives of our troops, 'other assets' & foreign relations." Normally, The Jester preferred to disrupt sites he viewed as being used by jihadist groups and other Islamist revolutionaries; every time he succeeded he sent the same delighted message: "TANGO DOWN". Believed to be a former US military recruit, The Jester appeared to have decided on this occasion to target Assange.

The Jester's attack was the first intriguing skirmish in what turned into a serious cyber-fight. Big US corporations tried to push Assange off the internet. But he was defended by a committed online group of underage libertarians and cyber-freaks. In this warfare, some would discern the beginnings of a decentralised global protest movement. Others would dismiss it as the antics of a handful of sexually frustrated young men. But there was no doubt WikiLeaks was under siege.

To dodge the DDOS attacks, Assange diverted the site's main WikiLeaks page – though not the one with the diplomatic cables on it – to run on Amazon's EC2 or "Elastic Cloud Computing" service. The cablegate.wikileaks.org directory and its contents remained outside Amazon, on a server located in France. Amazon's commercial service was big enough to absorb DDOS attacks. On Tuesday 30 November there were more attacks against Amazon's main site and WikiLeaks' France-hosted cables site. Using machines in Russia, eastern Europe and Thailand, the assaults were larger and more sophisticated. Nonetheless, WikiLeaks managed to weather the storm, aided by Amazon's powerful EC2 servers. Assange publicised that he was hiring them.

Senator Lieberman upped his campaign. He called Amazon and urged them to stop hosting WikiLeaks. Lieberman's browbeating worked. Amazon removed WikiLeaks from its servers. Instead of admitting it had come under political pressure, the firm claimed in weasel tones that WikiLeaks had breached its "terms of service". "It's clear that WikiLeaks doesn't own or otherwise control all the rights to this classified content," Amazon said. "Further, it is not credible that the extraordinary volume of 250,000 classified documents that WikiLeaks is publishing could have been carefully redacted in such a way to ensure they weren't putting innocent people in jeopardy."

This was a statement Amazon had no factual basis to make. Only a tiny proportion of the 250,000 cables had been published, and each one was, in fact, being carefully redacted. It seemed plain that Amazon executives were regurgitating lines fed to them by politicians.

The senator hailed Amazon's "right decision" and urged "any other company or organisation that is hosting WikiLeaks to immediately terminate its relationship with them". He went on: "WikiLeaks' illegal, outrageous, and reckless acts have compromised our national security and put lives at risk around the world. No responsible company – whether American or foreign – should assist WikiLeaks in its efforts to disseminate these stolen materials."

The WikiLeaks team had used free software to generate a graphic display showing an overview of the cables' classification, number and other general data. The small company that licensed it, Tableau Software, removed the graphic from its public site – also feeling the pressure (though there was no direct contact) from Lieberman's office. The dominoes then started to fall. The company EveryDNS, which provides free routing services (translating human-readable addresses such as wikileaks.org into machine readable internet addresses such as 64.64.12.170) terminated the wikileaks.org domain name. It also deleted all email addresses associated with it. Justifying the move, EveryDNS said the constant hacker attacks on WikiLeaks were inconveniencing other customers.

In effect, WikiLeaks had now vanished from the web for anyone who couldn't work out how to discover a numeric address for the site. WikiLeaks shifted to an alternative address, www.wikileaks.ch, registered in Switzerland but hosted in a Swedish bunker built to withstand a nuclear war.

Fresh problems surfaced: PostFinance, the Swiss postal system, closed Assange's bank account, on the basis that he was not living in Geneva, as required by the rules. PayPal, owned by the US auction site eBay, said it would suspend WikiLeaks' account there, due to "violation of the PayPal acceptable use policy". A spokesman said the account "cannot be used for any activities that encourage, promote, facilitate or instruct others to engage in illegal activity". It later emerged that the US state department had written to the company on 27 November – the eve of the cables' launch – declaring that WikiLeaks was deemed illegal in the US. On Monday 6 December, the credit card giant MasterCard followed suit, saying that WikiLeaks "contravened rules". On Tuesday, Visa Europe did the same. These were popular and easy methods of donating online; seeing both closed down shut off much of WikiLeaks' funding. (Critics pointed out that, while WikiLeaks was judged off-limits, the Ku Klux Klan's website still directed would-be donors to a site that takes both MasterCard and Visa.) It was a wounding blow and left Assange struggling to pay his and WikiLeaks' growing legal bills.

These salvoes against WikiLeaks did not go unanswered: they triggered a backlash against the backlash. Fury raged online at such a demonstration of political pressure and US corporate self-interest. While polls suggested many Americans backed a shutdown of WikiLeaks, others were angered by the suppression of free speech; and far more outside the US thought the company cave-ins were a bad portent for free expression on the internet.

Into the arena stepped "Anonymous", a grouping of around 3,000 people. Some were expert hackers in control of small-scale botnets: others were net newbies seeking a cause to rally around. It was a loose collective, mainly of teenagers with time on their hands, and older people (almost all men) with more nous and technical skills. The Anonymous crowd was only a group in the loosest sense, the *Guardian*'s technology editor Charles Arthur wrote: "It's more like a stampeding herd, not sure quite what it wants but certain that it's not going to put up with any obstacles, until it reaches an obstacle which it can't hurdle, in which case it moves on to something else."

Anonymous – which grew out of the equally chaotic "/b/" messageboard on the discussion site 4chan.org – had in the past tormented the Scientologists, reposting videos and leaking secret documents that the cult hoped to suppress. Anonymous's broad manifesto is to fight against the suppression of information – but its members were not above childish actions simply to annoy and frustrate web users for their own amusement (known as "doing it for the lulz"). Anonymous supporters turned up at demonstrations from time to time – some of them wearing the same spooky Guy Fawkes mask that adorned the group's Anony_Ops Twitter page. "It's complex, puerile, bizarre and chaotic," one of them told Arthur.

Operation Payback had previously been directed against the websites of law firms that pursued online music pirates, as well as against the Recording Industry Association of America (RIAA). Now it was the online payment firms' turn for "payback". Despite having no hierarchy or recognisable leader, on Wednesday 8 December Anonymous hackers forced the main website of MasterCard offline for several hours. They temporarily disrupted Sarah Palin's credit card account. Anonymous also claimed to have knocked out PostFinance's site and that of the Swedish prosecutor's office. Some Anonymous supporters posted a "manifesto". "We support the free flow of information. Anonymous is actively campaigning for this goal everywhere in all forms. This necessitates the freedom of expression for the internet, for journalism and journalists, and citizens of the world. Though we recognise you may disagree, we believe that Anonymous is campaigning for you so that your voice may never be silenced."

What effect the attack had on MasterCard's actual financial operations is unclear: the company did not say whether transactions (which would be carried out over secure lines to its main computers) were affected. It largely ignored the attack, hoping not to inflame the attackers. The tactic worked; Anonymous next considered turning its ire on Amazon and PayPal, but the disorganised nature of the group meant they could not muster enough firepower to knock either site offline; Amazon was too big, while PayPal withstood some attacks. The suggestion made privately was that the powerful hackers who had acted against MasterCard did not want to inconvenience themselves by taking out PayPal, which they used themselves all the time.

This event was something new – the internet equivalent of a noisy political demonstration. What had begun with a couple of teenage nerds had morphed into a cyber-uprising against attempts to restrict information. As they put it in one portentous YouTube video, upon a soundtrack of thrashing guitars: "We are everywhere." They were certainly in the Netherlands, at least, where, in December, police arrested a 16-year-old and a 19-year-old. Some Anonymous supporters without sufficient computer skills had overlooked the fact that the software – called LOIC – being offered to them to run attacks would give away their internet location. Police could, given time, tie that to a physical user.

Behind all this online turbulence, however, a much more serious game was afoot. President Obama's attorney general, Eric Holder, called a press conference to announce there was now an "active, ongoing, criminal investigation" into the leaking of classified information. He promised to hold those who broke US law "accountable", and said: "To the extent that there are gaps in our laws, we will move to close those gaps, which is not to say that anybody at this point, because of their citizenship or residence, is not a target or a subject of an investigation that is ongoing." In Alexandria, Virginia, just outside Washington, rumours began to spread that a secret grand jury had been empanelled, and many subpoenas were being prepared for issue. Bradley Manning, the young soldier who had by now spent seven months in virtual solitary confinement, would only see an end to his harsh treatment, his friends started to believe, if he was willing to implicate Julian Assange and WikiLeaks in some serious crimes.

It seemed clear that prosecuting Assange – an Australian citizen now living in the UK – for espionage or conspiracy was going to be an uphill affair, not least because of the old-fashioned nature of the US Espionage Act. But it was also clear that an exasperated White House wanted to be seen vigorously pursuing this option. Would the justice department try and winkle Assange out of his hideaway in the English countryside? And was there not a still unresolved police investigation into his behaviour in Sweden? The threat of extradition – and the possibility of several decades in a US supermax jail – began to loom over Assange, as the rest of the world sought to digest the significance of the cascade of documents he had released.

CHAPTER 16

The biggest leak in history

Cyberspace
30 November 2010

"It is the historian's dream. It is the diplomat's nightmare"
TIMOTHY GARTON ASH, HISTORIAN

What did we learn from WikiLeaks? The question, as with virtually everything else to do with the leaks, was polarising. There was, from the start, a metropolitan yawn from *bien pensants* who felt they knew it all. Arabs don't like Iran? The Russian government is corrupt? Some African countries are kleptocracies? Go on, astonish us. You'll be telling us next that the pope is Catholic.

According to this critique the disclosures stated the obvious, and amounted to no more than "humdrum diplomatic pillow talk". (This was from the *London Review of Books*. Academic Glen Newey said he was unimpressed by the revelation that French leader Nicolas Sarkozy "is a short man with a Napoleon complex".)

Then there were the people who argued that the cables did not reveal enough bad behaviour by Americans. On the left this was a cause for disappointment – and, sometimes, suspicion. A small cabal began poring over the cables for evidence of ideological editing or censorship. And why so little on Israel? On the right, and from government, this served as fuel for the argument that there was no public interest in publication. This was not the Pentagon papers, they reasoned. There was little malfeasance in American foreign policy revealed in the documents, so where's the justification for revealing all? Then there was the US government's insistence that the leaks were endangering lives, wrecking Washington's ability to do business with its allies and partners, and helping terrorists.

What these arguments missed was the hunger for the cables in countries that didn't have fully functioning democracies or the sort of free expression enjoyed in London, Paris or New York. Within hours of the first cables being posted the *Guardian* started receiving a steady stream of pleading requests from editors and journalists around the world wanting to know what the cables revealed about their own countries and rulers. It was easier to call the revelations unstartling, dull even, if one lived in western Europe, rather than in Belarus, Tunisia, or in any other oppressive regime.

This was as powerful a case for the WikiLeaks disclosures as any. It was not particularly edifying to see western commentators and politicians decrying the public interest in the publication of information which was being avidly, even desperately, sought after by people in far off countries of which they doubtless knew little. Who was to say what effect these disclosures would have, even if, on one level, they were revealing things that were in some sense known? The very fact of publication often served as authentication and verification of things that were suspected.

In fact, far from being routine, the leak was unprecedented, if only in size. WikiLeaks called it, accurately, "the largest set of confidential documents ever to be released into the public domain". There were 251,287 internal state department communiqués, written by 280 embassies and consulates in 180 different countries. Among them were frank, and often unflattering, assessments of world leaders; analysis, much of it good quality; as well as comments, reports of meetings, summations, and gossip. There were accounts of vodka-fuelled dinners, meetings with oligarchs, encounters in Chinese restaurants and even that Saudi Arabian sex party. Some cables were long essays, offering fresh thinking on historically knotty problems, such as Chechnya; others simple requests to Washington.

They highlighted the geopolitical interests and preoccupations of the US superpower: nuclear proliferation; the supposed threat from Iran; the hard-to-control military situation in Kabul and Islamabad. The American embassy cables came from established power centres (London and Paris) but also the far-off margins (Ashgabat, Yerevan and Bishkek). Boring they are not. On the contrary, they offer an incomparably detailed mosaic of life and politics in the early 21st century.

But more importantly than this, they included disclosures of things citizens are entitled to know. This is true for Americans and non-Americans. The cables discussed human rights abuses, corruption, and dubious financial ties between G8 leaders. They spoke of corporate espionage, dirty tricks and hidden bank accounts. In their private exchanges US diplomats dispense with the platitudes that characterise much of their public job; they give relatively frank, unmediated assessments, offering a window into the mental processes at the top of US power. The cables were, in a way, the truth.

The constant principle that underpinned the *Guardian*'s selection – what to print and what not – was whether a cable contained material that was in the larger public interest. Nowhere was this more clear-cut than with a classified directive from July 2009 that revealed the US government was spying on the United Nations, and its low-key South Korean secretary general, Ban Ki-moon. The cable began by requesting predictable diplomatic information about positions and views on hot topics such as Darfur, Somalia,

Afghanistan, Iran and North Korea. But read more closely it clearly blurred the line between diplomacy and spying.

The directive from Washington asked for sensitive communications information – passwords, encryption codes. It called for detailed biometric information "on key UN officials, to include undersecretaries, heads of specialised agencies and their chief advisers, top SYG [secretary general] aides, heads of peace operations and political field missions, including force commanders", as well as intelligence on Ban's "management and decision-making style and his influence on the secretariat". Washington also wanted credit card numbers, email addresses, phone, fax and pager numbers and frequent-flyer account numbers for UN figures. It was also after "biographic and biometric information on UN security council permanent representatives".

The "national human intelligence collection directive" was distributed to US missions at the UN in New York, Vienna and Rome; and to 33 embassies and consulates, including those in London, Paris and Moscow. All of Washington's main intelligence agencies – the CIA's clandestine service, the US Secret Service and the FBI – as well as the state department, were circulated with these "reporting and collection needs".

The UN has long been the victim of bugging and espionage operations. Veteran diplomats are used to conducting their most sensitive discussions outside its walls, and not everyone was surprised at the disclosures. Robert Baer, a former CIA field officer in the Middle East, remarked: "There is a reason the CIA station is usually next door to the political section in our embassies. There are ambassadors who love that stuff. In the American system it sloshes over from side to side."

But the cable – signed "CLINTON" – illuminated a cynical spying campaign. American diplomatic staff enjoy immunity and can operate without suspicion. The British historian and *Guardian* columnist Timothy Garton Ash was one of many disturbed by the directive. Garton Ash remarked that "regular American diplomats are being asked to do stuff you would normally expect of low-level spooks".

Experts on international law were also affronted. The cable seemed to show the US breaching three of the founding treaties of the UN. Ban's spokesman, Farhan Haq, sent off a letter reminding member states to respect the UN's inviolability: "The UN charter, the headquarters agreement and the 1946 convention contain provisions relating to the privileges and immunities of the organisation. The UN relies on the adherence by member states to these various undertakings."

The American cables held numerous other secrets that it was right to disclose in the public interest. Memo after memo from US stations across the Middle East exposed widespread behind-the-scenes pressures to contain President Ahmadinejad's Iran, which the US, Arab states and Israel believed to be close to acquiring nuclear weapons. Startlingly, the cables showed King Abdullah of Saudi Arabia urging the United States to attack Iran to destroy its nuclear programme. Other Arab allies, too, had secretly been agitating for military action against Tehran. Bombing Iranian nuclear facilities had hitherto been publicly viewed as a desperate last resort that could ignite a far wider war – one that was not seriously on anyone's diplomatic table except possibly that of the Israelis.

The Saudi king was recorded as having "frequently exhorted the US to attack Iran to put an end to its nuclear weapons programme". He "told you [Americans] to cut off the head of the snake", the Saudi ambassador to Washington, Adel al-Jubeir, said, according to a report on Abdullah's meeting with the US general David Petraeus in April 2008.

The cables further highlighted Israel's anxiety to preserve its regional nuclear monopoly, its readiness to go it alone against Iran – and its relentless attempts to influence American policy. The defence minister, Ehud Barak, claimed, for example, in June 2009, that there was a window of "between six and 18 months from now in which stopping Iran from acquiring nuclear weapons might still be viable". Thereafter, Barak said, "any military solution would result in unacceptable collateral damage".

The true scale also emerged of America's covert military involvement in Yemen, the Arab world's poorest nation. Washington's concern that Yemen has become a haven for Al-Qaida in the Arabian Peninsula (Aqap) was understandable. The group had carried out a series of attacks on western targets, including a failed airline cargo bomb plot in October 2010 and an attempt the previous year to bring down a US passenger jet over Detroit. Less justifiable, perhaps, was why the US agreed to a secret deal with Yemen's president, Ali Abdullah Saleh, to pass off US attacks on al-Qaida targets as his own.

The cables showed Saleh gave the Americans an "open door" to conduct counter-terrorist missions in Yemen, and to launch cruise missile strikes on Yemeni territory. The first in December 2009 killed dozens of civilians along with alleged militants. Saleh presented it as Yemen's own work, supported by US intelligence. In a meeting with Gen Petraeus, the head of US central command, Saleh admitted lying to his population about the strikes, and deceiving parliament. "We'll continue saying the bombs are ours and not yours," he told Petraeus. It was a lie the US seemed ready to condone.

As the *New York Times*'s Bill Keller put it, the documents advanced our knowledge of the world not in great leaps but by small degrees. For those interested in foreign policy, they provided nuance, texture and drama. For those who followed stories less closely, they were able to learn more about international affairs in a lively way. But the cables also included a few jaw-dropping moments, when an entire curtain seemed swept aside to reveal what a country is really like.

The most dramatic such disclosures came not from the Middle East but Russia. It is widely known that Russia – nominally under the control of President Dmitry Medvedev but in reality run by the prime minister, Vladimir Putin – is corrupt and undemocratic. But the cables went much further. They painted a bleak and despairing picture of a kleptocracy centred on Putin's leadership, in which officials, oligarchs and organised crime are bound together in a "virtual mafia state".

Arms trafficking, money laundering, personal enrichment, protection for gangsters, extortion and kickbacks, suitcases full of money and secret offshore accounts – the American embassy cables unpicked a political system in which bribery totals an estimated $300bn year, and in which it is often hard to distinguish between the activities of government and organised crime. Read together, the collection of cables offered a rare moment of truth-telling about a regime normally accorded international respectability.

Despite the improvement in US-Russian relations since President Obama took power, the Americans are under no illusions about their Russian interlocutors. The cables stated that Russian spies use senior mafia bosses to carry out criminal operations such as arms trafficking. Law enforcement agencies, meanwhile, such as the police, spy agencies and the prosecutor's office, run a de facto protection racket for criminal networks. Moscow's former mayor, Yuri Luzhkov, sacked in 2010 by Medvedev for political reasons, presided over a "pyramid of corruption", US officials suggested. (Luzkov's billionaire wife, Yelena Baturina, dismissed the accusations as "total rubbish".)

Russia's bureaucracy is so corrupt that it operates what is in effect a parallel tax system for the private enrichment of police, officials, and the KGB's successor, the federal security service (FSB), the cables said. There have been rumours for years that Putin has personally amassed a secret fortune, hidden overseas. The cables made clear that US diplomats treat the rumours as true: they speculate that Putin deliberately picked a weak successor when he stepped down as Russian president in 2008 because he could be worried about losing his "illicit proceeds" to law enforcement investigations. In Rome, meanwhile, US diplomats relayed suspicions that the Italian prime minister, Silvio Berlusconi, could be "profiting personally and handsomely" by taking a cut from clandestine energy deals with Putin.

A particularly damning cable about Russia was sent from Madrid. Dated 8 February 2010, it fed back to Washington a briefing by a Spanish prosecutor. Jose Gonzalez spent more than a decade trying to unravel the activities of Russian organised crime in Spain. He met US officials in January and told them that Russia had become a "virtual mafia state" in which "one cannot differentiate between the activities of the government and OC [organised crime] groups." Gonzalez said he had evidence – thousands of wiretaps have been used in the last 10 years – that certain political parties in Russia worked hand in hand with mafia gangs. He said that intelligence officers orchestrated gun shipments to Kurdish groups to destabilise Turkey and were pulling the strings behind the 2009 case of the Arctic Sea cargo ship suspected of carrying missiles destined for Iran. Gangsters enjoyed support and protection and, in effect, worked "as a complement to state structures", he told US officials.

Gonzalez said the disaffected Russian intelligence services officer Alexander Litvinenko secretly met Spanish security officials in May 2006, six months before he was murdered in London with radioactive polonium. Litvinenko told the Spanish that Russia's intelligence and security services controlled the country's organised crime network. A separate cable from Paris from December 2006 disclosed that US diplomats believed Putin was likely to have known about Litvinenko's murder. Daniel Fried, then the most senior US diplomat in Europe, claimed it would be remarkable if Russia's leader knew nothing about the plot given his "attention to detail". The Russians were behaving with "increasing self-confidence to the point of arrogance", Fried noted.

The *Guardian* published WikiLeaks' Russia disclosures on 2 December 2010, over five pages and under the striking headline: "Inside Putin's 'mafia state'". The front-page photo showed Putin, a former KGB foreign intelligence officer, wearing a pair of dark glasses. For many, the Russia WikiLeaks disclosures were the most vivid to emerge. Janine Gibson, the *Guardian*'s website editor, was struck by the online response: "The Russia day was brilliant and hugely well read. It was the best day. We were able to say everything you might want to say, but you could never previously say because everybody is so terrified. It was an extraordinary thing." She went on: "You can tell what the internet thinks about things. You could tell what everyone thought. There was an enormous sense of, 'Ah-hah!'"

(Across the Atlantic, however, as though determined to cement its reputation for understatement, the *New York Times* published the same material under a studiedly diffident headline: "In cables, US takes a dim view of Russia". The contrast between US and British journalistic practices could give future media studies students much to ponder.)

Undoubtedly, the cables showed the dysfunctional nature of the modern Russian state. But they also showcased the state department's literary strengths. Among many fine writers in the US foreign service, William Burns – Washington's ambassador to Moscow and now its top diplomat – emerged as the most gifted. Burns has a Rolls-Royce mind. His dispatches on diverse subjects such as Stalin or Solzhenitsyn are gripping, precise and nuanced, combining far-reaching analysis with historical depth. Were it not for the fact that they were supposed to be secret, his musings might have earned him a Pulitzer prize.

In one glorious dispatch Burns described how Chechnya's ruler Ramzan Kadyrov was the star guest at a raucous Dagestani wedding and "danced clumsily with his gold-plated automatic stuck down the back of his jeans". During the "lavish" reception Kadyrov showered dancers with $100 notes and gave the happy couple an unusual wedding present – "a five kilo lump of gold". The ambassador was one of more than 1,000 guests invited to the wedding in Dagestan of the son of the local politician and powerful oil chief Gadzhi Makhachev.

Burns went to dinner at Gadzhi's "enormous summer house on the balmy shores of the Caspian Sea". The cast of guests he describes is almost worthy of Evelyn Waugh. They included a Chechen commander (later assassinated), sports and cultural celebrities, "wizened brown peasants", a nanophysicist, "a drunken wrestler" called Vakha and a first-rank submarine captain. Some were slick, he noted, but others "Jurassic".

"Most of the tables were set with the usual dishes plus whole roast sturgeons and sheep. But at 8pm the compound was invaded by dozens of heavily armed mujahideen for the grand entrance of the Chechen leader Ramzan Kadyrov, dressed in jeans and a T-shirt, looking shorter and less muscular than his photos, and with a somewhat cock-eyed expression on his face." Kadyrov and his retinue sat at the tables eating and listening to "Benya the Accordion King", Burns reported. There was a fireworks display followed by *lezginka* – a traditional Caucasus dance performed by two girls and three small boys. "First Gadzhi joined them and then Ramzan ... Both Gadzhi and Ramzan showered the children with $100 bills; the dancers probably picked upwards of $5,000 off the cobblestones."

This was entertaining and telling stuff, about a region – the north Caucasus – that had fallen off the world's radar. It was reportage of the best kind.

But there were also disclosures from other troublesome areas that had long been of concern in Washington. Far from being firm, natural allies, for example, as many people had assumed, China had an astonishingly fractious relationship with North Korea. Beijing had even signalled its readiness to accept Korean reunification and was privately distancing itself from the North Korean regime, the cables showed. The Chinese were no longer willing to offer support for Kim Jong-il's bizarre dictatorship, it seemed.

China's emerging position was revealed in sensitive discussions between Kathleen Stephens, the US ambassador to Seoul, and South Korea's vice foreign minister, Chun Yung-woo. Citing two high-ranking Chinese officials, Chun told the ambassador that younger-generation Chinese Communist Party leaders no longer regarded North Korea as a useful or reliable ally. Moreover, they would not risk renewed armed conflict on the peninsula, he stated. The cable read: "The two officials, Chun said, were ready to 'face the new reality' that the DPRK [North Korea] now had little value to China as a buffer state – a view that, since North Korea's first nuclear test in 2006, had reportedly gained traction among senior PRC [People's Republic of China] leaders."

It is astonishing to hear the Chinese position described in this way. Envisaging North Korea's collapse, the cable said, "the PRC would be comfortable with a reunified Korea controlled by Seoul and anchored to the United States in a 'benign alliance' – as long as Korea was not hostile towards China." The Chinese, in short, were fed up with their troublesome North Korean neighbours. In April 2009 Pyongyang blasted a three-stage rocket over Japan and into the Pacific in an act of pure belligerence. China's vice foreign minister He Yafei was unimpressed. He told US embassy officials that the North Koreans were behaving like a "spoiled child" to get Washington's attention. This was all new.

The cables also disclosed, ominously for the internet future, that Google had been forced to withdraw from mainland China merely because of an unfortunate piece of bad luck. A senior member of the Communist Party used the search engine to look for his own name. He was unhappy with what he found: several articles criticising him personally. As a result Google was forced to drop a link from its Chinese-language search engine to its uncensored Google.com page and – as the cable put it – "walk away from a potential market of 400 million internet users".

*

As far as the UK was concerned, the cables made distinctly uncomfortable reading. Educated Americans frequently regard Britain's royal family with amused disdain, as a Ruritanian throwback. Rob Evans of the *Guardian* realised that, and had rapidly discovered a pen portrait which shed painful light on Prince Andrew, one of the Queen's sons. Andrew, who was regularly flown around the world at the British taxpayers' expense as a "special trade representative", was the subject of an acid cable back to Washington from faraway Kyrgyzstan. He emerged as rude, blustering, guffawing about local bribery, and – to the shocked delight of reporters at the *Guardian* – highly offensive about their own newspaper's exposures of corruption. The US ambassador quoted him denouncing "these (expletive) reporters, especially from the National [sic] Guardian, who poke their noses everywhere' and (presumably) make it harder for British businessmen to do business."

Less comic was the overall tone adopted by the Americans towards their junior UK allies, who craved a "special relationship". While there was evidence everywhere of the intimacy and intelligence-sharing which went on worldwide between the two Anglophone states, there were also signs of a condescending attitude. The cables showed that the US superpower was mainly interested in its own priorities: it wanted unrestricted use of British military bases; it wanted British politicians to send troops for its wars and aid its sanctions campaigns, against Iran in particular; and it wanted the UK to buy American arms and commercial products. Richard LeBaron, the US charge d'affaires at the Grosvenor Square embassy in London, recommended that the US continue to pander to British fantasies that their relationship was special: "Though tempting to argue that keeping HMG [Her Majesty's government] off balance about its current standing with us might make London more willing to respond favourably when pressed for assistance, in the long run it is not in US interests to have the UK public concluding the relationship is weakening, on either side. The UK's commitment of resources – financial, military, diplomatic – in support of US global priorities remains unparalleled."

In the leaked cables, the unequal relationship between senior and junior partners was visibly played out. When then British foreign secretary David Miliband tried to hamper secret US spy flights from Britain's Cyprus base, he was peremptorily yanked back into line. When Britain similarly thought of barring US cluster bombs from its own territory on Diego Garcia, the Americans soon put a stop to it. Britain even offered to declare the area around the US Diego Garcia base a marine nature reserve, so the evicted islanders could never go back. However, when Gordon Brown, as British prime minister, personally pleaded in return for compassion for Gary McKinnon, a British youthful computer hacker wanted for extradition, his plea was humiliatingly ignored. The incoming British Conservative administration, headed by foreign secretary-designate William Hague, lined up cravenly to promise the US ambassador a "pro-American regime".

Sifting through this huge database of diplomatic documents, it was hard not to come away with a depressing view of human nature. Mankind, the world over, seemed revealed as a base, grasping species. Many political leaders showed remarkable greed and venality. One of the most egregious examples was Omar al-Bashir, the Sudanese president. He was reported to have siphoned as much as $9 billion out of the country, and stashed much of it in London banks. A conversation with the chief prosecutor of the international criminal court said some of the funds may be held by Lloyds Bank in London. The bank denied any connection.

It was a similar story in Afghanistan, a regime – like Russia – sliding into kleptocracy. The cables show fears of rampant government corruption; the US is apparently powerless to do anything about it. In one astonishing alleged incident in October 2009, US diplomats claimed that the then vice-president Ahmad Zia Massoud was stopped and questioned in Dubai, after flying into the emirate carrying $52 million in cash. Officials trying to stop money laundering interviewed him. Then they let him go. (Massoud denies this happened.)

The US was also deeply frustrated by Hamid Karzai, Afghanistan's leader. It regarded him as erratic, emotional, prone to believing conspiracy theories – and linked to criminal warlords. US diplomats spelled out their conviction that Ahmed Wali Karzai, the president's younger half brother and a senior figure in Kandahar, is corrupt.

Some of the world's biggest companies have also been involved in dubious practices and dirty tricks, the communiqués alleged. Shell's vice-president for sub-Saharan Africa boasted that the oil giant had successfully inserted staff into all of the main ministries of Nigeria's government. Shell was so well placed that it knew of the government's plans to invite bids for oil concessions. The Shell executive, Anne Pickard, told the US ambassador Robin Renee Sanders that Shell had seconded employees to every government department so knew "everything that was being done in those ministries".

The revelations appeared to confirm what campaigners had long been saying: that there were intersecting links between the oil giant and politicians in a country where, despite billions of dollars in oil revenue, 70% of people still lived below the poverty line.

Pfizer, the world's biggest pharmaceutical company, was also identified in Africa dispatches. According to a leaked cable from the US embassy in Abuja, Nigeria's capital, Pfizer hired investigators to unearth evidence of corruption against the country's attorney general. The drug firm wanted to pressure him to drop legal action over a controversial drug trial involving children with meningitis. Pfizer denies wrongdoing. It says it has now resolved a case brought in 2009 by Nigeria's government and Kano state, where the drug was used during a meningitis outbreak.

*

What did this worldwide pattern of diplomatic secrets actually all mean? Some commentators saw it as proof that the United States was struggling to get its way in the world, a superpower entering a long period of relative decline. Others thought the revelations at least showed the bureaucracy of the state department in a fairly good light. In the *Guardian*, Timothy Garton Ash confessed he had been impressed by the professionalism of the US diplomatic corps – a hard-working and committed bunch. "My personal opinion of the state department has gone up several notches," he wrote. "For the most part ... what we see here is diplomats doing their proper job: finding out what is happening in places to which they are posted, working to advance their nation's interests and their government's policies."

Some world leaders brushed off the embarrassing revelations, at least in public, while others went on the attack. Iran's President Mahmoud Ahmadinejad, who did not come out well in the disclosures of his regional unpopularity, dismissed the WikiLeaks data drop as "psychological warfare". He claimed the US must have deliberately leaked its own files in a plot to discredit him. Turkey's prime minister, Recep Tayyip Erdoğan, reacted furiously to cables that suggested he was a corrupt closet Islamist. But in countries where there is no free press – Eritrea is a good example, but there are lots of them – there was no reaction at all, only silence.

The Russians executed a remarkable handbrake turn. President Medvedev at first dismissed the Russia cables as "not worthy" of comment. But when it became clear that the leak was far more damaging in the long-term to the US and its multilateral interests, one of Medvedev's aides proposed, tongue-in-cheek, that Julian Assange should be nominated for the Nobel peace prize.

It was Assange himself that dominated the coverage in Australia. The *Sydney Morning Herald* hailed Assange as the "Ned Kelly of the internet age", in reference to the country's 19th-century outlaw folk hero. However, Australia's prime minister, Julia Gillard, behaved more like the rest of the irritated world leaders:

she condemned the publication as illegal, and Assange's actions as "grossly irresponsible". The cables themselves revealed an unflattering view of Australia's political class. The former prime minister – now foreign minister – Kevin Rudd was called an abrasive, impulsive "control freak" presiding over a series of foreign policy blunders.

Was the Big Leak of the cables changing anything? As the year ended, it was for the most part too early to say. The short-term fall-out in some cases was certainly rapid, with diplomats shuffled and officials made to walk the plank. *Der Spiegel* reported that a "well-placed source" within the Free Democratic Party had been briefing the US embassy about secret coalition negotiations in the immediate aftermath of the German general election in 2009. The mysterious man was quickly outed as Helmut Metzner, head of the office of party chairman and vice-chancellor Guido Westerwelle. Metzner lost his job.

In January 2011 Washington was forced to withdraw its ambassador from Libya, Gene Cretz. Colonel Gadaffi had clearly been stung by comments concerning his long-time Ukrainian nurse – a "voluptuous blonde", as Cretz put it. Other US diplomatic staff were also quietly told to pack their bags and move on. Sylvia Reed Curran, the charge d'affaires in Ashgabat, was reassigned after penning an excoriating profile of Turkmenistan's president, Gurbanguly Berdymukhamedov. She described him as "vain, suspicious, guarded, strict, very conservative", a "micro-manager" and "a practised liar". She added, memorably: "Berdymukhamedov does not like people who are smarter than he is. Since he's not a very bright guy, our source offered, he is suspicious of a lot of people."

Curran's fate? She was sent to Vladivostok, where the sun rarely shines.

Some other developments were positive and suggested that WikiLeaks' mission to winkle out secrets might help bring results. One cable, from the US embassy in Bangladesh, showed the British government was training a paramilitary force condemned by human rights organisations as a "government death squad", held responsible for hundreds of extrajudicial killings. The British were revealed to be training the "Rapid Action Battalion" in investigative interviewing techniques and "rules of engagement". Since the squad's exposure in the cables, no more deaths have been announced.

In Tunisia, the country's repressive president, Zine al-Abidine Ben Ali, blocked the website of a Lebanese newspaper that published cables about his regime. The reports from the US embassy in Tunis were deeply unflattering, and made no bones about the sclerotic state of the small Maghreb country, widely considered one of the the most repressive in a repressive region. "The problem is clear," wrote ambassador Robert Godec in July 2009, in a secret dispatch released by Beirut's *al-Akhbar* newspaper. "Tunisia has been ruled by the same president for 22 years. He has no successor. And, while President Ben Ali deserves credit for continuing many of the progressive policies of [predecessor] President Bourguiba, he and his regime have lost touch with the Tunisian people. They tolerate no advice or criticism, whether domestic or international. Increasingly, they rely on the police for control and focus on preserving power."

The cable went on: "Corruption in the inner circle is growing. Even average Tunisians are keenly aware of it, and the chorus of complaints is rising. Tunisians intensely dislike, even hate, first lady Leila Trabelsi and her family. In private, regime opponents mock her; even those close to the government express dismay at her reported behaviour. Meanwhile, anger is growing at Tunisia's high unemployment and regional inequities. As a consequence, the risks to the regime's long-term stability are increasing."

The ambassador's comments were prescient. Within a month of the cable's publication, Tunisia was in the grip of what some were calling the first WikiLeaks revolution.

CHAPTER 17

The ballad of Wandsworth jail

City of Westminster magistrates court,
Horseferry Road, London
7 December 2010

"I walked, with other souls in pain"
OSCAR WILDE, *BALLAD OF READING GAOL*

If aliens had landed their spaceship outside, they might have presumed that one of God's saints was about to ascend. Julian Assange had just become, in many eyes, the St Sebastian of the internet age, a martyr pierced by the many arrows of the unbelievers. A scrum of cameramen thronged the gates of the City of Westminster magistrates court. On the pavement a polyglot huddle of journalists waited impatiently to get in. Other reporters had managed to sneak inside and they milled around the ground-floor vestibule.

The previous evening Swedish prosecutors had decided to issue a warrant for Assange's arrest, over the still unresolved investigation into allegations he had assaulted two women in Stockholm. He was listed as a wanted man by Interpol – wanted, the Red List notice said, for "sex crimes". That night, sitting in the Georgian surroundings of Ellingham Hall, and with his options rapidly narrowing, Assange had concluded that he was going to have to hand himself in. He had scarcely slept for days; he was under siege from the world's media; the way forward must have seemed rocky and difficult. According to his WikiLeaks associates, after taking the decision to go to the police Assange at last fell heavily asleep.

Early that morning he drove to London. There, he met at 9.30am with officers from the Metropolitan police's extradition unit. The meeting had been arranged in advance; Assange was with his lawyers Mark Stephens and Jennifer Robinson. The officers promptly arrested him. They explained they were acting on behalf of the Swedish authorities. The Swedes had issued a European arrest warrant, valid in Britain. It accused Assange of one count of unlawful coercion, two counts of sexual molestation and one count of rape, all allegedly committed in August 2010. Westminster magistrates court would decide later that afternoon whether to grant him bail, they said.

News of his arrest prompted some rejoicing in Washington, which had found little to cheer about in recent days, as the contents of its private diplomatic dispatches were sprayed around the world. "That sounds like good news to me," said the US defence secretary, Robert Gates, speaking from Afghanistan. There was a big smirk on his face.

At 12.47pm Assange slipped into court via a back entrance. Stephens told the waiting media his client was "fine". He had held a successful meeting with police. "It was very cordial. They verified his identify. They are satisfied he is the real Julian Assange and we are ready to go into court." But the rest of the afternoon's proceedings didn't go according to plan. In a beige upstairs courtroom, the district judge Howard Riddle asked Assange whether he consented to his extradition to Sweden. Was he ready to answer the charges in the arrest warrant? "I understand that, and do not consent," Assange replied. The judge then asked Assange to give his address. Assange fired back: "PO Box 4080."

It was the kind of apparently flippant answer you might expect from a global nomad. Assange was, after all, an international man of mystery who moved from country to country, carrying only a couple of rucksacks with computer gear and a slightly rank T-shirt. As his friends well knew, getting hold of Assange was exceptionally difficult. But in fact, his answer may not have been as flippant as it sounded. He had not known what to expect in the courtroom, and was nervous about giving away his location in public for fear of ill-wishers. He would have been better-advised to ask to submit his true current address written down on a piece of paper. That would have been perfectly normal.

As it was, his answer entertained the gallery, but dissatisfied the court. Riddle made it clear he was not here to pass judgment on Assange's Manichean struggle with the Pentagon or other dark forces: "This case isn't about WikiLeaks." After hearing a brief outline of the evidence from Sweden the judge concluded that Assange's community ties in the UK were weak. The prosecution also claimed – unreasonably as it later turned out – that it was unclear how Assange had entered Britain. Judge Riddle concluded there was a risk Assange might not show up for his extradition hearing – or, in colloquial British parlance, do a runner. He refused Assange bail.

The decision at 3.30pm was an unexpected hammer-blow. Assange had confidently expected he would be free to walk out of court. He had even failed to bring a toothbrush. There would be no triumphant press conference, however; instead Assange was carted off in a "meat wagon" to HM Wandsworth prison, his new home. This forbidding ensemble of grey Victorian buildings might have come from the pages of Charles Dickens. It proved to be an excellent setting for another reel in what would surely become Assange's biopic. His life story already had the trajectory of a thriller. But now it had an unexpected change of pace, with a sequence to come on its protagonist's suffering and martyrdom.

Nelson Mandela, Oscar Wilde, Alexander Solzhenitsyn (Assange's hero), all had spent time in prison. They had used their confinement to meditate and reflect on the transitory nature of human existence and – in Solzhenitsyn's case – on the brutalities of Soviet power. Now it was Assange's turn to be incarcerated, as some saw it, in a dank British gulag.

Assange's situation attracted a group of glamorous left-wing Assangistas, many initially rounded up by his lawyers to offer sureties for bail. They included John Pilger, the campaigning UK-based Australian journalist, the British film director Ken Loach, and Bianca Jagger (former wife of Mick), the human rights activist and onetime model. Also present was Jemima Goldsmith, generally described as a socialite. She was to complain about this appellation, tweeting indignantly "'Socialite' is an insult to any self respecting person." From the US, the left-wing documentary maker Michael Moore had pledged to contribute $20,000 bail money, while urging observers "not [to] be naive about how the government works when it decides to go after its prey". Other well-wishers who would attend subsequent court hearings included Gavin MacFadyen, the former TV producer from City University's Bureau for Investigative Journalism who over the summer had given Assange a bed in his London townhouse. Some knew Assange personally; others did not. Some seemed convinced that the court case was unconnected with what happened in a Swedish bedroom. Instead, as they saw it, it was an attempt to imprison Assange for his real "crime": releasing secret documents that humiliated the United States.

For a certain kind of radical, Assange had extraordinary appeal: he was brave, uncompromising and dangerous. Did Pilger and Loach, perhaps, see in Assange the ghosts of their own revolutionary youth? Assange's targets were those that the original 60s radicals had themselves struggled against – chiefly US imperialism, then in Vietnam, but now in Afghanistan and Iraq. There were other secret abuses Assange had revealed, too: the callousness of the US military, and the widespread use of torture. But the proceedings at Horseferry Road had, strictly speaking, little to do with this.

Several of the broadcasters outside court were also bemused by the celebrities' spontaneous appearance. When the grey-haired Loach emerged from court, reporters from CNN, broadcasting live, had no idea who he was. "Who was that gentleman? It may be Julian Assange's attorney; we're trying to find out," the stumped CNN anchor said. Jemima Goldsmith's attendance was even more bizarre. Goldsmith admitted she didn't know Assange, but said she was offering support for him because of her backing for freedom of speech. This cause had not been one that appealed much to her late father, James Goldsmith, an eccentric right-wing billionaire with a fondness for making libel threats.

For some of Assange's supporters, the series of extradition and bail proceedings brought by Sweden seemed proof of the US conspiracy. Assange's lawyer Mark Stephens hinted as much afterwards on the steps of the court. Having compared the Swedish prosecutor Marianne Ny to the murderous Soviet ogre Lavrentiy Beria, Stephens dismissed the sex allegations as "very thin indeed". He was subsequently to assert that Assange was being imprisoned in the very same cell once occupied by the 19th-century playwright Oscar Wilde, who had been martyred for his sexuality. The homosexual Wilde was later shipped on to a second prison where he wrote his famous *Ballad of Reading Gaol*. Stephens said many people believed the charges against Assange to be politically motivated. He also referred to a "honeytrap", implying that Assange had been set up. Assange himself fulminated about what he called the unseen constellation of interests – personal, domestic and foreign – he felt were driving the case forward. The judge's refusal to grant bail provoked a swirl of more or less ill-informed online outrage.

In the eyes of critics, Assange's team was embarking on a PR strategy. The effect was to elide Assange's struggle to bring governments to account (which was a good thing) with allegations of sexual misconduct (which were an entirely separate matter for the courts). Over the ensuing months, these two unrelated issues – the universal principle of freedom of speech, and Assange's personal struggle to prevent extradition to Sweden – would become entangled. This blurring may have served Assange's interests. But the talk of honeytraps had a nasty air: it fuelled a global campaign of vilification against the two complaining Swedish women, whose identities rapidly became known around the world.

In Wandsworth, Assange did his best to adjust to his new life as an inmate. He had been remanded in custody for a week. For a man used to spending 16 hours a day in front of a laptop, the underground corridors and clanking Victorian cells must have been a distressing experience. His legal team went away hoping to devise a more successful line of attack. Their job was to get Assange out of jail as soon as possible, certainly in time for Christmas.

Assange's fame had reached what seemed like galactic proportions by the time of his second appearance in court on 14 December, when a maverick member of the British establishment was at last to ride to his rescue. The crowd outside Westminster court had grown even bigger, with the first reporters setting up their equipment at dawn. Obtaining a pass for the hearing was a bit like getting hold of one of Willy Wonka's golden tickets; the usual humour and tribal solidarity among journalists gave away to flagrant pushing in and shoving. The court was overflowing by the time Assange – flanked by two private Serco company prison guards – was escorted into the glass-fronted dock. He gave a thumbs-up sign to Kristinn Hrafnsson, his faithful lieutenant. But for the rest of the hearing he sat quietly.

Gemma Lindfield, acting for the Swedish authorities, set out the charges once again. She concluded: "He [Assange] remains a significant flight risk." It was then the turn of Geoffrey Robertson QC, the prominent human rights lawyer and Assange's newly hired Australian-born barrister. Standing to address the judge, Robertson began seductively. In melodious tones he described the WikiLeaks founder as a "free-speech philosopher and lecturer". The idea that he would try and escape was preposterous, he said. Robertson announced that Vaughan Smith of the Frontline Club, Assange's previous secret hideout host throughout November, was willing to take responsibility for his good behaviour. "Captain Smith", as Robertson winningly described him, was prepared to house Assange once again up at Ellingham Hall in Norfolk, should the judge agree to give him bail.

The WikiLeaks arrest saga had so far been short of jokes. But Robertson had one ready-made. It would not be so much "house arrest as mansion arrest", he quipped. Not only that, but it was inconceivable Assange would attempt to escape "since darkness descends rather early in that area of Britain". Additionally, Assange was willing to give up his Australian passport and wear an electronic tag. Finally, he wasn't likely to get very far given that "media exposure" had made him "well-known around the world".

Robertson invited Smith to give his own assessment of WikiLeaks' controversial founder. "He is a very honourable person, hugely courageous, self-deprecatory and warm. Not the kind of things you read about," Captain Smith said, loyally.

After establishing that Smith was a former Guards officer and one-time captain of the British army's shooting team, the QC asked for details of Smith's family home. That, it appeared, was the clincher. "It has 10 bedrooms and 60 acres." Better still, there was even a police station. "It's a short distance on a bicycle. I can cycle it in about 15 minutes ... It's about a mile. Perhaps a little bit more." Smith added helpfully: "It's an environment where he would be surrounded. We have members of staff. My parents live in proximity as well. My father was a Queen's Messenger and a colonel in the Grenadier Guards. He patrols the estate." Smith added that his housekeeper, too, could keep a beady eye on the Australian: "My staff will be reporting to me, sir."

If the judge had class instincts, there could hardly have been a more pitch-perfect appeal. The prosecution had by this stage also conceded that Assange had arrived legitimately in Britain from Sweden on 27 September. Outside the crowded courtroom, celebrity supporters had gathered on the second floor next to the coffee machine. Pilger, Goldsmith and Loach were there again – Bianca Jagger had successfully got herself a courtoom seat. Jagger later told friends that women fans had been a similar problem for her rock star ex-husband. "It was much worse with Mick. When you are world-famous other women throw themselves at you," she mused. Despite their show of support, the celebrities' presence was much less crucial than their money. All had offered to provide sureties of £20,000.

Inside the courtroom, Robertson moved to paint a picture of Assange's time in prison. His conditions inside Wandsworth were a pure living hell: "He can't read any newspapers other than the *Daily Express*! This is the kind of Victorian situation he finds himself in." He went on: "*Time* magazine sent him a magazine with his picture on the cover but all they would allow him to have was the envelope!"

The judge announced that, after all, bail would be "granted under certain conditions". These turned out to be relatively onerous: an electronic tag, an afternoon and night curfew, and a requirement to report to Bungay police station near Ellingham between 6pm and 8pm every evening. Oh, and £200,000 in cash. Assange's lawyers asked if the court would take cheques. No. It would have to be money up front.

The news – communicated via Twitter, of course – of Assange's bail brought a loud cheer from the 150 people who had gathered opposite the court to cheer on their hero and brandish their banners and placards to the world. One read: "Sex crimes – my arse!" Another: "That's just what we need – another innocent man in jail". And a third: "Sweden: muppets of the US". Three young activists were so thrilled they broke into an impromptu chorus of *We Wish You a Leaky Christmas*.

Their jubilation was premature. Lindfield and the Crown Prosecution Service predictably appealed the judge's decision up to the high court, leaving Assange still temporarily jailed. But in the dock, he seemed in good spirits. As the warders led him away, he managed a thumbs up for the dusky-haired Turkish TV reporter sitting in the gallery. She boasted: "I had an exclusive interview with him a month ago."

Two days later, on 16 December, all gathered again at the Royal Courts of Justice in the Strand, for Assange's third hearing. Outside court number four a queue of journalists waited in a more orderly line than before, drinking coffee and leafing through the morning papers. Among them was a group of Australian reporters, who in nasal tones lamented their country's overnight collapse at the hands of England in the Ashes. But Assange's own prospects were looking brighter. At 11.30am Mr Justice Ouseley strode into a courtroom decorated with leather-bound legal tomes and portentous Gothic wood panelling.

The judge's first concern wasn't Assange but the fourth estate – specifically the international journalists sitting on the packed wooden benches in front of him. Several were already playing furtively with their BlackBerry handhelds. They were micro-blogging the hearing live to the outside world. Mr Justice Ouseley made clear that tweeting – although allowed by Howard Riddle two days earlier in Assange's previous hearing – would not take place in the high court. Twitter was banned, he said. Immediately, several journalists tweeted his ruling. It was probably the quickest contempt of court in the history of justice.

Lindfield reprised the allegations. She warned that if Assange was bailed he might not flee the country but simply vanish in the UK. The judge appeared unconvinced. He seemed to accept the claim that the Stockholm prosecutor had originally decided there was no case to answer, before a second prosecutor agreed to pursue the allegations. "The history of the way it was dealt with by the Swedish prosecutor would give Mr Assange some basis that he might be acquitted following a trial." For Assange, sitting in the dock behind ornate bars, this was encouraging stuff.

Robertson got to his feet again. Next to him were several of Assange's supporters – Smith, Loach, Pilger and the Marchioness of Worcester, a former actress turned eco-activist. In the third row sat Assange's frizzy-haired mother, Christine, who had been brought from Australia. Robertson declared it was sheer speculation that Assange would try and abscond, or that his wealthy supporters would spring him from Britain.

"Is it really suggested that Mr Michael Moore is going to slip through customs wearing a baseball hat, go to Norfolk in the middle of the night and plan to transport this gentleman we know not where?"

It was ridiculous to describe Assange as "some kind of Houdini figure". Even if Assange did attempt to bolt from Ellingham Hall he wouldn't get far, what with the "gamekeepers looking after him and Mr Smith". Robertson claimed Assange had co-operated with Swedish investigators. He also defined three categories of rape under Swedish law: gross rape – four to 10 years in prison; ordinary rape – two to six; and minor rape – up to a maximum of four years. Assange had been charged with minor rape, he said. If convicted he was likely to get "eight to 12 months, with two-thirds off for good behaviour".

The judge said he was concerned that some of Assange's supporters might think going into hiding was a "legitimate response" to his predicament. "I'm troubled by the extent to which support [for Assange] is based on support for WikiLeaks." But shortly before lunch, Mr Justice Ouseley decided Assange could return to Ellingham Hall. He upheld the decision by the City of Westminster magistrates court to grant bail. But he also warned him that he was likely to be sent back to Sweden at the end of his two-day extradition hearing, set for 7-8 February 2011.

The judge imposed strict conditions. (It emerged that the nearest police station to Smith's estate, in the town of Bungay, had permanently closed. Assange would have to report instead to Beccles, where the station was open only in the afternoon – and not at all over Christmas and the new year.) The bail conditions were a £200,000 cash deposit, with a further £40,000 guaranteed in two sureties.

Over the next few hours the race was on to get Assange's guarantors to deliver the cash, without which Assange was going to spend another night back in Wandsworth. His legal team proposed five new sureties: the distinguished retired investigative journalist and author of *The First Casualty*, Sir Philip Knightley; millionaire magazine publisher Felix Dennis; Nobel prize winner Sir John Sulston; former Labour minister and chairman of Faber & Faber publishing house Lord Matthew Evans; and Professor Patricia David, a retired educationalist.

The WikiLeaks team spilled out of the Gothic architecture of the British court in high spirits. Vaughan Smith promised Assange a rustic dinner of stew and dumplings, and said there was no prospect he would escape from his Norfolk manor: "He isn't good at map reading. He's very topographically unaware. If he runs off into the woods I will find him." Kristinn Hrafnsson, Assange's lieutenant, also welcomed the release: "I'm delighted by this decision. It will be excellent to have Julian back with us again." But it was Pilger who articulated the deeper worry among Assange's supporters: that the US would charge him with espionage. Pilger, who had been rejected by the judge as a surety because he was "another peripatetic Australian", hailed the grant of bail as "a glimpse of British justice". But he went on: "I think we should be looking not so much to the extradition to Sweden but to the US. It's the great unspoken in this case. The spectre we are all aware of is that he might end up in some maximum security prison in the US. That is a real possibility."

Just before close of play, the bail conditions were met. At 5.48pm Assange emerged on to the steps of the high court into the flash-flare of TV cameras and photographers – clutching his bail papers, his right arm raised in triumph. There were whoops and cheers from his supporters. He had been in prison a mere nine days. But the atmosphere was as if he was had made the long walk to freedom, just like Nelson Mandela. Assange addressed the crowd:

It's great to smell [the] fresh air of London again … First, some thank-yous. To all the people around the world who had faith in me, who have supported my team while I have been away. To my lawyers, who have put up a brave and ultimately successful fight, to our sureties and people who have provided money in the face of great difficulty and aversion. And to members of the press who are not all taken in and considered to look deeper in their work. And, I guess, finally, to the British justice system itself, where if justice is not always the outcome at least it is not dead yet.

During my time in solitary confinement in the bottom of a Victorian prison I had time to reflect on the conditions of those people around the world also in solitary confinement, also on remand, in conditions that are more difficult than those faced by me. Those people need your attention and support. And with that I hope to continue my work and continue to protest my innocence in this matter and to reveal, as we get it, which we have not yet, the evidence from these allegations. Thank you.

It was a strange little speech, executed in curiously looping phrases and odd syntax. But as a piece of TV theatre it was perfect – with Assange identifying himself with freedom and justice, while expressing a virtuous concern for his fellow man. His lawyers standing to his side – Robertson, Robinson, and Stephens – seemed to be trying to radiate both solemnity and delight. In the long run, the court's decision was unlikely to change much: Assange had yet to confront his accusers in Sweden; the prospect of extradition to the US loomed like a dark ghost. But for the moment Assange and WikiLeaks were back in business.

He swept out of the court in Smith's old armour-plated Land Rover, originally driven by him all the way back from Bosnia and more usually parked – sometimes with a flat tyre – outside the Frontline Club. With snow beginning to fall, the Guards officer and the internet subversive set off together on the latest step of their big adventure. For Smith there had previously been the Balkans and Iraq and the mountains of central Afghanistan, where the temperatures fall below freezing at night. This was something new, which also had several ingredients in common with wars and war reporting. There was adrenaline, lots of it. There was a sense of living for the moment. But, above all, there was uncertainty. Nobody quite knew what would happen next.

CHAPTER 18

The future of WikiLeaks

Ellingham Hall, Norfolk, England
Christmas 2010

*"Julian is a spectacular showman for the youngsters of the
internet era who are disgusted with the seniors"*
JOHN YOUNG, CRYPTOME.ORG, 15 JULY 2010

Sitting in the kitchen of his temporary country home with the
Guardian's Ian Katz and Luke Harding, Assange contemplated the
uncertain long-term future of WikiLeaks. He was looking better –
still somewhat wrung out after his brief ordeal in Wandsworth
prison, but cheerful and composed. It was a pleasant English scene:
stilton cheese and fruitcake were on the table; two female kitchen
workers were chopping up beef for dinner; his host Vaughan
Smith's father was once more protectively prowling the grounds
with his rifle and deerstalker hat; and sacks full of Christmas cards
and fan mail for Assange were arriving daily for the mantelpiece.

But anxiety was never far away. The previous night, yet
another grandstanding commentator on Fox News had called for
Assange's death. "It's quite dangerous actually. I'm known to be
in a particular place at a particular time," he said, casting a glance
out of the window and across the estate. He had been thinking

about how he would handle life in an American jail if they ever sought to extradite him: "I would ... have a high chance of being killed in the US prison system, Jack Ruby style, given the continual calls for my murder by senior and influential US politicians."

Even in his moments of gloom, Assange could not resist painting himself on a canvas of historical importance: in 1963 Jack Ruby shot to death Lee Harvey Oswald, days after Oswald was arrested for the assassination of President John F Kennedy. Many people at the time thought Oswald had to be silenced, because he Knew Too Much.

Assange's counsel, Geoffrey Robertson, was even more extreme in his predictions. He told one British court: "There is a real risk ... of him being detained at Guantánamo Bay ... There is a real risk that he could be made the subject of the death penalty."

By Christmas, there were indeed some reasons to wonder whether the WikiLeaks phenomenon might not be on the way out. Was it a brief comet that had streaked across the sky throughout 2010, thanks to an extraordinarily audacious act by one young soldier, but was now likely to be extinguished? The supposed leaker of the tsunami of documents, Bradley Manning, could only look forward to his court martial in the spring, followed, no doubt, by many grim years in a US brig. Meanwhile, anyone who typed in the URL "wikileaks.org" got a message that the operation was not functioning: "At the moment WikiLeaks is not accepting new submissions."

There were money uncertainties, too. The Germany-based Wau Holland Foundation, WikiLeaks' main financial arm, for the first time released some data about revenue from donations at the end of the year. It showed that Assange was trying to put his team on a more regular footing, with salaries for key employees costing €100,000 a year, including €66,000 annually to go to him. Another €380,000 was going on expenses, including hardware and travel. Thanks to the global publicity generated with his newspaper partnership, WikiLeaks had acquired an impressive €1 million in donations in 2010. But closer analysis showed donations had dropped off significantly in the second half of the year: by August, the site had raised about €765,000, meaning it only collected about €235,000 subsequently.

Assange said the "political interference" by the US, which had led corporations such as Visa and MasterCard to stop donations to WikiLeaks, had dealt his organisation a blow. It was "economic censorship outside the judicial system". By his estimate, pulling these financial plugs cost WikiLeaks half a million euros in donations – a war chest that could have funded its operations for another six months. Assange added that his own defence fund had been "totally paralysed". "We don't have enough money to pay our legal bills," he said. At this point WikiLeaks' projected legal costs had risen to £200,000, with his own personal legal bill at another £200,000. It even cost him £16,000 to have the Swedish material in his case translated into English, he claimed.

These legal difficulties over his Swedish sex case were yet another brake on WikiLeaks' future. The nomadic Assange was grounded. Because of his bail conditions, he was shackled to Ellingham Hall – almost literally so, since he had to wear an electronic tag round his ankle, even in the bath. He hated that, describing it in an interview with *Paris Match* magazine as "emasculating" and a "chastity belt". He also had to turn out and report in person daily to the local police station. The future held the possibility of a wearying legal fight to avoid extradition to Sweden, and perhaps a long-lasting shadow over his reputation because he was not willing to face his accusers.

With another court hearing scheduled for the new year, Assange was still seething at the bad publicity when he met the two *Guardian* journalists, and smouldering at what he characterised as a plot to bring him down. There had been a leak from the Swedish prosecutor's report, containing witness statements about his encounters with both women. The dossier did not support the idea of a "CIA honeytrap". The *Guardian*'s Nick Davies had published an article in December itemising those details – to Assange's complaints, and the chagrin of his celebrity supporters.

John Humphrys, the veteran anchorman of BBC Radio 4's agenda-setting *Today* programme, followed up by demanding to know whether he was a "sexual predator".

Assange replied: "Of course not."

Humphrys sought to probe further: "How many women have you slept with?"

Assange, somewhat cornered: "A gentleman doesn't count!"

He described this encounter with Humphreys as "awful" – it was further proof of his black-and-white insistence that there were only two kinds of journalist out there – the "honest" and the "dishonest".

Ominously perhaps for the long-term future of Assange's brainchild, it also looked as though there was a danger WikiLeaks could lose its cyber-leaking monopoly, thanks to the emergence of a crowd of imitators. Over in Germany, in December 2010, the former WikiLeaks No 2 Daniel Domscheit-Berg unveiled OpenLeaks, a rival platform. Domscheit-Berg had fallen out with Assange, accusing him of imperious behaviour. Assange's personal control of the organisation had additionally created technical "bottlenecks", he argued, with data not properly analysed or released. At a presentation in Berlin in December, Domscheit-Berg promised OpenLeaks would be more transparent and democratic.

He offered to work systematically alongside mainstream media, with a relatively modest and logical goal for his own "transparency organisation". He said that OpenLeaks.org could confine its technical activities to "cleaning" leaks so that they could be submitted safely and anonymously online. That specialised task performed, the leaks would be turned over to newspapers and broadcasters, who would then do what the traditional media was good at, bringing resources, analysis and context. Finally, there was publication. Domscheit-Berg argued it was realistic that the mainstream media should generally be allowed to publish leaked material first, in return for the time and effort spent in editing it.

The breakaway organisation was described by one technology website as "hoping to do what WikiLeaks is trying to do but without the drama". If Domscheit-Berg, or indeed other imitators, could develop workable clones of WikiLeaks, then there was little doubt that many other mainstream editors would be attracted to them.

Meanwhile, for all its high profile, WikiLeaks lacked a coherent organisation. One of his most stalwart helpers, Kristinn Hrafnsson, went back to Iceland for Christmas. Team Assange was only slowly moving from its origins as a rather chaotic insurgency towards a more structured organisation. Beseeched by his friends to enlist professional aides, Assange invited London PR professional Mark Borkowski to prepare him a public relations plan. After a day spent at Ellingham Hall, however, the elaborate Borkowski deal failed to materialise. Assange compromised by attempting to get in his own spokesmen to deal with the torrent of media demands. In January he advertised for some novel vacancies: "Four graduates wanted to staff newly established WikiLeaks press office. Appropriate remuneration. Successful candidates will be disciplined, articulate, quick-witted, capable of multi-tasking and accustomed to lack of sleep. Ability to start immediately is essential."

Assange thus faced a formidable list of challenges as he sat around the Christmas Day lunch table with Vaughan Smith and his family – though you might not have guessed it from his decision to sport a Santa suit and play up to the camera lens for a gossipy *Newsweek* photo-shoot. But the man who had caused such a worldwide commotion had not lost his strengths.

He promptly succeeded in obtaining a contract to write his memoirs for more than a million pounds ($1.6m). This deal, brokered by literary agent Caroline Michel with Knopf in the US and Canongate in the UK, plus several foreign publishers, assuaged some of his money worries. "I don't want to write this book but I have to," he explained. He was liable to get more than £250,000 immediately in advances, although a six-figure chunk would have to be set aside to hire a ghostwriter. Michel's agency also set up a meeting with Paul Greengrass, acclaimed director of *The Bourne Ultimatum*, with a view to him turning Assange's life-story into a secret-agent escapade. The book, *WikiLeaks Versus the World: My Story*, was scheduled for release in April 2011 – an ambitious deadline.

Another piece of good news was the diminishing prospect that Assange would personally become the victim of some kind of vengeful US drone-strike. The US department of justice had issued secret subpoenas on 14 December for the Twitter accounts of Manning, Assange and his friends. This led to unwelcome publicity when Twitter robustly went to court and got the subpoena unsealed. Icelandic MP and WikiLeaks supporter Birgitta Jónsdóttir made a political fuss. "It sort of feels to me as if they've become quite desperate," Jónsdóttir said. The investigation was fruitless, she added, since "none of us would ever use Twitter messaging to say anything sensitive". If the US was reduced to chasing tweets, their legal pursuit appeared to have become slightly less menacing.

Contrary to the bloodcurdling claims made in public about the crimes of WikiLeaks, senior state department officials in fact appeared to have concluded by mid-January that the WikiLeaks controversy had caused little real and lasting damage to American diplomacy. The Reuters news agency reported on 19 January 2011 that in private briefings to Congress top US diplomats admitted the fall-out from the release of thousands of private diplomatic cables across the globe had not been especially bad. One congressional official briefed on the reviews told Reuters that the administration felt compelled to say publicly that the revelations had seriously damaged American interests in order to bolster legal efforts to shut down the WikiLeaks website and bring charges against the leakers. "I think they want to present the toughest front they can muster," the officials said.

The tacit retraction of Hillary Clinton's lurid claim that the release of the WikiLeaks cables had been an attack on the entire international community followed the equally low-key admission that Assange did not in fact have "blood on his hands" from the release of the earlier Iraq and Afghan war logs.

But the publicity – and the controversy – had achieved something very valuable for him. WikiLeaks had, as a result of the rows, become a stupendous global brand. Writing in the *New York Times*, Evgeny Morozov, the cyber-analyst from Stanford University, saw a wonderful possible future. He argued that WikiLeaks could have two major advantages over any of its imitators: a widely and easily recognisable brand and an extensive network of contacts in the media. Following several years in "relative obscurity" it had now become the "media's darling". He envisaged that WikiLeaks could "morph into a gigantic media intermediary", as a journalistic clearing-house: "Under this model, WikiLeaks staffers would act as idea salesmen relying on one very impressive digital Rolodex."

Ian Katz, the *Guardian*'s deputy editor, put the position trenchantly at a debate organised by the Frontline Club in mid-January. "I think Julian has used his profile very cleverly and what he is doing is trying to make himself the brand, if you like, that is synonymous with whistleblowing ... He wants you to think if you are a pissed off analyst in [the military] or wherever and you have got something you want to share with the world, 'I will send it to that Assange fellow, not to the *Guardian*.' Which poses a really interesting question for traditional media partners like us – have we helped to create, as it were, a brand which people will go to in place of traditional media?"

WikiLeaks had also spawned a host of clone sites which were not so much competitors as admiring tributes: IndoLeaks, BrusselsLeaks, BalkanLeaks, ThaiLeaks, PinoyLeaks. Some were reposting American embassy cables. Others were publishing material from their own sources. Assange's concept of an online site for anonymous whistleblowing activists seemed to be going viral – as, perhaps, he always believed it might – while he continued his own plan to spend months sending leaked cables to journalists in an ever-widening range of countries.

One of the most interesting – and subtle – immediate positive outcomes of the WikiLeaks saga was in one of those normally obscure countries. Following the publication of excoriating leaked cables from the US mission in Tunisia, about the corruption and excess of the ruling family, tens of thousands of protesters rose up and overthrew the country's hated president, Zine al-Abidine Ben Ali.

Was this a WikiLeaks revolution? Not quite. It began after an unemployed 26-year-old university graduate, Mohammed Bouazizi, set fire to himself in desperation. Officials had prevented him from selling vegetables. His death triggered nationwide rioting over joblessness and political repression. It was long-simmering frustrations with the Ben Ali regime which were behind the revolt. The Tunisians were the first people in the Arab world to take to the streets and oust a leader for a generation. But they already knew their ruling family was debauched; they didn't need WikiLeaks for that.

There was, however, a genuinely extraordinary WikiLeaks effect. "Sam", a pseudonymous young Tunisian writing on the *Guardian*'s Comment is Free site in mid-January, specifically referenced WikiLeaks as he described how a resigned cynicism about the regime under which he'd grown up turned to hope:

The internet is blocked, and censored pages are referred to as pages "not found" – as if they had never existed. School-children are exchanging proxies and the word becomes cult: "You got a proxy that works?" ... We love our country and we want things to change, but there is no organised movement: the tribe is willing, but the leader is missing. The corruption, the bribes – we simply want to leave. We begin to apply to study in France, or Canada. It is cowardice, and we know it. Leaving the country to "the rest of them". We go to France and forget, then come back for the holidays. Tunisia? It is the beaches of Sousse and Hammamet, the nightclubs and restaurants. A giant Club Med.

And then, WikiLeaks reveals what everyone was whispering. And then, a young man immolates himself. And then, 20 Tunisians are killed in one day. And for the first time, we see the opportunity to rebel, to take revenge on the "royal" family, who have taken everything, to overturn the established order that has accompanied our youth. An educated youth, which is tired and ready to sacrifice all the symbols of the former autocratic Tunisia with a new revolution: the jasmine revolution – the true one.

Paradoxically the leaked comments by the US ambassador in Tunis, widely read across the region, played a major role in boosting Washington's image on the Arab street. Ordinary Tunisians liked the way in which the Americans – unlike the French – had so frankly highlighted corruption. They now wanted the US to support their on-going jasmine revolution. They asked Washington to exert pressure on neighbouring Arab leaders, and prevent them from interfering.

Muammar Gaddafi, the despot in neighbouring Libya, had no problem in acknowledging a link between events in Tunis and WikiLeaks – a demonic link, so far as he was concerned. Gaddafi said he was pained by Ben Ali's overthrow and "concerned for the people of Tunisia, whose sons are dying each day". He warned Tunisians not to be tricked by WikiLeaks, "which publishes information written by lying ambassadors in order to create chaos". Gaddafi himself was soon overthrown and killed in October 2011.

The US secretary of state, Hillary Clinton, had previously denounced the leak of the cables, because it had "undermined our efforts to work with other countries to solve shared problems". But the same leak was now helping to repair America's battered reputation in the Middle East, damaged by the Iraq war, and to advance the White House's lofty goals of democratisation and modernisation. Assange had unwittingly helped restore American influence in a place where it had lost credibility. It was ironic. By increasing the amount of information in the system, WikiLeaks had generated unpredictable effects.

For all the ironies and ambiguities of his campaign, and for all the problematic nature of his personality, Assange himself now seems to have acquired a vast worldwide fan-base – at any rate, outside the United States. Despite the hostility of government officials, and the "latex gloves" (as *Vanity Fair* put it) with which the main stream media have handled him, much of the world has nothing but admiration for WikiLeaks and Julian Assange. In his native Australia and elsewhere he is regarded by many unreservedly as a hero, as someone whose war on secrecy has created something genuinely new and exciting.

His own preferences remain subversive. He personally helped fund a humorous rap video about WikiLeaks which he played to the visitors to Ellingham Hall, tapping out the address on his MacBook Pro. It is by Robert Foster, a performance poet living in Australia. The spoof news bulletin is titled, "RAP NEWS – WikiLeaks' Cablegate: the truth is out there." Foster raps while dressed up in a variety of roles: TV anchor, Hillary Clinton, Silvio

Berlusconi, and Gadaffi, as well as the right-wing conspiracy theo-rist and American radio host Alex Jones. A voluptuous blonde nurse with a stethoscope sidles up to Gadaffi. Meanwhile, Berlus-coni, flanked by two young women in underwear, says: "Hey Robert, how much for your news show? I pay cash! I just got some roubles!"

Assange loves this stuff: as it plays, he can be seen smiling and wiggling his feet to the music. There is something else which has also recently given him pleasure: Italy's *Rolling Stone* magazine made him their cover-boy, depicting him – shirtless – with the legend, in a nod to David Bowie, "The Man who Fell (from the web) to Earth … a platinum villain who endangers the powerful of the planet, passing himself off as a cyberpunk". The magazine named him "Rockstar of the Year".

CHAPTER 19

The Simon Bolivar of SW1

Ecuadorian embassy, Knightsbridge, London
19 June 2012

"Are you enjoying the interview, Julian?"
ECUADORIAN PRESIDENT RAFAEL CORREA ON *THE JULIAN ASSANGE SHOW*,
RUSSIA TODAY, MAY 2012

It was Tuesday afternoon when there was a ring at the doorbell of the Ecuadorian Embassy. No one was expected. The embassy is situated immediately behind Harrods, London's most famous department store. The surrounding enclave, Knightsbridge, is the capital's wealthiest. No longer the preserve of the British upper classes, SW1 has become the haunt of the international super-rich, many of whom have snapped up property here to safeguard their capital.

But the figure who rang the bell at the embassy's address – Flat 3b, 3 Hans Crescent – wasn't a Kazakh oligarch or a confused shopper. It was none other than Julian Assange.

Days earlier, Assange's lengthy attempts to evade extradition to Sweden had ended in disappointing failure. Britain's Supreme Court had ruled that the warrant issued by the Swedish authorities was valid. Assange should be extradited to answer the August

2010 accusations that he sexually assaulted one Swedish woman and raped another, it said.

At this point the WikiLeaks founder had exhausted all UK legal options. The best barristers in the land had appealed the case right up to the highest court.

A further appeal to the European court of human rights in Strasbourg was theoretically possible. (Assange had until 28 June to lodge one.) But his chances of success were slim, most commentators believed. Assange's pursuers, then, had finally caught up with him.

It was against this backdrop that Assange took a typically bold and surprising step: to seek refuge and diplomatic protection inside the Ecuadorian embassy.

The tactic wasn't new. During the Cold War, various dissidents found refuge in western embassies to escape communist persecution. The most celebrated, Hungary's Cardinal Mindszenty, spent 15 years in the cramped US embassy in Budapest.

But this was 2012, not 1956. And Assange's plight didn't exactly equate to Mindszenty's, who faced a second communist show trial if captured and probable death. There were no Soviet tanks outside Harrods; and on the manicured surrounding streets filled with Bentleys and Porsches, few signs of state brutality.

After entering, Assange calmly explained that he was seeking political asylum from Ecuador's progressive government. He mentioned the UN's declaration on human rights.

Assange had picked one of Latin America's smaller nations. But his choice made sense. The country's president Rafael Correa is a charismatic populist, and a leading member of South America's leftist bloc. Like Assange, Correa views US influence critically. In 2011, Correa threw out the US's ambassador in Quito, Heather Hodges, after a cable leaked by WikiLeaks alleged corruption inside the country's police force. In power since 2007, Correa enjoys strong support – in 2013 he won a third term.

Assange's request created an immediate problem for Ecuador's ambassador in London, Ana Alban, and her small team: what to do with their new house guest? The embassy's mansion home looked grand. But in reality it comprised a modest suite of ground-floor rooms.

Inside is a reception area, several white-painted offices hung with paintings, and a tiny balcony overlooking the street. There was no bedroom. Or shower. The sprawling red-brick house had multiple occupants; outside was a taxi rank; round the corner Harrods' noisy loading bay.

Alban later insisted she had no foreknowledge of Assange's dramatic asylum plan. "There were no pre-negotiations," she claimed. She had been as stunned as anybody when the fugitive Australian turned up, she told the *Guardian*, adding, "It was a big surprise."

Alban rang the foreign ministry in Quito. She then went home to fetch a blow-up mattress so Assange had something to sleep on. (In a subsequent briefing to journalists the ambassador said she had gone out to find something for Assange to sleep 'with'; horrified aides swiftly corrected her.)

Assange's extraordinary move would precipitate a bitter stand-off between Britain – an ex-colonial power – and Ecuador, a nation with growing regional and international aspirations. The Ecuadorian government said it would consider Assange's asylum request. In the meantime, it added, he could remain at the embassy under its "protection". Quito wasn't trying to interfere in the judicial processes of either the UK or Sweden, it stated.

The British foreign office disagreed. Viewed from London, Correa appeared to be abusing the asylum process for cynical reasons. His real motive, the FCO felt, was to bolster his anti-US credentials ahead of elections. And perhaps to stake a claim to pan-American leadership. (Correa's close ally, Venezuela's Hugo Chavez, was seriously ill and would die nine months later.)

Assange's action also created an expensive headache for Scotland Yard. Its detectives now had the task of arresting him – or trying to. Under the 1961 Vienna Convention, the Metropolitan police weren't allowed to storm the building and drag Assange away. It was protected diplomatic property. Or was it?

William Hague, the British foreign secretary, begin exploring legal loopholes. The UK was legally bound to extradite Assange to Sweden, he said. Perhaps there was a way to nab him after all?

In the meantime, staff converted a small back-office for Assange into an impromptu bedroom. The room was less than five metres wide. There was space for a single bed, a bookshelf, a small round table and chairs. The embassy bought a larger fridge.

Assange's conditions weren't exactly luxurious. But nor were they quite as grim as the cell he had had in Wandsworth prison. Most importantly he had a computer and fast internet connection. WikiLeaks could function.

Ten days after his walk-in, the Met wrote to Assange. It asked him to leave the embassy forthwith and to report to Belgravia police station. Assange declined.

He justified this by citing the US's ongoing "investigation" against WikiLeaks. Washington's attempts to prosecute him for espionage were active and real, he said. It was "only a matter of time" before the US authorities tried to extradite him from Sweden or elsewhere.

By August this UK–Ecuador crisis reached boiling point. A British official in Quito handed a letter to the Ecuadorian government. In blunt terms, it warned that if Ecuador refused to hand Assange over, the UK would "take actions" to arrest him on diplomatic territory: in other words break into the embassy.

In 1980 the SAS had famously stormed the Iranian embassy in nearby South Kensington, shooting dead five hostage-takers. TV footage of the incident, often replayed, cemented Britain's reputation for using brute solutions when required.

The letter invoked a little-known British law, the Diplomatic and Consular Premises Act of 1987. It ended: "We sincerely hope that we do not reach that point, but if you are not capable of resolving this matter of Mr Assange's presence in your premises, this is an option open for us."

Correa and his foreign minister Ricardo Patino were furious. An indignant Patino pointed out: "We are not a British colony." If the UK did storm the embassy Ecuador would view this as a "hostile and intolerable act", he said.

The minister appealed for solidarity from other South American nations. He further dubbed Britain's hardball tactics "a blatant disregard of the Vienna Convention" and a "dangerous precedent" for diplomats everywhere, including UK ones.

Britain – a nation that under the late Margaret Thatcher evicted Argentina from the Falkland Islands – was cast again as a bully and imperial aggressor. Not much was said about Assange's alleged Swedish victims.

In mid-August tensions spiralled further. Citing sources inside Ecuador's government, the *Guardian*'s Quito stringer, Irene Caselli, reported that Correa had decided to give Assange political asylum. It followed a visit to Ecuador by Assange's mother Christine, who met the president. Correa took to Twitter to say no ruling had been made.

Nevertheless, the *Guardian*'s exclusive prompted the FCO and Scotland Yard to panic. Late on Wednesday night, 15 August, three police trucks screeched into Hans Crescent. Dozens of officers swarmed up the building's communal internal staircase; one copper even stood guard outside the window of the embassy's toilet.

Assange and the South American diplomats waited nervously inside, wondering what would happen next. "It was amazing," Alban said later. She added: "When Mr Assange was first here we had just four policemen."

Despite this clumsy show of force, the London government failed to make good on its threat to storm the premises. The next day Patino confirmed that Ecuador was indeed granting Assange asylum. The minister citied "political persecution" against WikiLeaks and its self-styled editor-in-chief. He said Assange couldn't expect a fair trial in the US and might face the death penalty.

The British were disappointed; Sweden's foreign minister Carl Bildt said his country's democratic system guaranteed everybody's rights – including Assange's. Claes Borgström, the lawyer for the two women, said his clients thought the decision absurd. "Assange is a coward," he suggested.

Coward or not, on Sunday 19 August 2012, Assange made a triumphant public appearance – his first since vanishing inside the building two months earlier.

Addressing his followers from the pavement was out of the question; he would be arrested. So Assange delivered his speech from the embassy's balcony – a mere ten feet above street level. Theoretically speaking, it might have been possible for a tall Metropolitan police officer to have grabbed Assange by the leg. Or possibly his foot. They could have wrestled.

As it was, Scotland Yard was out in large numbers. Before Assange appeared, officers comprehensively sealed off the area. Several lurked at the side of the building. Others stood grim-faced in front of a scrum of media and WikiLeaks supporters packing the upscale neighbourhood. There was even a police helicopter, which circled noisily overhead. If Assange had planned to escape by hot-air balloon – well, the Met had it covered.

At around 2.30pm Assange emerged, a pallid figure dressed in a blue shirt and maroon tie. There was an enormous roar. Assange gave a thumbs-up, tapped the microphone and inquired: "Can you hear me?" This was surely the moment for someone to shout, Monty Python-style: "'E's not the Messiah! 'E's a very naughty boy!" But from the police officers there was a gloomy silence.

As part of his asylum deal, Assange had agreed not to make political statements. In reality the manner of his appearance – next to a large, colourful Ecuadorian flag, watched by the world's media, and yards from police – amounted to a giant, taunting raspberry blown in Hague's face.

In a ten-minute speech, Assange thanked all of those who had made his escape from Sweden's grasp possible: Correa; Ecuador – a "courageous Latin American nation"; staff at the embassy; the plucky sovereign countries of South America. He mentioned most of them by name, Argentina twice.

Unsurprisingly, Assange reserved his harshest words for the US. He urged President Obama to stop his "witch-hunt against WikiLeaks". And he called for Bradley Manning – "one of the world's foremost political prisoners" – to be released from military jail.

Assange's supporters were out in force. They included the left-winger Tariq Ali and Britain's former ambassador to Uzbekistan, Craig Murray. (Speaking in a megaphone Ali said Europe should change its gaze, and learn from South America. Someone shouted back: "So should you, mate").

The good news for Assange was that he was at liberty, if confined. The bad news was that the Andes were a long way away. And as one police officer pointed out, as the crowds melted away in the weekend rain: "He's not going anywhere." Quito, often grey and cool, set in a valley bowl with neighbourhoods climbing up its slopes, was as distant as the moon.

To his critics Assange's speech – with its portentous references to oppressed citizens "whispering in the dark" – was another attempt to confuse a possible US plot against him with his personal woes in Sweden. Assange said nothing about the allegations against him. These were unrelated to any potential US indictment.

In Washington, meanwhile, the Obama administration gave out mixed messages over its intentions towards Assange. US officials told Reuters the White House was divided over the wisdom of prosecuting him, with the likelihood of criminal charges now receding rather than growing.

Other officials, however, told the *New York Times* an investigation was ongoing and that tens of thousands of pages of evidence had been gathered against him, with the US seeking information from at least four former members of WikiLeaks.

Assange's defence of Bradley Manning and other persecuted whistleblowers was admirable. But two years after his ill-fated trip to Stockholm, other more obnoxious trends were visible to many.

Assange was quick to criticise the US and other western countries – notably the UK and Sweden – when they behaved badly in the international arena, or compromised on principle. But he seemed reluctant to speak out against governments that supported him personally. This was true even if these governments had egregious human rights records arguably far worse than in the EU and US.

This was glaringly true of Assange and Russia. Assange had surely read the US cables on Vladimir Putin's Kremlin. They argued that the Russian government, its powerful spy agencies, and organised crime had become practically indistinguishable, with Russia in effect a "virtual mafia state".

And yet in 2011 Assange signed a lucrative TV deal with Russia Today (RT), Putin's English-language propaganda channel. Launched in 2005, RT's mission was to accuse the west of hypocrisy while staying mute about Russia's own failings, especially in the fields of freedom of speech and fair elections.

The fate of whistleblowers inside Russia was grimly clear to everyone – you would have thought. The investigative reporter and Kremlin critic Anna Politkovskaya was shot dead in 2006; the Chechnya-based human rights activist Natalia Estemirova murdered in 2009. The list of Russians and opposition journalists killed in murky circumstances grew ever longer.

When *The Julian Assange Show* aired on RT in March 2012 it included interviews with ten guests – among them Hezbollah's Hassan Nasrallah, the Slovenian philosopher Slavoj Žižek and Ecuador's Correa. But there were no interviews with any members of Russia's opposition.

Assange did talk to WikiLeaks' supporter Jacob Applebaum, and two other "cypherpunks", who co-authored a 2012 book with the WikiLeaks publisher. It advocated encryption against state snooping.

Critics concluded Assange was the latest in a line of western "useful idiots", exploited by Moscow for its own PR purposes. Assange shrugged off the charge. Clearly, though, the Kremlin's American-bashing agenda sat comfortably with Assange's own.

In retrospect his interview with Correa, which took place just months before he sought asylum from Ecuador, looks like a piece of bromance. Assange spoke to Ecuador's leader by video from Ellingham Hall. It was engaging stuff. Correa accused the US ambassador of "loftiness, insolence, grandeur and imperial airs". Correa also defended his decision to close Ecuador's US base, teasing that Ecuador should get its own military base in Miami, Florida.

At one point the president asked Assange: "Are you enjoying the interview, Julian?"

Assange nodded, grinned and replied: "I'm enjoying your jokes a great deal."

By Christmas 2012, Assange must have got used to his strange new life – to some a parody of dissidence, to others a justified response to US hounding.

The embassy had become home. His friend the film director Ken Loach gave him a treadmill; a personal trainer stopped by; Julian reportedly ran an average of four miles each day. WikiLeaks staffers brought him clean clothes and food, with take-aways from the branch of Wasabi next to Harrods.

His biggest problem was lack of natural daylight. Assange compared his plight to living in a space station. As the *Guardian*'s Esther Addley reported, Assange's room was so dim he used a lamp that imitated blue sky, set to a timer. It would go off at night to stop him working through the early hours. He also made use of a sun lamp to combat his ghostly pallor; on one occasion he burned his face so badly his skin blistered.

Six months after he first entered, in December 2012, Assange made a second balcony appearance and delivered a festive Christmas message to friends and supporters. Embassy staff had hung fairy lights around the ornate white railings. Despite a large police presence again the mood was mellow.

Fans sang Christmas Carols – Bob Dylan's "I Shall Be Released" wafted across Knightsbridge, and a version of "Santa Claus is Comin' To Town". (Its lyrics went: "You better watch out/You better not cry/Better not pout I'm telling you why/WikiLeaks is coming to town." There was also a pretty terrible WikiLeaks-ised version of "On the First Day of Christmas".)

Some Assange enthusiasts wore Anonymous masks, now a global symbol of protest. A woman in a mink coat asked them to clear off her doorstep; some people waved candles. In his speech Assange thanked the Ecuadorian government and called the embassy his "refuge". "I came here in summer. It's winter now," he observed.

He also talked in gnomic terms about the struggle for transparency worldwide: "True democracy is the sum of our resistance." A noisy chant went up in Spanish. It went: "Julian, my friend/The people are with you."

And so it went on. By summer 2013 the first anniversary of Assange's stay in the embassy loomed. True, there had been no diplomatic breakthrough in his case. But several celebrities had dropped in to cheer his spirits. Lady Gaga spent five hours inside; Vivienne Westwood came by too, as did the lead singer of a Puerto Rican rap duo.

Many of Assange's high-profile backers had lost large sums of money when Assange broke his bail conditions. (Assange's electronic tag had disappeared; someone presumably sawed it off.) The sum forfeited came collectively to £293,500. Most, including Vaughan Smith, nonetheless remained loyal.

But not Jemima Khan. The pair fell out when Assange took vehement objection to a documentary on WikiLeaks which Khan executive-produced. In a long, sorrowful essay for the *New Statesman* magazine she traced her own journey of admiration then disillusionment and finally "demoralisation" with Julian. It was, as she noted, a familiar path which many of his former allies had already trodden. "The problem with Camp Assange is that, in the words of George W Bush, it sees the world as being 'with us or against us'," she wrote.

Her critique was surely correct. Khan listed WikiLeaks' many accomplishments – its exposure of war crimes, torture, corruption and cover ups. She also recognised the polarised nature of the debate Assange provoked, and agreed that anyone leading a radical transparency movement "was bound to be a bit different".

But Khan also remarked that Assange had a bad habit of falling out with his closest supporters. As well as early collaborators like Domscheit-Berg, and news organisations such as the *Guardian* and *New York Times*, Assange had parted ways with his lawyer Mark Stephens and his publisher, Jamie Byng of Canongate Books.

Byng reportedly stumped up £500,000 in total for Assange's ghostwritten autobiography. Assange took the money to pay his legal bills, but then – after long sessions with his ghostwriter Andrew O'Hagan in Ellingham Hall – changed his mind and withdrew cooperation. In an attempt to recoup its loss, in 2011 Canongate brought out a draft memoir, *Julian Assange: The Unauthorised Autobiography*. Julian promptly disowned it. Sales were poor.

The first-person story begins with Assange's Wandsworth stint in solitary as prisoner A9379AY and ends with a stinging attack on his erstwhile media partners. It is not a bad book. But the tone – devoid of humour and prone to grandiosity – makes it difficult to love.

Khan also said she had tried to raise with Assange the opinion of legal experts – that he was no more vulnerable to extradition from Sweden to the US than from the UK. But Assange refused to talk about it. She freely conceded that there were "troubling aspects" about the behaviour of Swedish prosecutors towards Assange. Even so, Assange was in danger of ending up as Australia's L Ron Hubbard, the founder of the Scientology cult, she warned:

"The problem is that WikiLeaks – whose mission statement was 'to produce ... a more just society ... based upon truth' – has been guilty of the same obfuscation and misinformation as those it sought to expose, while its supporters are expected to follow, unquestioningly, in blinkered, cultish devotion."

By the spring of 2013 WikiLeaks was still functioning, just about. Assange made another surprise announcement: that he would stand for election to Australia's federal parliament. His plan was to win the seat for Victoria in the Senate, the Upper House. Assange's biological father John Shipton helped to organise his son's political campaign for the newly formed WikiLeaks party.

Since the 2010 disclosure of classified US communiqués, Assange had released some new material. It included secret files from Guantanamo Bay, emails from the global intelligence company Stratfor, and communications from inside Syrian government ministries.

But there was nothing on the scale of Manning's revelations. And much of Assange's daily endeavour seemed devoted to attacking his critics on Twitter. In March 2013, Assange released the "Kissinger files", US diplomatic cables dating from 1973–6. The US government, however, had already declassified them. They were old news, reheated.

If Ecuador was growing fed up with Julian, there were no signs of it at this point. Back in Quito a decision was made to recall Ana Alban from London. Some whispered the ambassador was being moved because of her failure to end the Assange saga. Ecuador denied this.

True or not, her attempts to make progress in the case were stunningly unsuccessful. During one meeting with the UK foreign office minister Hugo Swire, Alban reportedly asked: "What are we going to do about the stone in the shoe?" To which Swire replied: "Not my stone, not my shoe."

Ecuador's foreign minister arrived in London two days before the first anniversary of Assange's self-imposed detention. The two men met in the embassy and stayed up talking until 4am. Patino said he found Assange fit, in good spirits, and ready to remain inside if necessary for another five years.

"We are not going to smuggle Mr Assange out in the boot of a car or through an underground tunnel or something," he said. Patino subsequently met William Hague. Their encounter yielded nothing of substance.

One year on, Assange appeared stuck indefinitely in a small but comfortable prison of his own making. WikiLeaks was slipping from the headlines.

Was it, some wondered, after months of fire and fury, becoming slowly irrelevant?

CHAPTER 20

The court martial

Fort Meade, near Washington DC
3 June 2013

"Not a typical soldier"
DEFENCE LAWYER, DAVID COOMBS

Jihrleah Showman, from Tulsa, Oklahoma, is a big woman. As she said, her biceps literally measure 15 inches. She called Bradley Manning "faggotty" once whilst they were training in the same unit, and when the diminutive soldier finally lost it in Iraq and punched her, she wasted no time in wrestling him to the ground.

She recounted that story expansively to film-maker Alex Gibney for his WikiLeaks documentary, "We Steal Secrets":

> I was off shift, and I had to come in, to find something that
> *he* should have been able to find; and he was pacing back and
> forth, saying smart comments to me; and I blatantly said:
> "Manning, how about you fix your shit before you try to fix
> mine?" And he screamed and punched me in the face, while
> I was sitting down. My adrenaline immediately hit overload.
> I stood up, pushed my chair back. He continued to try to
> fight me, but I ... pulled him on the floor and laid on top of

him and pinned his arms, you know, beside his head. At that time, I can't believe that he'd mess with me ... I was the last person he probably should have punched.

Three years later, the US army put Jihrleah Showman on the witness stand to claim that Manning was, right from the outset, a disloyal character with no respect for the American flag. Manning's lawyer, David Coombs, accused her of inventing this story "to make my client look bad". It was a rare moment of courtroom combat that relieved the usual grim tedium of the proceedings. It also marked something of an evidential low point in the military's attempt to demonise the person who leaked so many of their classified files to Assange.

Showman informed army judge Colonel Denise Lind that while Manning was in training:

> I tapped the flag on my shoulder and I asked him what the flag meant to him ... He said the flag meant nothing to him. And he did not consider himself part of – did not consider himself to have allegiance to this country or any people ... As an American and as a fellow soldier, I was distraught by the statements he made.

She had even thought he was a "possible spy".

Manning's own lawyer put it to her that the argumentative junior soldier had in fact responded that he was against "blind allegiance" to a flag. That certainly sounded in character. It also transpired that, although Showman was his supervisor, she had never written up the allegedly shocking event. Her own superiors could not recall her saying anything. But she denied being personally hostile to Manning, who had once made an official complaint about her, and who characterised her in his chat-logs as "a dyke".

Coombs produced a legal mini-coup at this point: he unexpectedly played untransmitted out-takes he had obtained of her recent interview with the documentary film-maker. It turned out that she had indeed said hostile things to Gibney's camera:

> That's not a whistleblower, that's somebody who, in my opinion, has no allegiance to this country and in my opinion has no desire for our country's well-being. [He] has a desire for the outside sources to possibly do damage to our country.

The reason for the spat over this essentially flimsy testimony was that, as Assange's name began fading out of the headlines, the US military were finally bringing Bradley Manning to a court martial. He was the true source of all Assange's sensational leaked material and there was only one real question at stake: how long would he spend in jail? For his was to be a show trial.

Coombs, Manning's civilian lawyer, originally told his family the best result to aim for was that Manning would get away with 10 years – a hefty sentence, but not one that would utterly destroy the young private's life. If Coombs was going to achieve that limited outcome, however, the defence lawyer had a legal mountain to climb.

The US army was vengeful. Faced with this new phenomenon of "hacktivism", they refused to accept Manning's initial offer of a plea-bargain. He admitted wrongfully leaking the classified data to Assange and therefore faced a possible maximum sentence of 20 years. But the army sought to convict him in addition on the novel and far more serious charge of "aiding the enemy".

ARTICLE 104. AIDING THE ENEMY
Any person who–
(1) aids, or attempts to aid, the enemy with arms, ammunition, supplies, money, or other things; or

(2) without proper authority, knowingly harbors or protects
or gives intelligence to or communicates or corresponds with
or holds any intercourse with the enemy, either directly or
indirectly;
shall suffer death or such other punishment as a court martial
or military commission may direct.

Unlike its civilian equivalent in the Espionage Act, the wording
of this military charge did not seem to require any specific trea-
sonable intent. This was the loophole the army sought to exploit.
They also piled on a total of 21 other variegated charges, including theft of government property worth more than $5 million:
this was what they alleged was the current black-market rate for
such international espionage. Their sole concession was that they
would not seek Manning's death. He thus faced the prospect that
he could be imprisoned for life without parole.

In the summer of 2013, Manning's very small figure, somewhat unconvincingly encased in full-dress ceremonial uniform, was
handcuffed between two burly guards, and brought into eight
weeks of hearings beneath that US flag in a room at Fort Meade,
so a parade of military witnesses could document his un-American
history. He had already been imprisoned for more than three years.

Manning's solitary confinement at Quantico had seen him
prevented from sleep and made to stand naked, supposedly in
order to prevent him attempting suicide. The state department's
own assistant secretary for public affairs, PJ Crowley, publicly
called the Pentagon's harsh treatment of their prisoner "ridiculous and stupid and counterproductive". He wrote in the
Guardian: "Based on 30 years of government experience, if you
have to explain why a guy is standing naked in the middle of a jail
cell, you have a policy in need of urgent review."

The Pentagon's reputation fell further when in March 2012
the UN special rapporteur on torture, Juan Mendez announced:

"I believe Bradley Manning was subjected to cruel, inhuman and degrading treatment in the excessive and prolonged isolation he was put in during the nine months he was in Quantico."

By then, the sceptical Crowley had been forced to resign from the state department for stepping out of line and uttering criticisms. But Manning himself had been quietly moved to less uncivilised conditions at the Fort Leavenworth army prison in Kansas. As compensation for proven mistreatment, the judge granted him a token 112-day reduction in future jail time.

To get that inevitable sentence down further, Manning's legal team had, above all, to knock out the frightening count that Manning had "aided the enemy". Coombs' first attempt to strike it out came in April 2012 at a pre-trial hearing. He tried to argue that the prosecutors were violating the constitutional right to free speech. Manning never showed "general evil intent" to give the information to enemies, Coombs said. Crucially, he compared Manning's actions to those of a soldier speaking to the *Washington Post* or the *New York Times*.

At worst, his client could be accused of negligence in letting the leaked material indirectly fall into enemy hands, Coombs said. "They're really trying to say he should have known better," he added.

However, the military judge, Colonel Denise Lind, refused to throw out the charge. She ruled that it would be enough if the prosecution could prove that the nation's enemies actually accessed the online leaks, and that Manning knew for a fact that such a thing would happen.

The judge's initial ruling could be criticised as strained, or even perverse. Whatever its wording, Article 104 is plainly aimed at a disloyal soldier who deliberately communicates with the enemy, not one like Manning who just wanted to make everything public. Manning had not gone over to the other side. Nor had he sold military secrets to adversaries for money. On the face of it, the allegation of treason was absurd.

But Lind claimed the legal pathway she was authorising was not unconstitutionally broad because it would not endanger all soldiers who committed unauthorised disclosures – they would not automatically have the knowledge that it would "aid the enemy" in the way that a trained intelligence analyst like Manning might.

Evidently the US army was trying to fashion a sword which could be used against members of the military who passed information not just to the allegedly disreputable WikiLeaks crowd, but also to the mainstream media:

> The Court: I have asked this question of the government before, and I'll ask it one more time. Does it make any difference if it's WikiLeaks or any other news organisation – *New York Times*, *Washington Post*, or *Wall Street Journal*?
> Captain Overgaard: ... As I said, no, it would not. It would not potentially make a difference.

There was thus to be no distinction between leaking and spying. But at the same time the prosecutors also tried to shore up their novel case by repeatedly claiming that WikiLeaks was not "a legitimate news organization", but something more sinister.

There was a further logical disconnect in the military's approach. Any number of pieces of ordinary published information could be construed, in a way, as "aid to the enemy". A street map of New York would be of clear use, for example. That is why, during the second world war, the British took down all their signposts. On the other hand, a highly classified military document might be of no use at all. An instruction manual for a submarine-launched nuclear ballistic missile is undoubtedly classified top secret – but would probably be of no help to al-Qaida in Afghanistan. In the real world of battle, quite a lot depended on the actual aims of a mole and the actual needs of an "enemy".

No plausible evidence existed that Manning had swapped his allegiance and signed up for al-Qaida, because he obviously had not. Nor was any evidence presented in public that any soldier, or indeed any significant US military interest, had in fact come to harm as a result of Manning's massive leaks of historical material. The increasingly outspoken Crowley tweeted: "While supporting the #BradleyManning prosecution, it's hard to credibly argue as we exit #Iraq and #Afghanistan that he 'aided the enemy'."

Nonetheless, thanks to the legalisms initially accepted by the judge at Fort Meade, the prosecution got the go-ahead to construct an "aiding the enemy" case.

Their *pièce de résistance* was a demonstration that the demon king of all American nightmares, Osama bin Laden himself, personally read Manning's disclosures while holed up in the months before he was killed by a squad of US Navy Seals. The headline news, recorded in the unofficial transcripts diligently compiled by the Freedom of the Press Foundation, was that:

On 2 May 2011, United States government officials raided UBL's [Osama bin Laden's] compound located in Abbottabad, Pakistan and collected several items of digital media. From the items of digital media, the following items were obtained: One, a letter from UBL to a member of al-Qaida requesting the member gather Department of Defense material posted to WikiLeaks; two, a letter from the same member of al-Qaida to UBL, attached to which was the Afghanistan War Log as posted by WikiLeaks; and, three, Department of State information released by WikiLeaks.

All this boiled down to in reality was the fact that al-Qaida read the newspapers, just like everybody else. But it was used to promote a case theory that could convict Manning of the gravest crime in the military book.

The shaven-headed Captain Joe Morrow, from the Pentagon legal team, was given the job of making an aggressive prosecution opening statement, while a group of protestors demonstrated outside the Fort Meade gates with sporadic shouts of "Free Bradley Manning". While most US media ignored much of the trial, some dedicated bloggers provided daily commentary: one slept in her car to keep up the coverage.

Morrow announced: "The accused knowingly gave intelligence to the enemy." Manning deliberately sought out WikiLeaks from the beginning, he said, and fully "understood the nature of the organisation", whose internet disclosures, as the army had previously warned in an internal report, would be made use of by al-Qaida. "You will hear that enemies of the United States reviewed information provided by PFC Manning ... Manning knew the dangers of unauthorised disclosure to an organisation like WikiLeaks and he ignored those dangers."

Manning was: "a soldier who systematically harvested hundreds of thousands of documents from classified databases and then literally dumped that information on to the internet and into the hands of the enemy. Material he knew, based on his training and experience, could put the lives and welfare of his fellow soldiers at risk."

The prosecutor went on to insist: "There were massive, massive downloads ... This massive amount of information has great value to our adversaries." And in a strike at Assange's own self-regard, Morrow witheringly chose to describe the WikiLeaks group who acquired this document dump from the young soldier as nothing more than "random opportunists".

Overall, the government case was to be that Manning had no "noble motive", but was, in effect, a solitary attention-seeking misfit of no social consequence. His reasons for his revolt against the rules were held to be simply "arrogance", "self-interest", and "the notoriety he craved".

Confronted by this deflating portrait, Coombs and his defence team had from the outset two possible strategies. One was the psychiatric route – to portray Manning entirely as a nervous wreck, not really aware of what he was doing. But they eventually chose a mostly political defence. They presented Manning as a discriminating public-interest activist and whistleblower.

Coombs said that although Manning was tormented by "a very private struggle with his gender", he had also struggled over the bloodshed in Iraq and felt obliged to try and do something about it "to make a difference in this world". Coombs sought to fix a date for his client's moment of truth – Christmas Eve 2009, shortly after his arrival at Camp Hammer and just before he admitted leaking his first batch of material.

That night, he said, Manning's soldier colleagues were celebrating because a US convoy had escaped injury from a roadside bomb. But the bomb had in fact destroyed a civilian car that had pulled over in front. Inside was an innocent Iraqi family with three children. They were injured: one died.

> Everyone … was celebrating. Everyone was happy. Everyone but PFC Manning. He couldn't celebrate. He couldn't be happy. The reason why is he couldn't forget about the life that was lost on that day. He couldn't forget about the lives and the family that was impacted on that Christmas Eve. And from that moment forward PFC Manning started a struggle. You see, PFC Manning is not a typical soldier … Things started to change for him … And the evidence will show the reason why he started to struggle was no longer could he read … reports, and just see a name or number, and not think about that family on Christmas Eve who had just pulled over their car to let the convoy go by.

Coombs maintained that Manning then started to select sets of relatively non-sensitive information that he knew would do no harm to fellow-soldiers, in order to have them made public. He was not following instructions from WikiLeaks.

> He released these documents because he was hoping to make the world a better place ... He was a little naive in believing that the information that he selected could actually make a difference. But he was good intentioned.

This benign portrait got some support from a previously unknown witness. Before being sent out to Iraq, he had corresponded via AOL Instant Messenger with Laura McNamara, someone who had successfully "transitioned" from male to female. She came to court with a set of contemporaneous chat-logs, which once again proved their novel evidential value in the internet age.

Manning told her he was reading a lot:

> Delving deeper into philosophy, arts, physics, biology, politics than I ever did in school. What's even better with my current position is I can apply what I learn to provide more information to my officers and commanders and hopefully save lives ... I'm more concerned about making sure that everyone – soldiers, Marines, contractors, even the local nationals, get home to their families.

The 21-year-old had originally joined up, like so many others, in order to get government money to go on to college. But he was thoughtful:

> I actually believe what the army tries to make itself out to be. A diverse place full of people defending the country: male, female, black, white, gay, straight, Christian, Jewish, Asian, old or young, it doesn't matter to me. We all wear the same green uniform. But it's still a male-dominated,

Christian right, oppressive organisation, with a few hidden gems of diversity.

The chat logs show him already troubled:

Sometimes I wish it were all black and white like the media and politicians presented: "Him, he's the bad guy, and oh, he's the good guy." It's all shades of blurry grey.

Would this insight into a junior soldier's uneasy state of mind help provide him with a practical defence to the charge of "aiding the enemy"? Coombs tried again to get the charge thrown out, at the end of the prosecution case. This time, he argued that the prosecutors had failed to prove Manning had actual knowledge his leaks would reach the likes of bin Laden.

Colonel Lind, a career military lawyer since the day she left law school 30 years earlier, appeared unmoved. She ruled that concrete evidence did exist that was worth her consideration. It suggested Manning did know the dangers of WikiLeaks and of posting sensitive material on the internet. Captain Angel Overgaard from the prosecution team therefore succeeded for the time being in her contention that "PFC Manning is distinct from an infantryman or a truck driver because he had all the training".

The court martial ended faster than expected. Coombs did not put his client in the witness box to be cross-examined. The only time the world actually heard from him was the previous February, in an illicitly leaked audio recording. He uttered a 70-minute unchallenged pre-trial statement "written in confinement". He read it out quickly, nasally and unemotionally, but one phrase made an impact. He had leaked the Apache helicopter video, he said, because of the "seemingly delightful bloodlust" with which the pilots had dehumanised and slaughtered those who turned out to be innocent civilians.

The army's lead prosecutor, Major Ashden Fein, now made his own pitch for the limelight. Watching inside the courtroom, the *Guardian*'s Ed Pilkington described how Fein "unleashed a wave of rhetoric" for several hours. He accused Manning of in fact leaking the Apache video merely because it was "cool" to do so. He asserted that the US flag meant nothing to the army recruit. "He was interested in making a name for himself ... The only human PFC Manning ever actually cared about was himself."

> Manning pulled as much information as possible to please Julian Assange ... Manning thought the video was cool and decided to release it to a bunch of anti-government activists and anarchists ...
>
> PFC Manning was an anarchist ... not a humanist. He was a hacker. A hacker who described his fellow soldiers as dykes, a bunch of hyper-masculine, trigger-happy, ignorant rednecks or gullible idiots ... He was not a troubled young soul; he was a determined soldier with the ability, knowledge and desire to harm the US in its war effort ... He was not a whistleblower. He was a traitor.

That morning's *New York Times* carried a $52,000 full-page ad, from 850 donors including Daniel Ellsberg, Noam Chomsky and Joan Baez. It said: "We Are Bradley Manning". About 35 Manning supporters, many wearing T-shirts with the word "truth" on them, were in court, and at this peroration, one man announced aloud, "You're a hero, Bradley, as far as I'm concerned." There was a loud buzz as several others voiced support. Lind, standing up to leave as the courtroom day ended, angrily shouted, "Gallery, that's enough!"

Outside, Coombs reassured Manning's supporters. "If it takes six, seven hours to go on a diatribe and try to piece together some convoluted story ... If it takes you that long to get your point across, you know it isn't true."

Fein had been using his hot rhetoric to blur the biggest political and legal problem of his "aiding the enemy" case – that leaks to the media were now being called treason. He was attempting to portray "information anarchists", as he called them, as fundamentally different from journalists.

He quoted a snippet from one of the recovered chat logs between Manning and Assange: "The more the government controls information, the harder the government tries, the more violently the information wants to get out." Fein maintained: "Manning saw WikiLeaks as anything but a traditional journalistic organisation ... He identified WikiLeaks as the first intelligence agency for the general public."

One of Fein's key facts was also evidentially thin. To uphold his narrative that Manning was "evil", Fein needed to destroy the defence picture of the "good-intentioned" private with a crisis of conscience on Christmas Eve 2009 because of the cruel killings he saw in Iraq. Fein therefore asserted that Manning must have already leaked a video well before this date – of another calamitous airstrike on civilians, at Garani.

There was circumstantial evidence, he said, that an encrypted version of the Garani airstrike had found its way to another hacker, Jason Katz, much earlier in December. If it had emanated from Manning, this showed him acting as a dedicated WikiLeaks mole from the very beginning, and not having a crisis of conscience at all.

No positive proof existed that Manning had done such a thing, responded his defence team. Instead, Coombs did his best to focus the judge's mind elsewhere, on to the more notorious Apache helicopter video. During his final speech, he replayed to her the deeply disturbing Baghdad clips, in which a wounded, crawling, Reuters employee and the children in a van are zapped by an invisible storm of bullets, fired by pilots safely hovering a kilometre up in the sky.

You have to look at this through the eyes of a young man who cares about human life … You can no longer just ignore the fact that these are real lives being lost. These are real people dying … What do you do when these images are burned into your mind?

Lind delivered her verdict on Tuesday 30 July 2013. She refused to convict Manning of aiding the enemy and also of leaking the disputed Garani video. She did convict him, however, on most of the raft of other grave charges under the espionage act, and of the wholesale theft of government property.

Bradley Manning bowed to the inevitable ruin of his young life. To the dismay of some of his more belligerent supporters, he made a sad little statement of apology to the judge. He said he was sorry he had hurt the United States, and he realized that he would have to pay a price.

"When I made these decisions I believed I was going to help people, not hurt people," he said. "Unfortunately, I can't go back and change things".

The BBC's Tara McKelvey reported from the courtroom:

"It was a prepared script, and he had a hard time delivering it. His hands were shaking so much that he could not hold the paper still. He swallowed hard, trying to maintain his composure".

Manning was sentenced to 35 years in prison. The purpose of the extraordinary, no-holds-barred, US prosecution of this computer geek was clearly to ensure nothing of the kind would ever happen again.

Top secret

National Security Agency (NSA)
regional operations centre, Hawaii
June 2013

"Truth is coming and it cannot be stopped"
EDWARD SNOWDEN

At the very moment the US government was organising its prosecution against Bradley Manning, someone else was preparing new disclosures. His name was Edward Snowden. He was 29 years old. He was about to change the world.

Like Manning, Snowden was a whistleblower. In the spring of 2013, as Manning's trial headed inexorably towards its gloomy conclusion, Snowden was working as a contractor for the National Security Agency (NSA) at its operations centre in Hawaii.

As he later recalled, he had the perfect life: a beautiful girlfriend, a job on a volcanic island "paradise" and a generous $200,000 salary package. And yet for some years he had been dismayed by the US government's vast and undisclosed surveillance programmes.

The NSA, based at Fort Meade in Maryland, is the biggest, most powerful, and most ferociously secretive intelligence-gathering organisation in history. Formally its role is to collect foreign intelligence. Its mandate isn't supposed to include snooping on American citizens.

In reality, Snowden would reveal, the NSA spied on pretty much everyone – including Americans, whose phone records and email meta-data were hoovered up in a series of top-secret programmes. These were being carried out with no public acknowledgement and with senior intelligence officials seemingly lying about them to Congress.

The NSA was also spying intensively on non-Americans – on Germans and other allies, and on EU and western embassies in Washington and elsewhere. The agency's ambitions seemed limitless. What's more, most of Silicon Valley was apparently colluding with the NSA, with varying degrees of enthusiasm.

Snowden's summer 2013 disclosures to the *Guardian* and its columnist Glenn Greenwald were even more incendiary than Manning's – lifting the lid on the innermost secrets of American power. In May, Snowden abandoned his job in Hawaii and flew to Hong Kong. He took with him encrypted access to thousands of secret documents from the NSA and its UK counterpart, GCHQ.

For Assange, Snowden's appearance from nowhere must have seemed like a golden gift from heaven. Assange had long warned that the surveillance state and its unaccountable spy agencies had hijacked the internet. Hence the need for "cypherpunks" – activists who use encryption to protect basic freedoms.

Assange's thesis may have sounded a little crazy, especially to those who lived in mature democratic societies. But following Snowden's revelations – of the existence of the PRISM programme, and the sucking up of domestic phone records from US telecoms giant Verizon, for example – Assange seemed bang on. Prophetic even.

Over the summer the *Guardian* published a series of stories based on Snowden's disclosures. The man himself was holed up in a Hong Kong hotel room. With him were Greenwald, the *Guardian*'s veteran Washington correspondent Ewen MacAskill and the Berlin-based American filmmaker Laura Poitras.

On Sunday 6 June the fugitive Snowden took another extraordinary step. As speculation over the identity of the NSA leaker reached fever pitch, he outed himself as the source. The *Guardian* released a 12-minute film interview with Snowden. In it he explained – lucidly, persuasively – why he had taken the life-changing decision to become a whistleblower, and to give up his comfortable existence for a life on the run.

It was at this delicate moment in Snowden's fortunes that Assange inserted himself into the drama. The details are opaque. What is known is that WikiLeaks had been making frantic efforts to connect with Snowden, directly, via intermediaries and through his Hong Kong lawyers.

From Assange's perspective the approach was logical. For six years WikiLeaks had faced down threats to its publishing operation. And before settling on the small Latin American nation of Ecuador, Assange had also considered which countries might give him asylum – the sort of asylum that Snowden now badly needed.

The Snowden story also opened up a tantalising opportunity – a chance for Assange to step back into the limelight instead of being, as the *New York Times* put it, "a forgotten man". Ideologically, Assange and Snowden had much in common. In terms of temperament they were different. Snowden was shy, and deeply reluctant to become the focus of media attention; Assange ... well, the opposite.

With the hunt for him on, Snowden slipped out of his hotel room and disappeared. Back at the Ecuadorian embassy Assange hatched a plan. It had two key elements. The first was to secure an offer of asylum for Snowden from the Ecuadorian government. The second was to get Snowden physically to Quito – something that had eluded Assange for over a year.

Secretly, Assange dispatched his close aide and sometime girl-friend Sarah Harrison to Hong Kong. He also began discussions with his friend Fidel Narvaez, Ecuador's London consul. The two had become close, with Narvaez sleeping in the embassy for the first two months of Julian's stay there in 2012.

At Assange's urgent request, Narvaez issued Snowden a temporary Ecuadorian travel document. The plan seemed straight-forward enough. Snowden would fly to Moscow. From there he would change planes, travelling first to Cuba and then on to Ecuador, all the time avoiding US airspace.

Was Moscow Assange's idea? Probably. Were Russia's spy agencies involved? Possibly – although there is no proof of this. Was Russia a good choice for Snowden? Hardly, but as Assange surely recognised there were few good options.

On 23 June, Snowden and Harrison flew out of Hong Kong together and arrived at Moscow's Sheremetyevo international airport. Back in London, Assange gave a press conference reveal-ing that WikiLeaks had paid for Snowden's ticket.

So far so good. But Snowden then mysteriously failed to get on the next Aeroflot flight to Havana. There was a problem: the US had cancelled his passport. Snowden was going nowhere – the Moscow airport, it turned out, was to be his home for the next five and a half weeks. Back in Quito Correa was also having second thoughts – about granting asylum to Snowden and, troublingly, about the fact that Assange now appeared to be running Ecuador's foreign policy from his improvised bedroom.

The US, meanwhile, was applying pressure behind the scenes. Vice president Joe Biden called Correa. Mixing charm with implicit threat, Biden urged the president to reject Snowden's request. Elements in Quito were already unhappy about what they regarded as Assange's grand-standing. Had their London guest now outstayed his welcome?

In late June, Correa declared that Snowden's safe conduct pass was unauthorised. Narvaez would be "sanctioned" for his mistake, the president said, adding that Snowden was essentially now Moscow's problem and not Ecuador's. A leaked memo from Ecuador's US ambassador, Nathalie Cely, revealed Quito's exasperation with Assange during these heady days. "I suggest talking to Assange to better control the communications," she wrote. "From outside, [Assange] appears to be running the show."

Despite his private irritation, Correa made clear that Ecuador and its embassy remained a safe haven for Assange. For his part, the WikiLeaks founder issued an uncharacteristic apology "if we have unwittingly [caused] Ecuador discomfort in the Snowden matter".

Assange continued: "There is a fog of war due to the rapid nature of events. If similar events arise you can be assured that they do not originate in any lack of respect or concern for Ecuador or its government."

Through late June and July, Snowden remained in Moscow airport – appearing just once to give a press conference to a group of Russian human rights activists. The US demanded Russia hand him over. Putin refused. Meanwhile the Bradley Manning trial rolled on.

And then on 1 August Snowden strolled out of Moscow's Sheremetyevo airport – grinning, carrying a rucksack and a large holdall, and accompanied by a delighted Harrison. He climbed into a grey car. He disappeared. Snowden's lawyer Anatoly Kucherena announced that his American client had been granted a year's asylum in Russia.

In London, Assange was quick to claim credit for Snowden's liberty. He tweeted: "Edward Snowden was granted temp asylum in Russia for a yr, has now left Moscow airport under care of WikiLeaks' Sarah Harrison." In a second tweet Assange thanked the Russian people for "protecting" Snowden. He declared: "We have won the battle – now the war."

Assange's remarks – as ever – mixed truth with a large dollop of fiction. The Russian people had little to do with the decision to grant Snowden asylum; Russia wasn't a democracy. Rather, after mulling the situation for some weeks, Putin concluded that Snowden's propaganda value for the Kremlin outweighed any possible repercussions from a furious Washington.

The battle hadn't exactly been won either. Snowden was, after all, stuck in a country with a dismal human rights record, a pawn in a 21st-century great game. And from now on, the FSB – the KGB's successor agency – would track his every move.

Still, some three years after Assange burst onto the world stage with a series of spectacular leaks about the wars in Afghanistan and Iraq and the conduct of US diplomacy, he was back in the game. Perhaps not quite as a world-historical figure. But certainly as a member of the celebrity establishment.

That summer, in July 2013, Assange posed for a *Hello!*-style photo-shoot for an Australian glossy magazine. The magazine, *Who*, featured a photo of Assange on the cover with the headline: "My Life in the Embassy". Its other stories included "Kate & George's First Days at Home" and "Stars Hit the Beach".

Back in 2010, Italy's *Rolling Stone* magazine had depicted Assange as a sort of cyberpunk David Bowie. For this latest photo-shoot Assange was wearing a dark suit, a red tie, his collar artfully unbuttoned. He was also clutching a mug advertising the Australian rock band AC/DC. The look hinted at rock star. But it also said politician.

ACKNOWLEDGEMENTS

The authors would like to thank:

James Ball

Ian Black

Julian Borger

Heather Brooke

Jon Casson

Lisa Darnell

Alastair Dant

Rob Evans

Harold Frayman

Paul Galbally

Janine Gibson

John Goetz

Ian Katz

Bill Keller

Francois Kunc

Gavin MacFadyen

Ewen MacAskill

Toby Manhire

Georg Mascolo

James Meek

Richard Norton-Taylor

Daithí Ó Crualaoich

Aron Pilhofer

Gill Phillips

Geraldine Proudler

Mark Rice-Oxley

Simon Rogers

Marcel Rosenbach

Alison Rourke

Paul Scruton

Eric Schmitt

Vaughan Smith

Holger Stark

Jonathan Steele

Oliver Taplin

Simon Tisdall

Jan Thompson

Declan Walsh

Helen Walmsley-Johnson

INDEX

(in subentries, JA = Julian Assange; *NYT* = *New York Times*; WL = WikiLeaks)